SO-AIV-996

"The *New York Times* is by far the most influential newspaper in the world and thus receives far too little journalistic scrutiny due to its power to affect careers. Any book that casts a critical eye on the Paper of Record's history, as this book does, is performing a valuable service."   —Glenn Greenwald

"In an account brimming with fascinating, if morbid, detail, Ashley Rindsberg rigorously exposes the dark side of the *New York Times*. For 99 years— since a 1922 description of Hitler as someone 'actuated by lofty, unselfish patriotism'—it has labored under the shadow of its dynastic owners' triad of problems: capitalist guilt, Jewish self-hatred, and an ambition for power, wealth, and status. The *Times*' importance means the family's issues have done much damage."   —Daniel Pipes

"With the researcher's eye for the damning detail and the novelist's feel for the egos and appetites that animate great characters, Ashley Rindsberg has produced an eminently readable account of why a formerly great American newspaper betrayed its principles and how its decline made us all the poorer. Anyone curious about the *New York Times*'s path to perdition would do well to begin with this well-crafted story of ideological convictions obscuring grim realities, big personalities obscuring dogged truth-tellers, and unearned reputations obscuring a slow and sad fall from grace."

—Liel Leibovitz, Editor-at-Large, *Tablet Magazine*

"Rindsberg's timely book deals with the abuse of information for political purposes. It is a brave piece of historical journey into the annals of the *New York Times*. It shows us how what is now considered to be a new phenomenon, Fake News, belonging to the social media era or to the Trump presidency, began much earlier, and does not belong to only one particular political camp. Rindsberg has an important story to tell to anyone who has ever opened the pages of the *New York Times*."   —Adi Schwartz, *The War of Return*

"This book is a bracing, urgent reminder of the devastating real-world consequences that arise when an important institution falls in love with the sound of its own voice and puts its power in the service of myth creation on behalf of elites."   —Jenny Holland, Author & Former *Times* Staffer

"We are all aware that the *New York Times* has its fair share of biases and more than a few disgraces. But Rindsberg exposes journalistic scandals well beyond what is commonly known. Studiously researched and eloquently written, this volume provides us with an indispensable antidote to the halo effect that the *Times* has enjoyed for so long."

—Benjamin Kerstein, Israel Correspondent, *The Algemeiner*

The
Gray
Lady
Winked

How *The New York Times*'s
Misreporting, Distortions, and Fabrications
Radically Alter History

by Ashley Rindsberg

Midnight Oil Publishers

Midnight Oil Publishers LLC

Copyright © 2021 by Ashley Rindsberg

All rights reserved. No part of this book may be reproduced or used in any manner without written permission of the copyright owner except for the use of quotations in a book review. For more information, address: info@midnightoilpublishers.com

Cover design: Jamie Keenan
Interior design: Julie Karen Hodgins

ISBN: 978-1-736-7033-1-1
FIRST EDITION

www.MidnightOilPublishers.com

"The basis of our governments
being the opinion of the people,
the very first object should be to keep that right;
and were it left to me to decide whether
we should have a government without newspapers,
or newspapers without a government,
I should not hesitate a moment to prefer the latter."

Thomas Jefferson

Acknowledgments

his book is the result of a years-long (almost decades-long) process. As such there are many people to whom I owe my gratitude. First and foremost are my parents, Steve and Denise Rindsberg, without whose love and support nothing would have been possible, let alone this book. I also have to thank the book's earliest readers and supporters—emotional, psychological and spiritual—my comrades in arms, Lionel Harkham, Daniel Fink and Rafi Harkham. The climb would not have been possible without their providing me a base camp. Jason Ressler offered invaluable and unstinting support along the way, particularly in helping shove the massive monolith that is a book out through the narrow window of publishing and into the world. My brother Tony Rindsberg generously lent me his expertise in connecting this book with its intended readers. And I extend my gratitude to my mother-in-law, Rachel Golding, who has offered her support and enthusiasm for this project.

Lastly and certainly mostly, I owe endless amounts of gratitude to my wife, Jane Rindsberg, who has borne every gripe, every hesitation, each moment of intellectual handwringing (and everything in between) with equanimity, love and generosity. Without her always there I don't know where I would ever be.

Contents

Foreword

𝕿 hose who still trust the *New York Times* to tell them all they need to know about the most important issues of the day, and who live their lives accordingly, should look into the Gray Lady's rich history of pumping out Big Lies—a history that will come as quite a shock to her devoted readers. The paper that, for over four years, feverishly likened Donald Trump to Adolf Hitler was unabashedly pro-Hitler in the Thirties, serving as a sturdy fount of Dr. Goebbels's propaganda ("reporting," just as his newspapers did, that *Poland* invaded *Germany* on Sept. 1, 1939). The paper that, for twenty years, has made Vladimir Putin out to be a second Stalin was unabashedly pro-Stalin in its coverage of the famine in Ukraine (there wasn't one, according to the *Times*) and the show trials (legitimate, according to the *Times*). And the paper that persistently envisions an imaginary Holocaust in Syria *blacked out* the real one at the time, having carefully downplayed the Nazis' persecution of the Jews from 1933.

These are just a few of the grave journalistic wrongs that the Gray Lady has perpetrated in her time, and that are cogently recounted here by Ashley Rindsberg, who also digs into her eerie celebration of the bombing of Hiroshima and Nagasaki (the reporter under contract with the Pentagon); its rock-star treatment of Fidel Castro as an ardent democrat; its fierce cheer-leading for the coup that killed Ngo Dinh Diem (an operation that prolonged the war in Vietnam); its amplifying outright fabrications in its coverage of the Second Intifada and the US occupation of Iraq (which it helped bring about, by stoutly echoing Bush/Cheney's scary lie about Saddam Hussein's "weapons of mass destruction"); and, more recently, its elaborate fantasy that the Americans who fought for independence from Great Britain were fighting mainly to keep slavery going (a crackpot notion that, despite historians' objections, the *Times* continues flogging in the nation's classrooms, its glossy "educational materials" presenting that "woke" fantasy as fact).

Some may argue with the author's thesis as to *why* the *Times* has such a spotty record, but no one can refute his cogent demonstration that America's "newspaper of record" has serially misinformed its readers, often with disastrous consequences; and that is why this book is so important at this moment, with the *New York Times* still riding high—and still routinely misinforming millions, on urgent subjects of all kinds. No paper with a past like the Gray Lady's can be trusted to deliver "all the news that's fit to print," or to identify "fake news." And so the time has come to knock her off her pedestal, by following Ashley Rindsberg's bold example. Whether we agree with it (or him) politically or not, we too must read that all-too-influential paper *critically*, seek out our daily news elsewhere, and thereby help to break her spell at last.

Mark Crispin Miller
Professor of Media Studies
New York University

Preface

The journey that has taken this book from its original inception to this point of landing in the hands of readers like you has been long and winding. When I initially began writing *The Gray Lady Winked*, I, in my naiveté as a twenty-five-year-old, the ink still drying on my university degree in philosophy, believed the world would be eager for a book that illuminated the somewhat harsh reality of a well-worn American myth. This was not to be. Almost before they were even opened, doors were slammed shut on the book—not because anyone contested the quality of its writing or accuracy of its claims (objections that never arose), but simply because the book risked angering the *New York Times*.

Over and over, decision makers in publishing told me explicitly, in no uncertain terms, that they could not support the project because the *New York Times* was simply too powerful. The executive editor of the most influential literary agency in the US said he could not risk his relationship with the paper, on which he depends for reviews and publicity for his authors. Publishers who are brand names in the industry balked. Even freelance designers and editors refused to work on the book, saying it was not a risk they could afford to take. On one occasion, I received a strongly worded email from someone in the industry who lambasted me as "irresponsible" (and worse) for my decision to publish this book. In my innocence, I'd protest that this book has never been about opposing the *New York Times* but about pursuing the same mission to which the paper is dedicated—unearthing the truth. But no matter how wholehearted it was, the strength of that argument could not overcome an evidently widespread fear of the cultural and political behemoth that is the *New York Times*. An idea I'd considered almost intuitively natural—that we should shine a light of truth where we can, especially where we think a lie might be lurking—suddenly became dangerous.

For a number of years, I acquiesced, thinking that publication would not be worth the trouble: It's not worth the fight, it's not worth the risk to my career. But the book stuck in my throat. I'd see news stories related to the ones presented in the following chapters covered in only the most superficial way, and I'd want to shout at my computer screen, "That's only a tiny piece of the bigger picture!" I'd watch scandals jolt the newspaper, leaving readers wondering how could this have happened at the *New York Times*, of all places, and I'd ache to show them that this kind of thing has been part and parcel of a deeply flawed organization for decades.

Finally, I realized I could no longer keep the book under wraps. One way or another, it had to see the light of day. My only choice was to go it alone. As I warmed to this idea, I began to understand that independent publishing is not what it was ten or fifteen years ago. No longer an anomaly, it increasingly looks like the way forward for all forms of content. Thanks to digital technologies, we now have endless new ways of reaching audiences. This is not only the case in music, film, and publishing, but in journalism itself. In recent years, some of our biggest and brightest journalists have struck out on their own as their traditional journalistic homes no longer found their ideas suitable. I look to these people, who have departed from major media outlets—the *Atlantic,* the *Intercept,* the *Washington Post* and, of course, the *New York Times* among them—with admiration for their courage and their boldness. Because of their example, I was inspired to do the same.

Through sheer belief in its importance, I was able to get the book to this point. But it will be readers like you who will determine the course it takes from here onward. My hope is that people will pick it up, read it, or read the chapters that touch on their interests, and not so much pass the book along (though, of course, I would deeply appreciate that gesture of confidence) but transfer the knowledge they've discovered from reading it to others around them. My hope is that they develop a more rounded understanding of this crucially important news outlet and, on that basis, emerge with a deeper impression of how truth is determined. More importantly, I hope they will look at journalism with a fresh perspective—one that does not cast various institutions or reporters in black-and-white, good-or-bad narratives but takes as its starting point the idea that, as with everything else in life, the field of journalism is characterized by shades of gray.

It's this color, gray, so key to the *New York Times*'s reputation, that might provide a hinge for us to create a healthier understanding of the newspaper—and of journalism in general. For decades, the *New York Times* proudly wore the moniker of the "Gray Lady" because that adjective, gray, spoke to a concrete objectivity, a kind of neutral take on the facts that testified to the bloodless accuracy of its reporting. But as this book shows, for at least the past century, that has not been the case. On many of the most important subjects of the day, the *New York Times* was neither disinterested nor dispassionate. In fact, as these pages attest, the paper staked a very definite position when it came to its coverage of major historical episodes.

My own view is that it's time for us to think differently about the concept of grayness in news reporting. Instead of understanding journalism as either a collection of neutral entities who process unassailable fact into truth or as partisan operators hacking away at an agenda, we should see the endeavor as encompassing a spectrum of ideas and opinions that approximate or come as close as possible to the truth. While this might feel paradoxical—after all, we tend to think that something is either true or it's not—the reality is that absolute truth is not available to the human mind. We do our best by putting in place processes that rely on a multitude of perspectives to come as close as possible to the truth. This doesn't mean there is no objective truth. I firmly believe there is. But just like in science, journalism done right attempts to come as close as possible to the truth while fully recognizing that it will never present a perfect picture. In fact, this is the idea that sits at the core of the ideal newsroom: alone, an outlet, reporter or news report is almost never completely right or wrong, but together, a multitude of institutions and individuals aiming for the truth come much closer to it than any one person ever can.

For too long, the *New York Times* has been seen as the sole (or at least the primary) arbiter of truth in journalism. It lost sight of the clichéd but very effective idea that journalism is the "rough draft" of history and instead strove to present the crystallized final version. Large swaths of the American public, and in particular the country's elite, certainly believed this to be the case (or, at least, they acted as if it were). The *New York Times* was not scrutinized the way any institution that serves a critical public function ought to be. No one was watching the watchdog.

The *New York Times* is not alone in suffering the effects of a great reputation. Like other major figures or organizations in history, at some point it began acting in certain instances as if it were above or beyond the truth. But the opposite is very much the case. The *New York Times* is not a manufacturer or crafter of truth, as it sometimes seems to suppose itself, but a receptacle for it. It does not shape the truth—it is shaped by it. If there is one lesson I hope readers take from this book, it is this.

Introduction

It was Election Day and war was raging. There wasn't a man or woman in the US who didn't have an opinion—who should be elected, who should run the war, or alternatively, who should end it. Amid the din of discontent and partisanship, one of the country's most influential newspapers was able to break through the noise with a ringing editorial. Entitled "The Momentous Day,"[1] its clear-sightedness and moral strength resound through history:

> The day has come—the day of fate. Before this morning's sun sets, the destinies of this republic, so far as depends on human agency, are to be settled for weal or for woe. An inevitable choice is this day to be made by the American people, between a policy of carrying out salvation or a policy of carrying ruin to the nation.

The newspaper and its editors were certain about who each of the two opposing candidates were and what each of them represented, as far as the years-long war was concerned:

> On the one hand is war, tremendous and terrible, yet ushering in at the very end national security and glory. On the other is the mocking shadow of a peace, tempting us to quit these sacrifices, and sink again

into indulgence, and yet sure to rob us of our birthright, and to entail upon our children a dissevered Union and ceaseless strife.

On the one side was a Democrat, a former general who believed the war had initially been justified but that it had gone on too long and that if it had been based on more limited goals, it could have been easily won. According to the Democratic candidate, if he were elected, he would "exhaust all the resources of statesmanship"[2] to end the horrible war.

On the other side was a candidate who, as president, had begun the war and refused to give it up until the country fought to the bitter end in order to achieve not limited aims but total victory. The leaders of this candidate's own party had urged him to talk to the enemy, to meet halfway at the negotiating table. He refused, knowing full well that this refusal would likely cost him his office. But he believed fervently it was the right thing—the only possible thing—to do. This was the candidate of war, "tremendous and terrible, yet ushering in at the very end national security and glory."

The Democratic candidate's name was George McClellan. He represented the "mocking shadow of a peace" the newspaper condemned. The war candidate the paper had thrown its weight behind was Abraham Lincoln. And the newspaper that unequivocally supported the incumbent, and the war he was directing, was the *New York Times*.

The election of 1864 between George McClellan and Abraham Lincoln took place little more than ten years after the founding of the *Times*. Yet through thick competition, the paper had managed to burst through the pack of American opinion makers and establish itself as one of the most important news outlets in the land. The *Times* was founded by an ambitious newspaper man named Henry Raymond, who had worked for Horace Greeley, owner and editor of what would become the archrival of the *Times*—the *New York Tribune*. Greeley was a staunch anti-slavery supporter in the early years of the Civil War but by the time of the 1864 election his zeal had started to fade. He, like so many others on both sides of the election, began to advocate talking to the Confederacy about ending the war and entering negotiations concerning the question of slavery.

For Lincoln, this line meant defeat. It meant the Union would be able to drive a hard line when it came to reunification and the restoration of the Constitution. But, in exchange, there would have to be serious compromises and concessions on ending slavery. In other words, the institution that Lincoln considered so odious and so despicable that he was willing to risk his presidency, his life, and the wellbeing of the Union in order to defeat would remain.

The *Times* vociferously opposed the line taken by Greeley and the *Tribune*. Instead of compromise, it thundered about military victories in historical terms. The paper understood that the Civil War was not—as many claimed then as they claim today—about money, political power, or even opposing ideologies. It was about right and wrong, the moral and the flagrantly immoral. This is the reason Lincoln could not abide talks with the enemy, even if they held a glimmer of hope for reconciliation and a cessation of the killing. For Lincoln, and for the *Times* standing behind him, the war was about what the nation's sixteenth president called the country's most "precious jewel"—freedom.

It's no coincidence that the great democratic leader and the great newspaper moved in parallel on the question of slavery and the Civil War. For well over a century since that day, both Lincoln and the *Times* have served as beacons of America's most fundamental ideals. They have emerged as bright symbols of the American promise. In Lincoln's case, America found an embodiment of liberty, not as a political slogan or bumper sticker and not as a rationale for self-serving behavior, but as a principle that requires huge self-sacrifice—one that, in many ways, is rooted in self-sacrifice. The *Times* came to represent a similar ideal: the principle that despite every consideration of expedience and ideology, the truth must always win out. Without this principle, which sits at the foundation of the proverbial fourth estate of governance—that is, a free press—liberty means nothing.

For much of the twentieth century, the *Times* was seen as a standard bearer of the truth. It is because of this unique standing that the seven words that constitute the *Times*'s famous slogan, "All the News That's Fit to Print," have been printed atop each day's edition since 1897 without irony or embarrassment. America believed in the *New York Times,* and the *New York Times* believed in America. But for many news consumers today, including some of the paper's most loyal readers, the picture of a truth-bearing newspaper that went to the ends of the earth to bring readers the unadorned facts feels like a quaint relic from a bygone era. Over the past years, the *Times* has increasingly become not only a point of political contention but a flashpoint of scandal. It often seems that not a week goes by in which the *Times* is not the subject of headlines, often its own, related to stories of journalistic failings, malfeasance, and internecine newsroom skirmishes. While these stories serve as appetizing table scraps for the millions of cultural critics (self-appointed and otherwise) who make up today's social media-fueled news environment, in reality, they point to deeper questions that cut to the core of our society.

Few questions today are more salient or more vital than the ones we're asking about truth. Who determines the truth? How do we know when it's true? Does it even matter? Can *my* truth be different from *your* truth? And what happens if it is? These issues have arisen alongside a parallel question about lies and falsehood. Google Trends shows that the popularity of the term "fake news" has exploded since the end of 2016, increasing tenfold right after the 2016 presidential election and peaking in January 2018 at a level *thirty times* greater than its baseline prior to the election. According to Google, the term is now used at a frequency that's three, four, and sometimes five times greater than what it was just a few short years ago. But what is fake news? What is the truth? And how do we know?

The seed for this book was planted when I stumbled across a footnote in a work of history about the Second World War, William Shirer's famed *The Rise and Fall of the Third Reich.* In the footnote, Shirer mentioned, almost casually, that on the eve of the outbreak of the Second World War, the *New York Times* reported that Poland had invaded Germany.[3] I was shocked by this barely noticed fact in the middle of a tome of history. It stopped me in my tracks. How could the great American newspaper, whose standards for excellence are known around the world, have reported the very opposite of what we now consider to be an unassailable fact, an idea fundamental to our understanding of the war—that Germany invaded Poland as the opening salvo of Hitler's scheme to conquer Europe? In reality, my first question was not "How could this have happened?" but whether it could possibly be true. To answer that question, I turned to one of the greatest historical resources online, the *New York Times*'s own digital archive, and I discovered that sure enough, the *Times* had reported that Poland invaded Germany, giving the Third Reich license to "retaliate" by subsequently invading Poland[4]. But this raised more questions than it answered. How did the *Times* arrive at this conclusion, and why? How could the *Times*'s journalists have ignored the decade of Nazi aggression leading up to the invasion of Poland? That story, which is told in detail in Chapter 1, opened my eyes to a different understanding of the *New York Times* than the one I had held for years as a reader of the paper.

Once my eyes were open, I could never close them again. I dug deeper and deeper, looking at some of the major historical events of modern history, including the Holocaust, the Vietnam War, the development and use of the first nuclear weapons, the Cuban Revolution, the rise of Soviet Russia, the Iraq War, the Second Intifada, and more recently, the emergence of race (and especially the historical impact of American slavery) as a defining issue of our time. In each case, my research churned up not mere errors or inaccuracies but whole-cloth falsehoods. In these instances, it was as if the *Times* had reported from a different dimension of reality, presenting narratives about unfolding history that were drastically divergent from the ones we now know—and, critically, what other key observers, including members of the *Times*'s own staff and management, knew then—to be true. Again, that terrible question arose: How could this be?

No institution is perfect. No human being is free from error. In some ways, error makes us human. This is especially the case when it comes to people whose Herculean job it is to capture the truth as it advances at a frightening speed and in the context of bewilderingly complex world events. But what I learned throughout my research is that, time and again, the journalistic errors examined in this book—the misreporting, fabrications, and distortions—were never the product of simple error. Nor were they solely the result of rogue reporters who took their journalistic fates into their own hands. Rather, they were the byproduct of a particular kind of system, a truth-producing machine that though built to purpose by the paper's original owners (first, Henry Raymond, and later, the man who would found the dynasty that owns and operates the paper to this day, a German Jewish immigrant named Adolph Ochs) was later tweaked and retrofitted to perform other functions, ones less noble and more murky in intention.

What this book shows is that the journalistic failure explored in each chapter occurred when politics, ideology, or institutional self-interest played too great a role in the shaping of a news story. Rather than fitting the pattern to the facts, the *Times* too often gave in to the temptation to fit the facts to a preconceived pattern. This is what we see over and over, and each time to devastating effect.

Returning to the idea of Abraham Lincoln, we can understand that what made the man great, what distinguished him for all history, was his willingness to bend and compromise on every issue except the one that mattered most. When it came to the question of ridding America of slavery, he refused—utterly and outright. As Lincoln wrote in his Second Inaugural Address:

> Fondly do we hope, fervently do we pray, that this mighty scourge of war may speedily pass away. Yet if God wills that it continue until all the wealth piled by the bondsman's 250 years of unrequited toil shall be sunk, and until every drop of blood drawn with the lash shall be paid by another drawn with the sword, as was said 3,000 years ago, so still, it must be said: "the judgments of the Lord are true and righteous altogether."[5]

No enticement—no amount of promised wealth, no amount of power—could sway Lincoln.

Just three decades later, Adolph Ochs made a statement of similar import (and there's little doubt that a newsman of that era would have been familiar with Lincoln's famed address) in a business announcement printed in the *Times* after he took control of the paper he'd recently bought:

> It will be my earnest aim that the *New York Times* give the news, all the news, in concise and attractive form, in language that is parliamentary

in good society, and give it as early, if not earlier, than it can be learned through any other reliable medium; to give the news impartially, without fear or favor, regardless of party, sect, or interests involved; to make the columns of the *New York Times* a forum for the consideration of all questions of public importance, and to that end to invite intelligent discussion from all shades of opinion.[6]

The announcement is as noble in its ideals as it is humble in their expression. "To give the news impartially, without fear or favor" reads like it could just as easily have come from the journalistic equivalent of the Hippocratic Oath. Ochs kept his word, including his dogged belief in using direct "parliamentary" language. But his successors did not. Over the course of the next century, Ochs would be succeeded by his son-in-law, Arthur Hays Sulzberger; the husband of his granddaughter, Orvil Dryfoos; his grandson, Arthur Ochs Sulzberger; his great-grandson, Arthur Ochs Sulzberger Jr.; and, most recently, his great-great-grandson, Arthur Gregg (A.G.) Sulzberger. For 120 years, this line has gone unbroken, constituting a literal patriarchy leading the world's most important and influential newspaper. It's the patriarch of this dynasty who selects the paper's top editors and managers. It's he—*always a he*—who leads decisions related to its infamous two-tiered stock structure, by which Class A common shares with no voting power are offered to the public, while privately held Class B stock, which *does* carry voting power, is available only to members of the *Times*'s controlling family.

This is where the question of how things went so wrong begins to find its answer. As we've seen throughout history, as well as in present-day politics, the founders of dynasties were always motivated by some specific and extrinsic aim, in this case, building a newspaper to bring the facts of world events, national politics, and local life to readers in an attractive format. However, the dynasty that follows the founder is at least partially (but often totally) devoted to maintaining its power, wealth, and position. And it's when this nearly irresistible trifecta of forces begins to compete with other priorities, such as digging up the unvarnished truth and delivering it to the public as simply as possible, that things tend to go horribly wrong.

Canned Goods:
"Minding the Nazis Less Than Most"

On December 21, 1924, the *New York Times* arguably made the worst prediction in the history of modern journalism: "His behavior during imprisonment convinced authorities that…[he] was no longer to be feared," the report stated. "It is believed he will retire to private life and return to Austria, the country of his birth." The "he" of the article was Adolf Hitler and, needless to say, he didn't return to private life or, for any real amount of time, to Austria. The man that the *Times* article reported as being both "sadder" and "wiser" than when he was first imprisoned went on to construct one of humanity's darkest regimes, ignited a war that killed tens of millions of people, and engineered the world's first program of mechanized genocide, making him the last person a reader of the *Times* should think "was no longer to be feared."[1]

The *Times* had been covering Hitler for more than two years by the time of the paper's disastrously wrong prediction about the future dictator's post-prison retirement. In those two years, Hitler had managed to raise a small army and had breathed an anti-Semitic fire into the hearts of people in Bavaria, where he first catapulted himself to power, as well as in many other parts of Germany. Two years before his release from prison, on November 20, 1922, the *Times* reported that Hitler had already organized a fanatical group of extremists, called National Socialists, which had begun "smouldering beneath the surface." But by the time of that November 1922 article, the *Times* reporter wrote that the movement had "eaten its way through, and a conflagration of course is not only possible but certain if this now free flame of fanatical patriotism finds sufficient popular combustible material to feed on."[2]

But even in the November 1922 article, the *Times* correspondent was eager to give Hitler the benefit of the doubt. "He is credibly credited with being actuated by lofty, unselfish patriotism," the *Times* reporter wrote. Then, as if he were deliberately ignoring the sentence about Hitler's "lofty, unselfish patriotism," the reporter added two sentences later: "The keynote of his propaganda in writing and speaking is violent anti-Semitism... So violent are Hitler's fulminations against the Jews that a number of prominent Jewish citizens are reported to have sought safe asylums in the Bavarian highlands..."

Which was it? The "lofty, unselfish" patriot or the mad, frothing anti-Semitic demagogue? The reporter couldn't seem to make up his mind. And as if to throw some more confusion into the mix, he followed up his paragraph on Hitler's violent "fulminations against the Jews" with an earnest disclaimer: "But several reliable, well-informed sources confirmed the idea that Hitler's anti-Semitism was not so violent or genuine as it sounded, and that he was merely using anti-Semitic propaganda to catch messes [*sic*] of followers and keep them aroused, enthusiastic, and in line for the time when his organization is perfected and sufficiently powerful to be employed effectively for political purposes."

And so, the *New York Times* delivered the second-worst prediction in the history of modern journalism, once again about Adolf Hitler. Seventeen years later, this split-the-difference reporting on Hitler and the Nazis would come home to roost. While in 1922, the *Times* had made the worst prediction in modern journalism, in 1939 this same approach to reporting on Nazi Germany resulted in what likely constitutes the single biggest, yet least recognized, journalistic failure on record.

◆ ◆ ◆

On August 31, 1939, Hitler put into action one of the most flagrant scams in the history of the modern world. In order to give Germany a reason and a right to begin its war of European conquest, he and a number of Gestapo propagandists and henchmen (including Heinrich Müller, who would be made head of the Gestapo a month later) concocted a scheme to make it seem as if neighboring Poland had attacked Germany. With a bit of crude but bold propaganda, the Second World War began.

The *New York Times* bought the Nazi dupe without flinching. Underneath its famous banner, "All the News That's Fit to Print," the paper reported that, according to "Chancellor Hitler," Germany had been attacked. Already in the second paragraph of the *Times*'s front-page article, the reporter, Otto Tolischus, went on to reprint verbatim Hitler's infamous war speech to the Reichstag, which the Führer used to justify to the world, as much as to the German people, his invasion of Poland.[3]

Between the pages, the *Times* went into detail, reporting that Polish attacks had been carried out against Germany at a German radio station in Gleiwitz—and other points along the border. The report was written in the *Times*'s characteristically deliberating and objective tone and presented the "facts" of the events that would lead to humanity's most horrifying war.

"At 8 P.M., according to the semi-official news agency," the *Times* report stated, "a group of Polish insurrectionists forced an entrance into the Gleiwitz radio station [in Germany], overpowering the watchmen and beating and generally mishandling the attendants. The Gleiwitz station was relaying a Breslau station's program, which was broken off by the Poles."

The problem, however, was that the times, places, names, and the events themselves, as they were reported by the *Times,* were all Nazi fabrications. With the publication of Nazi propaganda on the pages of the most trusted newspaper of the world's greatest democracy, the Führer and his top propagandists got more than they could have hoped for from "Operation Himmler."

Under the headline, "Hitler Gives Word," Otto Tolischus presented only the point of view of Hitler and the Nazis concerning the events along the German-Polish border. Tolischus wrote, "Charging that Germany had been attacked, Chancellor Hitler at 5:11 o'clock this morning issued a proclamation to the army declaring that from now on force will be met with force and calling on the armed forces 'to fulfill their duty to the end.'" In the very next paragraph, Tolischus reprinted Hitler's proclamation, which the dictator calculated as a way to fire up the German public for war. The proclamation and its reprint in the *Times* represented the next and possibly most damaging stage of Operation Himmler since the very first words of Hitler's widely published speech were coldly designed to deceive as much of Europe and America as possible: "To the defense forces: The Polish nation has refused my efforts for a peaceful regulation of neighborly relations; instead it has appealed to weapons," Hitler said. Tolischus printed the entirety of the proclamation in his front-page article and then went on to report German military restrictions and warnings. He never once mentioned the possibility that the Nazis, so well versed in propaganda and so ready to use that weapon, as they had proven many times by 1939, might be lying. For his error-ridden, propaganda-friendly reporting, Tolischus was awarded the Pulitzer Prize in 1940 "for his dispatches from Berlin."[4]

But the reality of the *Times*'s reporting was much more serious than Tolischus's blind reprint of Hitler's infamous speech or his failure to provide a smidgen of counterbalance in his report about the attack at Gleiwitz. When, on page three of that day's issue, the *Times* reported on the details of the supposed Polish attack that "according to the semi-official news agency, a group of Polish insurrectionists forced its way into the Gleiwitz radio station," the reporter and editors at the *Times* left out one critical fact that would have been known to them all: the "semi-official news agency" cited as the article's main source was one of the Nazis' central propaganda organs. In reality, by 1939 there was no such thing as a "semi-official news agency" in Germany. Propaganda minister Joseph Goebbels had brought the entirety of the media under his control when Hitler became Chancellor of Germany in 1933. There was no scrap or snippet of information published in any part of the news media that wasn't completely in line with his media guidelines.

However, as the *Times* article about the first attack of the Second World War went on, the use of Nazi sources masked by misleading terms like "semi-official news agency" (or lacking a citation at all) only grew worse. The article reported that "The Gleiwitz incident is alleged here to have been the signal 'for a general attack by Polish *frantireurs* [guerrillas] on German territory.'" That was quite a claim: Not only had Poland attacked Germany, but it had done so as the opening shot of a theater-sized war of aggression on all of German territory. An average American reader digesting the supposed facts of this story would no doubt have the impression that Poland's aggression warranted a strong German response, if not an all-out attack, by the victimized Germany which was only seeking to secure its border.

It is important to remember that in 1939, just as today, the *Times* was no metropolitan or even regional newspaper. Already by 1917, the New York Times News Service (similar to today's AP or Reuters newswire services) had become "the biggest newspaper syndicate in the United States."[5] By the mid-1920s, the paper had shrewdly leveraged its dominance in American reporting by branching out through investment in critical communications technologies and had come to hold "the most prominent position in foreign reporting, since its communications chief had built a super-heterodyne receiver for direct reception of press dispatches from Europe."[6] So when the *Times* printed the claim that the incident at the Gleiwitz radio station was "the signal for a general attack" by Poland, it wasn't just *Times* readers who were getting the information, but large swaths of the country. And all of these readers were deprived of yet another critical piece of information left out of the *Times*'s article about the start of the Second World War: the unsourced allegation that Poland's attack was the signal of a general assault on German territory was taken by the *Times* reporter directly from the Nazi Party newspaper *Volkischer Beobachter*.[7] Far from a "semi-official" news agency, this was the newspaper Hitler himself read while relaxing in his Bavarian retreat and which billed itself as the "fighting paper of the National Socialist movement of Greater Germany." Yet, the *Times* article failed to mention that its single source was the official newspaper of the NSDAP—the Nazi party in Germany.

At the time of the Gleiwitz Incident (as the propaganda scheme later became known), American public opinion was on a dangerous tightrope. A mere two decades after the end of the First World War, the US was awash in ambivalence about the notion of getting into what most Americans saw as another European war. Just as in the Civil War, the First World War, the Vietnam War, and of course, the more recent wars in Iraq and Afghanistan, the political fray had become polarized. On one side, there were those who saw a storm brewing as they watched the Third Reich arm itself to the teeth and brazenly begin aggressive campaigns to steal territory from neighboring countries while directing or attempting coups in others. These observers—President Roosevelt among them—knew that, eventually, the US would likely be drawn into a war with Nazi Germany. This group believed that each day the confrontation with Germany did not begin meant another day the Nazi monster could grow in size and strength.

On the other side of the political and public opinion spectrum was a loud chorus of anti-war activists who, on the whole, were by no means marginal or radical. Like today, many of the pre-Second World War anti-war activists were members of Congress, the State Department, academia, big business, and the most powerful masts of the mainstream media. Staunch war veterans and even former war planners, who were usually quick to a fight, were working hard in the late 1930s to prevent the US from getting sucked into what they thought of as "another British conflict." Additionally, swaths of corporate America, such as mega-conglomerate Standard Oil, enjoyed lucrative relationships with Hitler's regime and lobbied to keep things just as they were.[8] This movement had enough strength to keep FDR, who, with Winston Churchill, watched the Nazi rise with foreboding, constrained from taking the action he felt was necessary to prevent the all-out disaster that would soon become the Second World War.

American public opinion was in a delicate place at a critical time. Even as radio was transforming the media landscape, newspapers were still the primary outlet for news and opinion. And the *New York Times* was, as it is today, the flagship that led the American media fleet as it translated the daily tangle of pre-war events into the foundation of American political life: public opinion.

It was against this background that the Nazi leadership created and implemented Operation Himmler. Hitler's plan to start the war with an act of historical deception was calculated for a number of reasons. He first had to rally the German people who, on the eve of the war, were going about daily life as usual. According to firsthand accounts of public sentiment in Germany, they seemed to want things to stay that way.[9] Hitler had managed to dominate and then animate the political-military echelon, but as a leader, he had to deal with how the public felt, even if as demagogue and dictator his interest was in manipulating the public rather than in representing it.

The "Chancellor of Germany," as *Times* correspondent Otto Tolischus respectfully referred to Hitler at the time, also had his eye on the US when calculating his propaganda-based opening shot. Hitler knew that American production capabilities, resources, and military ingenuity could swing the coming war in either direction. His ultimate aim was to keep the US out of the war for as long as possible and then turn the wrath of the German military, backed by the natural resources, ports, fleets and arms of conquered Europe, to the Americas.[10] For Hitler, American delay meant German victory.

The Gleiwitz Incident, used to achieve this crucial delay, constituted a crude piece of propaganda. The operation was supervised directly by one of the Gestapo's darkest stars, Reinhard Heydrich, who had been handpicked by Himmler to lead the *Sicherheitsdienst*, comprising the Gestapo, the secret state police, and the Nazi criminal police organization, the *Kriminalpolizei*. Heydrich used a brutal pit bull of a man named Alfred Naujocks to organize the Polish-speaking Nazi officers who would raid the German radio station dressed up as Polish guerrillas. Heydrich and Naujocks also selected a few prisoners from one of the early Nazi concentration camps, dressed them up as German guards and executed them in order to make it seem as if the Polish invaders had actually killed Germans. It was on account of these executed prisoners, stuffed into German uniforms, that the Nazis who partook in organizing the Gleiwitz Incident referred to it with cruel humor as "Operation Canned Goods."

Any level of journalistic investigation would have, at minimum, raised some serious questions about what had actually happened at the Polish-German border. It can be argued that the lack of time and freedom of movement under the Nazi regime would have made this difficult, if not impossible, for foreign correspondents in Germany. However, in 1939, mass-scale Nazi propaganda was already well known. Since Hitler started gathering power in the early 1920s (when the *New York Times* was making bold predictions about him) and more seriously after 1933, when Hitler took control of Germany, the Nazis churned out one propaganda offensive after another. Over the course of this decade, the Nazis under Hitler employed the same tactic: pretend peace but pursue war. For nearly ten years, the *New York Times* reported many of these stories by simply reprinting Nazi claims, particularly when it came to Hitler's peaceful intentions. There was very little journalistic counterbalance in the *Times*'s reporting on Germany and even less editorial outrage when it came to the Nazi regime's early crimes. But a closer look at the *Times*'s coverage of Germany during the Nazi era—especially when compared to the accurate and incisive reporting of other American papers—raises more questions than it answers.

◆ ◆ ◆

The first major landmark in the *Times*'s pre-war reporting was its coverage of the now infamous Munich Conference of September 1938. During these talks, Germany managed to pull the wool over the eyes of many of the world's powers, thereby enabling the Nazi regime to continue to violate international treaties by re-arming and by provoking aggressive international disputes with its neighbors. By the time of the Munich Conference, Hitler had already unilaterally annexed Austria with the violent *Anschluss* campaign only six months beforehand. The process of the illegal annexation, however, began much earlier, in 1934, when Nazis in the Austrian government assassinated Austria's Chancellor Dollfuss. The German news agency denied that Germany had anything to do with the assassination, but most news sources, including the *Times*, recognized that

the murder of the Austrian head of government was a result of organized
Nazi aggression.[11]

Only two years after the German-directed assassination, the Nazi party
made a bold public relations move. In 1931, before the rise of the Nazi
party to power, Germany had been selected to host the 1936 Olympic
Games. The rise of Hitler and the Nazis was not something that would
stop the International Olympic Committee from going forward with
the scheduled games.[12] A number of American organizations supported
a boycott of the Berlin Games, arguing that participation would mean
endorsing what many Americans recognized as a terrifying and immoral
regime. The leader of the Amateur Athletic Union protested that the
Third Reich had broken Olympic Committee rules by instituting racial
and ethnic discrimination.[13] Other groups, like the American Jewish
Congress, the Jewish Labor Committee, and groups associated with the
Catholic journal, *Commonweal*, opposed the games on account of the
Nazis' virulent anti-Semitism and programmatic racism.[14] Unfortunately,
those on the other side of the Olympics question, including the head of the
American Olympic Committee, saw things differently. The Berlin Games
proceeded as planned.

If there is any one way to characterize the *New York Times*'s approach
to reporting on the Berlin Olympics in the lead-up to the games, it is by
comparing it to how the *Times* reported on Hitler in the early days of
the Nazi leader's rise. Back in 1922 and 1924, the *Times* wrote about
Hitler as if it could not decide whether he was good or bad, dangerous or
harmless, a "lofty patriot" or an anti-Semitic maniac. At the end of the
day, it was the notion that Hitler was a relatively harmless, if vociferously
nationalist, leader that prevailed in the Gray Lady's reporting. The same
is largely true of the approach to the Berlin Olympics in the lead-up to
the games, when the *Times* took a skeptical approach, with the paper
joining an effort led by *Commonweal* to boycott the Games.[15] However,
in the aftermath of the Games, the *Times*'s reporting was frighteningly
committed to a particular viewpoint, one that was so enthusiastic in its
adulation for the Nazi Olympics it almost defies explanation.

In July of 1935, one of the *Times*'s Berlin correspondents, Frederick Birchall, penned an article about the Olympics and what the world should think about them. This was a profoundly important question, especially given that Berlin had erupted into violent anti-Jewish riots just one year before the city was to host the international games dedicated to promoting brotherhood and mutual tolerance. In most cases, the Berlin riots were led by young, pro-Nazi Germans who were not necessarily members of the party. On one occasion, Nazi supporters showed up at one of Berlin's main shopping areas, the Kurfürstendamm, and began smashing windows, turning over tables, chanting "Sieg Heil!" and anti-Jewish slurs, and beating Jewish movie-goers and shoppers.[16] According to eyewitness reports, the police arrived and arrested a few of the pro-Nazi rioters, but the crowd turned against the police, demanding that they return their comrades. Eventually, a higher-ranking Nazi policeman showed up and released all the rioters, who continued to beat Jewish shoppers on the street as the police simply looked on. A large amount of destruction resulted, and one middle-aged Jewish man was left lying on the ground, unconscious, bloody, and unattended to by the German police or ambulance services until a private car picked him up and whisked him away.

Birchall wrote an article for the *Times* about what the riots might mean for the Olympics. The *Times* reporter could hardly have been more sympathetic—*to the Nazis*. While the article's headline was, "Berlin Riots Mar Olympic Planning," the report had almost nothing to do with the riots themselves and instead focused almost exclusively on the grand affair that the Olympics were sure to be.[17]

Not only Berlin but all Germany is looking forward [to the Olympics]... and is preparing for it with a thoroughness and a concentration such as few countries, if any, could manifest. It is to be the occasion for "showing the world what Germany really is."

The last statement was undoubtedly true. The Nazi Olympics were a full showing, a coming-out party of sorts, for the Third Reich, complete with boasts of German "racial superiority" and, of course, the exclusion of German Jewish athletes from participation. But for Birchall, who had earlier been a fairly senior editor at the *Times* before choosing to return to reporting, the Olympics would reveal the true nature of Nazi Germany.

In the eyes of the *Times* correspondent, that Germany was a misunderstood and quintessentially peaceful place. "The German authorities have given a pledge that there shall be no race discrimination in the selection of the country's official Olympians," Birchall reported in his article. This was almost laughably naïve for a reporter based in a country that would enact the Nuremberg Laws only two months later. But Birchall doubled down, this time not simply by reprinting Nazi claims but by asserting them as fact.

"Accordingly, one of the camps, that at Ettlingen, devoted its last three weeks to training Jewish candidates [for the Games]," Birchall wrote, assuring *Times* readers of the Nazis' good intentions. Ettlingen, however, was a well-known Nazi "sham" that was "part of the Reich's effort to deflect international criticism concerning discrimination against Jewish athletes."[18] Still, Birchall devoured the lies that had been spoon-fed to him by the Nazi propaganda machine. Like previous *Times* reporting on the Third Reich, Birchall went just as far as official German propagandists in his article to paint a pretty picture of the regime. After assuring readers that Germany was within the strict letter of the law regarding the participation of Jews in the games, Birchall went on to report: "In these circumstances, with Germany ready to invite the world in to see her at her best and with meticulous care to entertain her guests, both wonderment and consternation have been aroused by the manifestations of intolerance and race hatred last week."

In his article, Birchall raised the question of whether the riots were a "final gesture to the Jews to 'put them in their place'"—a message to Jewish and other "non-Aryan" athletes of Germany to stay out of the Games and leave them to the Aryans? For Birchall—and since he cited no source and provided no quotes in the article, for Birchall alone—the answer was astoundingly simple: They were not. "Apparently, while race persecution is assuredly no appropriate concomitant to a world invitation, none of the motives implied in these questions can be substantiated."

This was a convoluted way of giving the Nazis the benefit of the doubt. But Birchall went far beyond that, predicting that the coming German military draft meant:

> ...a great change will come into effect in the mental attitude of German youth. Thenceforward, the Nazi storm troops would count for nothing or less. Military discipline and army tradition will prevail in the land, and neither of these countenance rioting, whether racial or of another variety.

Thus, the *Times* entered another awesomely bad prediction into its growing register of dismal prognostications regarding Nazi Germany.

By this point, it is impossible to say which of the *Times*'s reports and hopeful predictions about the Nazis was the most disturbing. What can be said is that already by 1935, a clear pattern had emerged in the *New York Times*'s reporting on Nazi Germany. While reports from the 1920s might have taken a "split-the-difference" approach to Hitler, by the 1930s, the *Times* was struggling to ignore fifteen years of undisguised Nazi racism, jingoism, anti-Semitism, and predatory violence in order to maintain a delusion that maybe the Nazis were not so bad after all.

The final paragraph of Birchall's front-page story on the riots and the upcoming Olympics reveal the extent to which this trend had taken hold at the paper. Fifteen years of experience had revealed a violent, mythology-crazed Nazi regime. But even if it was not enough for Birchall to predict that the 1935 summer riots were the start of more systematic racist violence, the recent spate of violent events organized or supported by the Nazis should at least have prevented him from making a positive prediction about the regime's intentions. But not so. In fact, Birchall was so confident that the Nazis and their tyrant were more good than bad that he felt it appropriate to rationalize the anti-Jewish riots, saying, "This, perhaps, was the last chance for racial intolerance to raise its head and indulge its peculiar characteristics." Incredibly, he went even further, justifying the riots for political reasons. "And it may have been considered politic to permit the indulgence. There is something to this theory."

But the *New York Times*'s post-Olympics reporting made Birchall's Nazi-sympathizing article seem like hard-hitting anti-Nazi journalism. In no uncertain terms, the *New York Times* celebrated the Berlin Games—*after* the world had witnessed the despicable displays of racism at the Nazi Olympics and the brazen Fascist spectacle the regime orchestrated. The *Times* published a roundup article of the Berlin Games in December 1936. The headline of the 1,100-word article was a shocking claim about the Games: "Greatest Athletic Show in History," it blared. The article's subtitle hailed, of all things, the *diversity* of the games, with the headline: "They Came from Widely Scattered Lands to Win Glory in the Olympic Games at Berlin."[19]

The first sentence of the *Times*'s post-Olympics article said it all: "Perfect in setting, brilliant in presentation and unparalleled in performance, the Olympic Games of 1936 stand apart in history as the greatest sports event of all time."

"The greatest sports event of all times" is quite a claim to make. But the rest of the *Times* article went on to celebrate the Berlin Games in even more triumphant terms. In the entire article, the word "Nazi" did not appear. And needless to say, neither the writer nor the *New York Times* editors who approved the story felt it necessary to discuss—or even mention—the disqualification of Jewish athlete Gretel Bergmann for being "non-Aryan." Even the article's account of the flag-lined boulevards of Berlin failed to note that the single most prevalent flag was the one that bore the greatest symbol of human hatred in history—the swastika. To be fair, the writer did note that non-German audience members grew tired of hearing German fans shout the word "Deutschland." But that was his only complaint.

◆ ◆ ◆

It is not difficult to imagine Nazi leadership aglow at the propaganda opportunity an international sporting event would provide the party. Top Nazi officials envisioned a parade, in front of international eyes, of Germany's newly regained greatness in the form of clean boulevards bedecked with swastikas, stadiums full of enthusiastic German fans, and, of course, a grand display of Aryan racial superiority in the form of German athleticism. The Nazis got what they wanted, and then some. Germany won more medals than any other country at the Games. It enjoyed an influx of tourists and visitors from dozens of countries, in many cases ones against which it was already waging secret wars. Most importantly, the regime successfully controlled its own image, ordering German news outlets to avoid the race issue, such as the participation of what it called "Negro" athletes.

By this point, Germany's race policies were widely known. Even the disqualification of German high jumper, Gretel Bergmann, because she was Jewish, was no longer a secret. However, already on their political and military rise, which was achieved to a great extent by the power of propaganda, the Nazi leadership felt that it could not only do some public relations damage control when it came to the blight of its racial policies in the eyes of the West but that it could go further, transforming the Olympics, a symbol of human brotherly love and tolerance, into an international Nazi celebration. To this end, the German Ministry for Propaganda would have no problem controlling the German media. Through the Reich Press Chamber, it issued statements to news outlets to make sure the propaganda effort would be well coordinated: "Press coverage should not mention that there are two non-Aryans among the women: Helene Mayer (fencing) and Gretel Bergmann (high jump and all-around track-and-field competition)."[20]

In fact, by the time the Games came around, this propaganda directive was irrelevant, since the "offending" German athletes had been disqualified in any case. There was only one question confronting Nazi leaders: How would the international media portray the games—as the Nazi commandeering of an international tradition, as it was, or as a celebration of a rebuilt, beaming Germany, as Hitler wanted?

At this critical juncture just two years before the Nazi burning and looting of German Jewish stores and synagogues on Kristallnacht, three years before the German invasion of Poland and four years before the Nazi invasion of France, American public opinion of the Third Reich was more critical than ever. The American public was still unsure of what Nazi Germany intended to do and so waited for more information and a better understanding before it would call for action. Hitler understood this as well as Churchill and Roosevelt did. The German dictator knew that enough European nations would sell their allies down the river for him (which they did), but the United States was a different case. This was the reason why the Nazi leadership made such a concerted effort to conceal racist Nazi policies at the Olympics, especially concerning the participation of black athletes. (Contrary to the famous but apocryphal story that Hitler snubbed the star American runner Jesse Owens because he was black, no such event ever occurred.[21] Hitler was far too politically savvy to snub a black American athlete in the spotlight of the Games, since such an act would call global attention to Nazi Germany's racist policies. When the IOC presented him the choice of congratulating all winning athletes, including black athletes, or none, Hitler, under the guise of a pre-scheduled appointment, chose none.)

Directive after directive was issued by the Nazis to German press outlets emphasizing that in their coverage of the Games, no one should even mention race—especially the participation of black athletes in the Games. With the cooperation of German press outlets guaranteed—the Ministry for Propaganda's warning that German press outlets published stories about race "at their own risk" was insurance enough—Hitler and his propaganda chiefs had only to make sure that international (especially American) news outlets reported the Olympics the way the Nazis were presenting them: as a great international show of Germany's brotherly spirit, organizational capabilities, and athletic prowess.

The *New York Times*'s post-Olympics reporting was in lockstep with Nazi propaganda efforts, even if the paper's motives were not the same as the Reich's. While Birchall and reporters of the December article were praising the cleanliness of Berlin's streets, the hospitality of its citizens, and the air of tolerance and acceptance of the Games, the Jews of Germany were already lost in a downward spiral of persecution. Less than a year before the Games, Germany passed the Nuremberg Laws of 1935, which stripped Jews of their German citizenship and forbade marriage and sex between Jews and Aryans. The Nuremberg Laws had been preceded by the laws of 1933 and 1934 that locked Jews out of nearly every profession (including civil office, journalism, radio, farming, teaching, and stock trading) and by rounds of Nazi terror. But somehow, less than a year later, this had all been wished away by the *New York Times*, which reported on the Games as if Nazi Germany were nothing more or less than a model of a civilized European nation.

It's tempting to excuse this kind of distortion with the notion that the *New York Times* reporters who covered events in Nazi Germany did not have the benefit of hindsight, as we have today. But this explanation doesn't hold up to scrutiny when we consider the reporters at the time who reported the story very differently. Among these journalists was the prominent American reporter William Shirer, who went on to write some of the most widely read histories of the war in Germany. When it came to the Berlin Olympics, Shirer's reporting on the Games and their use as official propaganda shows just how skewed the *Times*'s reporting on the event had been. In a morbid and despairing tone, Shirer described what the Nazis had managed to accomplish in the summer of 1936:

> I'm afraid the Nazis have succeeded with their propaganda. First, the Nazis have run the Games on a lavish scale never before experienced, and this has appealed to the athletes. Second, the Nazis have put up a very good front for the general visitors, especially the big businessmen."[22]

The *Washington Post*, considered one of the *Times*'s main competitors, ran an editorial on the day of the opening ceremonies of the Berlin Olympics. Like William Shirer, the *Post* took a drastically different stance to the *New York Times*'s breathless praise of the Games, noting the violence in Germany instead of forgetting it and asking serious questions about what the Berlin Games meant for the tradition of the Olympics:

> Today the tyrant's tread is heard again in many parts of the world. Runners bearing the Olympic torch from Athens to Berlin were abused in Vienna… Hate and fear are known to be blowing hard on the Olympic flame in Berlin. Will there be any essence of fair play and sportsmanship left to illuminate the twelfth Olympics in Tokyo?[23]

The *New York Times* ran dozens of articles on the Berlin Olympics, and there were several pieces that also raised questions about the Games. But, while William Shirer, in his reporting, moved from considering the Berlin Games skeptically before they took place to lamenting the Nazi propaganda success in their wake, the *New York Times* went from raising hopeful questions in the lead-up to the games to giddily celebrating the Berlin Olympics in their aftermath.

Frederick Birchall wrote his own post-Olympics report in the *Times*, one that presented a version of the Nazi Olympics which could not have been more opposed to the one William Shirer offered. In a sprawling August 16 article entitled, "Visitors to Olympics Carrying Away Highly Favorable Impression," Birchall wrote glowingly about three main things: first, that Berlin was extremely clean; second, that the Games had been conducted smoothly; and third, that the German citizens made great hosts to their international guests. Birchall trumpeted the success of the Berlin Games at one point by declaring that "the great body of German people has cordially endorsed and carried out in spirit and letter this notion of national hospitality to strangers." This statement might have been true had Birchall added the phrase "except to Jews" to the end of the sentence—but he did not. That same day, the *Times* ran an editorial about the games written by Birchall, whose praise for the Berlin Games was unrestrained. He had only one concern about the Nazi displays during the summer of 1936: the German youth, according to the *New York Times* reporter, was being subjected to too much regimentation, making it absolutely essential that the Germans figure out "...how to limber it up and emancipate it from the goose-stepping tradition, which is obviously not suited to the development of speed and agility."

Rigid goose-stepping aside, Birchall wrote on the editorial page of the *New York Times* that foreigners who attended the Berlin Games would take home one overriding impression: "It is that this is a happy nation and prosperous almost beyond belief; that Hitler is one of the greatest, if not the greatest, political leaders in the world today, and that Germans are a much maligned, hospitable, wholly peaceful people who deserve the best the world can give them." This was not just the impression foreigners took away (at least according to the *New York Times*), but it was Birchall's own personal impression. He wrote in the subsequent paragraph that with all "political controversy side-tracked, all prejudice and all militarism put aside and forgotten, it is true."

The only thing really forgotten, or ignored, was the Nazi policies and actions: that they had forbidden one particular race from participating in the Games; that Hitler had not snubbed Jesse Owens by refusing to shake his hand but had made himself absent in order to avoid shaking the hand of any black athlete; that the shiny clean streets of Berlin were lined with swastika flags, and, more frightening than all of this, that for the past decade, Hitler had been overseeing an openly violent and racist policy, had ordered political assassinations, and conducted an illegal rearmament. The *New York Times* published Birchall's sympathetic editorializing as news articles and, maybe more egregiously, as opinion pieces. For Birchall and the *Times,* Hitler was one of the "greatest, if not the greatest, political leaders in the world," and the Nazi monster, which truly great leaders like Churchill and Roosevelt were watching with dread, was nothing more than a harmless figment of the world's collective imagination.

The 1936 Berlin Olympics were a Nazi triumph in the literal sense of the word—not because of the vast organization and building projects, the German athletes, or the positive experiences among attendees. The Olympics were a success for the Third Reich because those who should have been the first to condemn them—and in only the harshest terms of moral repugnance—were the first to celebrate them. The high praise sung by the *New York Times* rang in the ears of Americans, deepening their ambivalence, allowing the Nazi monster to lurch another inch forward toward its attempt at world conquest and genocide. The next Nazi victory was not long in coming, and tragically, the *New York Times* was there to once again usher it into the American political landscape.

◆ ◆ ◆

The years-long Nazi strategy of talking peace while acting war makes it surprising (to say the least) that the *New York Times* could continue to report on the Nazi propagandist bids for peace as if they were earnest efforts at diplomacy. But the *Times* did continue to do so, even following the disastrous Munich Conference, where Britain's Neville Chamberlain capitulated to Hitler, selling an ally to its enemy for the price of a non-existent peace.

For the *New York Times*, however, the 1938 Munich Agreement meant certain peace, and this is how the paper reported the appeasement of Hitler to its readers in the United States. After the Conference was announced, the *Times*'s Berlin bureau chief, a reporter named Guido Enderis, wrote a front-page story about the next day's "peace" conference under the headline "Berlin Is Relieved," as if the Nazi regime—which by that point had already unilaterally annexed Austria, flouted the most important treaty of the twentieth century, and demanded the territory (and, implicitly, the destruction) of its neighbor, Czechoslovakia—were desperate for peace and peace alone.[24]

The language of Enderis's front-page story helped set the tone of the Conference for the American public. In the first paragraph of the crucial article, the *Times*'s Berlin chief gushed that the announcement of the "four-power conference" had "burst in upon the stagnant political atmosphere like a freshening breeze." Enderis went on in the third paragraph to note that, "only a frank, intimate exchange across a conference table gave promise of breaking the deadlock" that had taken hold between Germany and the Allies. Though he made the bold, and odd, claim that the unfolding of the Nazi diplomatic strategies for war amounted to a "frank, intimate exchange," Enderis did not cite a single source for this viewpoint of the talks but only qualified the outrageous claim with the empty but journalistically convenient phrase "it was recognized that..."

"Chancellor Adolf Hitler," Enderis went on, still without identifying any source for the claim, "was reported determined not only to react to Mr. Chamberlain's appeal [for talks] but to expand the British Prime Minister's suggestion by making further conversations a four-power affair." Hitler, according to Enderis and the unnamed reports that he used as sources, not only cooperated with the peace-loving Neville Chamberlain but, *Times* readers were informed, the Führer had actually one-upped Chamberlain's peace proposal with the suggestion of a multilateral conference.

Enderis was definitely not the first journalist to make use of the passive voice ("recognized by" or "Hitler was reported determined") to pass off a personal viewpoint as an objective fact. Unfortunately, his use of dubious and possibly non-existent sources in his stories about Hitler and the lead-up to war was one of the most destructive instances of this kind of abuse in modern journalism. Enderis had used, and would continue to use, this kind of language on many occasions to treat Hitler and the Nazi regime very carefully in pivotal *Times* articles. In the case of Munich, one of Enderis's unnamed sources for the claim that Hitler was "determined" to not just cooperate but go further than Chamberlain in his peace attempts was almost certainly an official Nazi news outlet, as the view that Hitler staunchly desired peace but was resolute when it came to Germany's "rights" was exactly the one the Nazi propaganda machine was delivering. Enderis's moral cloudiness on the Munich Conference seems even more suspicious when the reports from reliable American reporters are considered. Once again, William Shirer's reporting provides an important ethical compass.

William Shirer was one of the most respected names in American journalism at that time. He started out with radio reports and news bulletins from Europe but quickly found himself on the fast track, as he was handpicked by Edward R. Murrow to be one of CBS's "Murrow's Boys." Shirer had made his way to Europe working as a hay-pitcher on a cattle boat in the mid-1920s. He arrived in Paris, began studying and covering the news, and was eventually hired in 1934 by the Universal News Service to report from Berlin, and then by Murrow, for whom he reported from Vienna and Germany. Shirer later went on to write a personal experience of the war, *Berlin Diary*, and one of the war's most widely read histories, *The Rise and Fall of the Third Reich*.

It was in *Berlin Diary* that Shirer offered a colorful, playful and honest description of some of the important foreign correspondents covering Europe in the lead-up to the war. When it came to the *Times*'s Guido Enderis, Shirer portrayed the *Times* Berlin chief as a dandified writer wearing a loud red tie who was noted for his tendency of "minding the Nazis less than most…"

Tellingly, Shirer's broadcast on the days before Munich presented an entirely different picture from the mix of fact and fiction being peddled by Enderis on the pages of the Gray Lady. On September 26, from the lengthening shadow of the Munich Conference only two days away, Shirer broadcast the following report:

> Well, at least on this fateful evening for Europe, we know where we stand. Most of you, I take it, heard Chancellor Adolf Hitler's speech five hours ago at the Berlin Sport Palace. If you did, you heard him say in a tone, and in words which left no doubt whatever, that he will not budge an inch from his position and that President Benes [of Czechoslovakia] must hand over to him Sudetenland by Saturday night, or take the consequences. Those consequences—in this critical hour you almost hesitate to use the word—are war. It's true Herr Hitler did not use the word himself. At least amidst the fanatical yelling and cheering in the Sport Palace I did not hear it, and I sat but fifty or sixty feet from him.[25]

Shirer also wrote about the Munich Agreement in his diary. The first line of the Munich entry began with the words, "It's all over." Chamberlain, who later called the Agreement the greatest mistake of his life,[26] and other pro-Munich actors who had deluded themselves about peace with Hitler, were also clamoring that "it's all over." However, for "pro-peace" and anti-war outlets like the *New York Times*, "It's all over" meant that war had been averted, that Hitler had been satisfied and would go back to sleep with his belly full of newly acquired territory. But for Shirer, "It's all over" meant that war had begun, that the possibility for peace had been slaughtered on the conference table that Guido Enderis, in his *Times* piece on the day before Munich, exalted as the only possibility for progress.

The *New York Times*'s coverage of the rest of Munich clearly took the Enderis path (even in reports not credited to Enderis) and never so much as stopped to consider the view that William Shirer and the "Murrow's Boys" were broadcasting from many of the same European locations as *Times* correspondents. The first line of the *New*

York Times's post-Munich article[27] proudly announced that "The war for which Europe had been feverishly preparing was averted early this morning when the leading statesmen of Britain, France, Germany and Italy, meeting in Munich, reached an agreement..." The *Times* had advanced an ideology when it ran the story that heralded, in a news report, no less, that talks with Adolf Hitler were a "freshening breeze." It fulfilled this prophecy in this front-page story, which ran only a day after the agreement was signed, with another starry-eyed prediction after the signing of the Munich Agreement by declaring (again in a news report) without the benefit of waiting even a week to measure the actual outcome that war had indeed been "averted." While William Shirer understood Munich to be the tragic end of peace, and Hitler saw it as the brilliant first triumph of war, the *New York Times* was still reporting the unqualified success of Europe's disastrous policy of appeasement. War had been "averted," the *Times* informed Americans. The "frank, intimate exchange" across a conference table had worked.

◆ ◆ ◆

Not many people know the name Guido Enderis. Unlike Turner Catledge, Gay Talese, or even Enderis's colleague Otto Tolischus, who have been the subjects of biographies, articles, and lengthy obituaries, Enderis seems to have slipped through the fingers of history. For the armies of reporters who covered a corporate beat or the metro section or minor league baseball, this is an understandable fate. For the chief Berlin correspondent of the *New York Times* during the most important war in modern history, it is almost impossible to understand—almost, that is, as if history wanted his fate to remain nameless.

It is easy to find reasons for this. Enderis's articles about Germany, the Nazis, and the Second World War go beyond some journalists' professional philosophy that reporting means providing facts, not morals. This kind of facts-only approach to American journalism continued well into the Vietnam War, during which American reporters avoided using terms like "massacre" and "genocide" for fear of crossing the fine line between reporting facts and making ethical judgments. But Enderis's articles, stuffed as they were with flowery, awkward expressions (the "freshening breeze" of above) and suggestive metaphors (the ill-fated "conference table" and its "frank, intimate exchange"), cannot be passed off as the product of a reporter who was too fastidious, too "gray," in *Times* terms, to make moral or ethical judgments. But even if this had been the case, and Guido Enderis was simply too literal about maintaining his standards as a journalist and too lacking in vision to see what was in front of him, the outcome was still a disaster. More importantly, it was a disaster that the *New York Times* as an institution did nothing to mitigate, correct, or even apologize for.

The truly strange thing is that it is not just hindsight that casts Guido Enderis in a troubling light. After everything that happened, after all the Nazi brutality, the Olympics propaganda, the eventual disaster of Munich, and the Gleiwitz Incident, Guido Enderis was still writing and assigning articles that were sympathetic, if not outright supportive, of the Nazi regime. It got so bad that, according to Laurel Leff's *Buried by The Times*,[28] members of the *New York Times*'s own staff started to protest *Times* reporting coming out of Germany. A city-desk reporter at the *Times* named Warren Irvin, who later became a part-time correspondent in Geneva, found Enderis's articles on Nazi Germany too much to handle. Irvin was so outraged by the articles that he did something the autocratically run *Times* considered almost blasphemous: Irvin wrote a letter to the *Times*'s then-publisher, and patriarch of the Ochs-Sulzberger family that owns the paper, Arthur Sulzberger. In the letter, Irvin asked the *Times* publisher a simple but daring question about Guido Enderis: "Don't you think it's time that the *New York Times* did something about it's [sic] Nazi correspondent in Berlin?"[29] Irvin went on in the letter to accuse Enderis of a "loud-mouthed defense of Nazism," which he found so damaging and offensive that he threatened to go public with the information. "I don't want to do anything to hurt my own paper; but I feel my loyalty to my country comes first, and if some action is not taken I shall feel compelled to publish these facts," Irvin wrote to Sulzberger. According to Leff,

Irvin later said the reason he was compelled to write the letter in the first place was that, listening to official Nazi broadcasts as part of his job reporting for the BBC, he continually heard Nazi news announcers citing *New York Times* articles by Enderis in their reports.

Sulzberger wrote back after receiving advice from another employee who told him that firing Enderis was not an option, since that would effectively shut down the *Times*'s Berlin operation. Instead, the publisher issued a strong response to Irvin, including a suggestion that if Irvin were to go public with his Nazi allegations about Enderis he might be slapped with a libel suit. Irvin wrote back saying that "Enderis has made no secret of his pro-Nazi sympathies." He went on: "I don't question the usefulness and value of Mr. Enderis to the *New York Times*. I *do* question the right of the greatest American newspaper to maintain a pro-Nazi as its chief correspondent in Berlin in times like these."[30]

Enderis had been running the Berlin bureau for the *New York Times* since 1929. For ten years, from the time of his appointment as head of Berlin reporting to the day of the Gleiwitz incident, he reported in a way that must have left Nazi propaganda minister Joseph Goebbels bewildered, but at the end of the day, extremely happy that an American newsman's reporting on the Third Reich could be so incredibly and volubly sympathetic.

Enderis's first big story on Hitler's rise was (or, at least, should have been) an embarrassment to the *Times*, as the report revealed the *Times*'s Berlin chief's tendency to make ridiculously bad predictions about the Nazi regime. The story ran on January 31, 1933, the day after Hitler became Chancellor of Germany. Enderis wrote a front-page *Times* article that began, "Adolf Hitler, leader of the National Socialist party, today was appointed Chancellor of Germany."[31] Enderis quickly moved to assure *Times* readers, who had been familiar with Hitler's name since the paper's numerous 1920s articles about a violent, Jew-hating fanatic, that this wasn't something to worry about. "The composition of the Cabinet," Enderis wrote, "leaves Herr Hitler no scope for gratification of any dictatorial ambition." Once again, the *Times* was reassuring its readers that, despite all evidence to the contrary,

Hitler was nothing to be concerned about. And, once again, a *Times* article about the world's most ruthless and destructive dictator was closer to wishful thinking in ink than honest or objective journalism.

For ten years, the *Times*'s Berlin bureau under Enderis took the soft tack on the Nazi regime, whitewashing its crimes and downplaying its dangerousness, all the while leading the American public, hungry for information about the new Germany, down a deadly path. That path ended in calamity. Germany declared war on the United States on December 11, 1941. As part of the Nazi war, all American journalists in Germany were rounded up and escorted by Nazi guards to a Berlin train station, where they were put on a train without being told their destination. They learned on the train that they were being placed under "house arrest" in a chateau in Bad Nauheim. There, the Americans lived under SS guard in a hotel that had been shut down. In the middle of the German winter, and with the hotel staff gone, heating pipes burst and food deliveries stopped. The interned American reporters lived in bone-chilling cold with little in the way of food, exercise, or personal freedom.[32] It was a prison in all but name.

The American journalists banded together and made the best of it, putting on plays, conducting group exercise in the small outdoor space the SS officers allowed them, and even starting an ad-hoc university where courses on topics like constitutional governance were taught and makeshift diplomas given to the "graduates."[33] It was a difficult time for the American reporters, though it could have been much worse. However, among all the American journalists who were arrested and interned at the freezing chateau, one was conspicuously absent. It wouldn't have taken long for the American journalists at Bad Nauheim to notice that the bureau chief of their country's largest and most influential newspaper was nowhere to be seen. Where was Guido Enderis?

Readers of the *New York Times* were fed a simple explanation for Enderis's absence among the interned American reporters at Bad Nauheim. In a December 15, 1941 article about the internment of the American reporters, the *Times* noted that the journalists and some US embassy staff had been taken to Bad Nauheim but that Enderis was ill with bronchial problems and "has been allowed to remain under doctor's treatment at his hotel, the Adlon."[34] But there was another explanation for Enderis's absence, one that the *New York Times* would under no circumstances have printed in its pages. Nazi Foreign Office Undersecretary Ernst Woermann was the German official responsible for overseeing the roundup and internment of the Americans in December 1941. Woermann issued an official Nazi memorandum declaring that the Americans were to be rounded up as a "reprisal" for actions taken against Nazi agents in the United States by the American government. However, Woermann noted, one American was to be left out of the roundup: Guido Enderis. Why? The Nazi undersecretary wrote in his official memorandum that the *New York Times* Berlin chief was to be left alone "because of his proved friendliness to Germany."[35]

◆ ◆ ◆

By the time Hitler and high-ranking Nazi party members decided in September 1939 to launch their propaganda mission to fake a Polish attack on German soil (Operation Himmler), the world had already witnessed an enormous amount of propaganda and ruthless violence perpetrated by the Nazi regime. The land grab at Munich, the racist Olympics, and even Kristallnacht, or "Night of the Broken Glass," when Germans burned Jewish stores and synagogues under the watchful, satisfied eye of the Nazi government, had already taken place.

From the Berlin Olympics, to the Munich Conference, to the events that took place on the eve of war, the *New York Times* failed its readers. Worse still, the very reasonable doubt about the integrity of its chief Berlin correspondent raises some very serious questions about why Enderis was not only selected to be the head of one of the most important *Times* bureaus but why he was kept on after ten years of reporting Nazi propaganda as objective fact. No matter what these questions or their answers may be, it is painfully clear—this time *with* the glaring clarity of hindsight—that just when the country and the world most needed the triumph of truth from America's flagship newspaper, the Gray Lady provided nothing more than a deadly string of devastating failure.

2

Broken Eggs:
"They're Only Russians"

"**B**ut—to put it brutally—you can't make an omelette without break- ing eggs…" These were the words that Walter Duranty, the *New York Times*'s correspondent in Russia during the early Soviet years, used to explain away the devastating Ukrainian famine of the 1930s perpetrated by Russia's communist government[1]. The famine was not a moderate temporary food shortage. It was not people substituting black bread for white bread, or eating grain instead of meat. It was a mass murder of starvation, in part a product of the new Soviet socialist system and its drive for collectivization, and in part a deliberate genocide.

In reality, the "broken eggs" that would supposedly make some kind of socialist omelet were the deaths of millions of people—mostly peasants. The more conservative estimates of Robert Conquest in his book on the famine, *The Harvest of Sorrow*, set the death toll of the Ukrainian famine at four million people. Other estimates place this number at six million, seven million, and even ten million deaths from starvation.[2] As many people as live in Los Angeles or Dallas were wiped out in two years. The primary target of the disastrous economic action and subsequent famine was a group of Russian peasants called *kulaks,* who had managed to create modest wealth for themselves through agriculture.[3] Their financially elevated status made them reviled by Russia's new socialist revolutionary elite, including the leader of the revolution, Vladimir Ilyich Lenin, who ignited this view by distinguishing between different classes of workers—agrarian and industrial, poor, middle-income, and so-called "wealthy" *kulaks*. The aim of this categorization was to identify all of the existing strata of working people in Russia so the differences could be obliterated and made into one larger class of "toiler." This toiler class would eventually become the platform for the creation of the "dictatorship of the proletariat." Even Lenin, the so-called idealist of Russia's socialist revolution, demanded that the *kulaks* should be "crushed" so that the lower peasantry could rise up and join the middle peasants in order to continue, strengthen, and, of course, spread the perpetual global revolution of communism that Lenin and his followers envisioned.

The Soviet revolution itself laid the groundwork for the famine. Early revolutionary violence and the ensuing civil war had caused a massive disruption in agricultural output.[4] After seizing power, the communists refused to allow even basic free market tendencies, such as variable prices and international trade of grain and other foodstuffs, a mistake that plunged the country into shortage. Already by the late 1920s (just a few years after the first major famine under communist rule), many feared the cities and the army would not have enough food. By the time Stalin came to power in 1924, the situation was dire. But it was the new Soviet dictator's economic ignorance combined with his barbaric hatred for the *kulaks* that set the famine in motion. Stalin began putting his disastrous plans into place in 1928 with the forced collectivization of group farms, called *kolkhozes*. As part of this second revolution in agriculture, Stalin intended to annihilate the *kulaks* as a class for reasons of Soviet revolutionary theory and on account of the more practical motivation—taking the entire *kulak* agricultural output, instead of allowing the *kulaks* to carry on their practice of holding onto or selling their agricultural surpluses on the open market.

Stalin, with characteristic brutality, planned to incite the poor villagers of the *kolkhozes* against the somewhat wealthier *kulaks*. But the peasants of the *kolkhozes* were more interested in struggling for a living than fighting for a theoretic concept of class. So Stalin resorted, as he would in every step of governance, to pure force and violence by killing, terrorizing, and exiling millions of *kulaks* to achieve his goal.

The loss of the *kulaks'* agricultural contribution was not the only result of this sinister policy. The *kolkhoz* workers, having recently lost their collective farms—the one thing that they could call their own—became despondent. A backlash ensued, and the *kolkhoz* peasants refused to till the land and even began slaughtering livestock in protest. In four years, starting in 1929, the number of horses in Russia was halved, making agriculture even more difficult. In addition to the slaughter of horses and the mass neglect of fertile fields, more than "30 million heads of cattle and 100 million sheep and goats were slaughtered," triggering more hardship for the peasant farmers and hurling the country deeper and deeper into distress.[5] Russia was plunged into dire shortages and, not long after, devastating famine. Sadly, the richly soiled lands of the Ukraine were among the hardest hit by the disaster. It was then that people began starving to death.

Nevertheless, Walter Duranty, who was the *New York Times*'s leading correspondent in Russia at the time, saw nothing particularly amiss. In his "breaking eggs" *Times* article of March 31, 1933,[6] Duranty flatly denied that there was a famine at all. "In short, conditions are definitely bad in certain sections—the Ukraine, North Caucasus and Lower Volga," he wrote. "The rest of the country is on short rations but nothing worse. These conditions are bad but there is no famine."

Duranty did not stop there. He went on in his article to attempt to discredit the statements of a Western journalist, British reporter Gareth Jones, who got the story of the famine painfully right.[7] Duranty told *New York Times* readers that he had initially believed Jones's account that there was "virtually no bread" in many villages but that Jones had not seen dead animals or people. However, Duranty claimed that after speaking with Jones, he went out and "made exhaustive inquiries about this alleged famine situation."[8] By his own account, Duranty's exhaustive inquiries amounted to speaking with official commissariats (the Soviet equivalent of a ministry of state), chatting with foreign embassies, gathering information from "Britons working as specialists" and "personal connections." While the information of the correspondent who had advanced the opposing view (that a famine actually was occurring) was firsthand, all of Duranty's information was secondhand.

Had the *New York Times*'s correspondent in Russia traveled to regions where the famine was, in his version of events, "allegedly" occurring, he would have seen for himself the march of death, disease, and starvation ravaging the countryside of Russia and the Ukraine. The pre-Soviet Russian general, Mikahil Alekseev, wrote in his novel *Bread is a Noun* that "After the *kulak* the middle peasant left the village, but voluntarily. In accordance with one order or another, all the grain and all the fodder were taken away. Horses began to die en masse, and in 1933 there was a terrible famine. Whole families died, houses fell apart, village streets grew empty, more and more windows became blind—sightless—those who went to the city boarded them up."[9]

In the historical novel, *Death*, Russian writer Vladimir Tendriakov (who was born in western Russia in 1923), wrote:

> Cattle died for lack of fodder, people ate bread made from nettles, biscuits made from one weed, porridge made from another... A year of hunger moved through the country, nineteen hundred and thirty-three. In Vokhrovo, the *raion* [administrative district] capital, in the little park by the station, dekulakized peasants expelled from the Ukraine lay down and died. You got used to seeing corpses there in the morning; a wagon would pull up and the hospital stable hand, Abram, would pile in the bodies. Not all died; many wandered through the dusty mean little streets, dragging bloodless blue legs, swollen from dropsy, feeling out each passer-by with doglike begging eyes..."[10]

Walter Duranty is still today widely associated with journalistic malfeasance on account of his attempt to cover up the Ukrainian famine. But the famine story, egregious as it is, is a symptom of a deeper cause. The 300-pound gorilla of a question that has gone unasked concerning Duranty is why he would cover up a famine so severe that it would have been obvious to even a casual observer, let alone a trained journalist. Why did he go to such lengths to deny that a famine was taking place?

◆ ◆ ◆

Just as Guido Enderis used Nazi news sources to report (or misreport) the onset of the Second World War, Walter Duranty relied on extremely dubious, vague, and unnamed sources ("Britons who are specialists and personal contacts") to report on one of the most consequential international stories of that decade. Ironically, right at the time when Guido Enderis was sending out reports about the rosy nature of the Third Reich and its peaceful intentions, Walter Duranty gave a lecture in New York in June 1934 about the dangers of Japan and Germany. The *New York Times* covered its Russia correspondent's lecture, entitled "Russia Since the Revolution," in a June 7 article that ran under the headline, "Duranty Predicts a Major War Soon."[11] The article reported on Duranty's lecture, saying the *Times* journalist "considered Germany and Japan 'the two most dangerous nations in the world.'" Duranty was perceptive enough to note that, "'If you will examine their imports—nickel, nitrate and other things used in munitions—you will see what I mean…I can't see how an explosion can be long postponed." It seems that America, or at least the *New York Times* and its readers, would have been better off if Walter Duranty and Guido Enderis had switched places. Nevertheless, though Walter Duranty managed to get a whiff of the German truth that Enderis adamantly ignored, Duranty's willful ignorance and repeated distortions make it doubtful that he would (or could) have reported honestly and accurately on any story, incident, or event.

The reason the *New York Times* devoted an entire article to a speech given by one of its regular correspondents is that Walter Duranty wasn't just a regular correspondent. He was a journalistic superstar, among the most famous reporters in America and possibly the world. Duranty could not have achieved this fame without the huge platform that the *Times* provided him, which not only legitimized his opinions but projected his voice onto an international stage. This is exactly why Duranty's reporting, like that of Guido Enderis, wasn't just "slovenly" (as the *Times* would later try to pass off the debacle of its famine reporting),[12] bad, or faulty—it was deadly.

The *New York Times* made another journalistically unusual move when it wrote a news report about one of its own correspondents meeting a state politician. That reporter was, of course, Walter Duranty. And the politician was New York Governor Franklin Delano Roosevelt. What made the meeting newsworthy, and what gives it historical value, was the fact that on that day, July 25, 1932, Roosevelt was just a little more than three months away from being elected president of the United States, and less than a decade away from being at the helm of the world's most powerful country during its most terrible war.

At stake in the meeting was the profoundly important question of whether the US should formally recognize the Soviet Union as the legitimate government of Russia. The Soviets had taken over Russia in a violent coup, without any democratic process or other formal transfer of sovereignty. Furthermore, the Soviets openly considered the capitalist system on which America was built to be the ultimate enemy and target of their ongoing global socialist revolution. A decision by the US to recognize the new regime would amount to the legitimization of not just the Soviets' ascendancy to power but of its ideological aims as a governing regime. Given this—and the Cold War that would persist for five decades, permanently re-shaping geopolitics at the price of the loss of liberty by as many as 300 million people who ended up living under Soviet rule[13]—it's difficult to think of a more consequential question for U.S. foreign policy at that time, or any time since.

It's not clear whether Roosevelt met with Duranty because he really wanted the journalist's advice on United States Soviet policy or if he was simply strengthening his pre-election foreign policy image. But Duranty's meeting with Roosevelt was positioned by the *Times* itself as being part of a campaign to convince the future president to take a more "friendly" approach to the communist government. The first sentence of the *Times* article about the event immediately put the meeting in context: "The value of a more friendly attitude toward Russia as an aid to international trade revival and to provide the United States with an extra weapon in international political negotiations is being suggested to Governor Roosevelt by a group of advisers, it was said today."

In this one sentence, the *Times* article (whose byline read only "From a Staff Correspondent") offered two major supposed benefits of "more friendly" relations with Russia and attributed this unproven view to a group of advisers. In the article's fifth paragraph, these advisers appeared again, this time to suggest that "the United States could profit by adopting an attitude different from that taken by the Republican [presidential] administrations of the last decade."

The problem was that the "advisers" who kept showing up in the piece remained unnamed. Only one adviser was actually identified in the entirety of the piece regarding the potential shift in United States relations with Soviet Russia—and that was Walter Duranty. This was an important fact, as the *Times* article itself made clear. While Duranty's meeting with Roosevelt was one in a "long chain of similar conferences," it was the meeting with Duranty, the article claimed, that "served to bring to the fore the report that the Governor is contemplating, in the event of his being elected President, a new policy toward the Soviet." According to the *Times*, Duranty, who had been awarded a Pulitzer Prize for his Russia reporting just two months beforehand, had been brought in to make the case for a pro-Soviet shift in American–Russian relations.

Regardless of the immediate outcome of the policy meeting, Roosevelt's invitation is a good reflection of Duranty's stature at the time. The sole reason for the invitation was Duranty's role in reporting on Russia for the *New York Times*, the newspaper where he had spent his entire career. A globetrotting, one-legged British writer known among journalists for his sexual philandering, openness to drugs, and the depth of his education (he could fluidly translate Latin, Greek, French and Russian, to name a few), Duranty had started out reporting from Paris during the First World War. But already by his first big story, which covered a zeppelin raid on Paris towards the end of the war, Duranty had departed from journalistic norms and began his trademark use of the first person, his sandwiching of facts between personal commentary, and his insertion of journalistic

jokes and ironic quips into his *New York Times* news reports. [14] He wrote
in his report on the zeppelin raid:

> At 7 o'clock last night I saw [British Secretary of State for War] Lloyd
> George and [Secretary of State for the Colonies] Bonar Law with a part
> of English officials enter the Hotel Crillon, and my companion remarked:
> "The zeppelins would have a good bag if they could drop a bomb on the
> hotel now." He spoke laughingly, but I remembered the raid on Epernay
> a few days ago. The night was fine and the German espionage service
> vigilant…Three hours later I was sitting in a boulevard café, when suddenly
> without the flourish of trumpets or the rushing of automobiles of a year
> ago almost to the day, the police and firemen began extinguishing lamps
> and the whisper was passed, "Zeppelins signaled approaching the city."

This was Gonzo Journalism fifty years before the world ever heard the
name Hunter Thompson.

From the time of his initial reporting, it would take the *Times* just five
years to hand Walter Duranty one of the top news department positions
at the paper—Russia correspondent.

Walter Duranty is now largely considered a media outlier or an anomaly, a reporter whose character flaws slipped through the editorial cracks
of his institution. But the reality is that Duranty fits a prominent pattern at
the *Times* of a star reporter whose celebrity enables him or her to commit
journalistic malfeasance in plain sight of his editors. While the pattern is
not unique to the *Times*, it's at the Gray Lady that the consequences of
his phenomenon stand out most starkly—and, maybe, most frequently.
As we'll see later in this book with figures like Jayson Blair and Judith
Miller reporting on the Iraq War, or Herbert Matthews reporting from
Castro, or David Halberstam in Vietnam, the journalistic stars of these
celebrity reporters shined so bright they all but blinded their editors. In
Duranty's case, a decade's worth of reporting for the prestigious *New York
Times* had earned the correspondent enough credibility and renown for
him to be considered qualified as an "adviser" to Roosevelt. Duranty's
fame only continued to grow. In 1935, his very appropriately titled book
I Write As I Please became a bestseller. However, more prestigious than

his brief meeting with FDR, more glamorous than a bestselling book, and more of an indicator of Duranty's influence and intellectual standing on account of his reporting and the flagship newspaper that carried it, was his Pulitzer Prize award of 1932.

Duranty was awarded the Pulitzer Prize in the category of correspondence: "for his series of dispatches on Russia, especially the working out of the Five-Year Plan." This Five-Year Plan was the collectivization and economic steps taken by the Soviet leadership. The "working out" the Five-Year Plan refers to the social, political, and economic impacts—famine, forced collectivization, political murder, and mass exile—on which Duranty reported. Looking back, the Pulitzer board's statement about Duranty's reporting sounds like satire:

> Mr. Duranty's dispatches show profound and intimate comprehension of conditions in Russia and of the causes of those conditions...They are marked by scholarship, profundity, impartiality, sound judgment, and exceptional clarity and are excellent examples of the best type of foreign correspondence.[15]

Strangely, Columbia University's famous journalism prize managed to honor Walter Duranty for almost every positive journalistic quality that he flouted and every norm he flagrantly violated. The *New York Times*'s reaction to Duranty and all of his success was predictable. In 1934, the paper reviewed his book, *Duranty Reports Russia*. Needless to say, the *Times* gave the book a glowing review, never once mentioning a single criticism of the correspondent, his book, or his reporting.

◆ ◆ ◆

Most accounts of Walter Duranty and his journalistic sins focus on the man himself. There are many theories that explain why Duranty botched a story that was so big right at a time when it was so critical. Duranty has been alternately accused of being a severe opportunist, an ardent communist, a reckless adventurer, and a philanderer. In truth, he was probably a mix of all these things, some to a greater degree than others. However, the single most direct and straightforward explanation for Duranty's absolute failure in reporting on Russia is the one that is the most downplayed: that once all the excuses and psycho-biographies are swept aside, the real failure did not belong to Walter Duranty—it belonged to his newspaper, the *New York Times*.

The *Times*'s slack or nonexistent oversight of Duranty's reporting put his false, unsourced stories on the pages of the Gray Lady. But it was his Pulitzer Prize that inducted Walter Duranty into a class of *New York Times* elites which gave the correspondent a virtual free pass that got even his most egregious news articles past *Times* editors without so much as a quick glance at the vague and often non-existing sources, the bizarre editorializing (such as the one about breaking eggs to make an omelet), and the factual claims that were contradicted by other journalists of international stature who were sending home eyewitness accounts of the famine and death-ravaged swaths of Russia and the Ukraine.

The more entangled Duranty became in his own web of lies, the more the *Times* became entangled with them. And with the 1932 Pulitzer Prize, the *Times* had even more of a reason to turn a blind eye to the fraud being perpetrated by Duranty against the victims of the terrible famine and against American newspaper readers who, unbeknownst to them, were also being dragged into a cynically crafted myth about Soviet Russia, one that—as we will soon see—had enormous political repercussions which changed the course of history.

Duranty's celebrity status led the *New York Times* to print a number of unusual articles about its reporter, such as the one that quotes the Russia correspondent on the issue of war with Japan and Germany. In 1936, *Times* editors dedicated an entire article to a talk Duranty gave to foreign correspondents. The headline of the article was "Duranty Talks of Job." The article's slug read, "Tells Foreign Correspondents How They Should Work." At that talk, Duranty managed to sum up the philosophy of journalism which drove him to craft a picture of the new Russia as an emerging socialist wonderland, rather than to simply deliver facts and straightforward reporting to the readers of the *Times* and the American public at large. Duranty opined at the talk:

There are two angles to a newspaper man's reporting, sensations and facts and between the two we are constantly torn. We must keep a close relationship to our job, to life and to truth, not forgetting the public which wants sensation to make reading less dull.[16]

Duranty lived up to this personal code of journalism—at least the second half of it. While he was not just *willing* to provide "sensation" but extremely skilled at it, he was less than worried if the truth had to be sacrificed here and there, or in its entirety, in order to "make reading less dull."

By 1934, Duranty was back to reporting in a way that would have put the most enthusiastic Soviet propagandists to shame. On May 9, the *New York Times*, which had now taken to reporting on the travel plans of its star journalist, ran a story reporting that Walter Duranty had made it back to the United States.[17] The *Times* even went so far as to specify the ship and the shipping line on which Duranty had traveled (the Bremen of the North German Lloyd line). The report cut quickly to Duranty's appraisal of the situation in Russia, which, to paraphrase it into two short words, was that things were very good. Duranty told the *Times* that "The health of the people has improved and the birth rate has doubled." While the first claim was too subjective to either confirm or contradict, the second one, that the birth rate had doubled in two years, would make a demographer chuckle. But it was the rest of Duranty's assessment of the situation in Russia, as reported by the *Times*, that would be truly laughable—if it had not been so damning.

The *Times*'s Russia man told the paper that "In Moscow there is a tendency among the officials to encourage the working class to shave, wash, and brush up when they go to a theater or the opera…There are plenty of theaters, cinemas, and dancing places…but otherwise life in Moscow is very dull." All this was true—there were theaters, cinemas, and "dancing places" in Moscow. But what Duranty and the *Times* left out of the "things-are-improved" story is that almost no one could afford them. Worse, Russia was still in a period when a pound of coffee was so scarce that even high-ranking embassy officials considered a cup of joe to be a relatively rare treat.

In his memoirs, the well-known Soviet dissident A.E. Kosterin spoke of a situation in 1933 and 1934 entirely different to the rosy picture of a Russia whose main fault was that it was sometimes "very dull." Kosterin wrote that between 1933 and 1934, he traveled through south-western Russia, where he witnessed "houses with boarded-up windows, empty barnyards, abandoned equipment in the fields. And terrifying mortality, especially in children."[18] But the *New York Times* rarely—if ever—published the accounts or stories of any of the millions of Russians who had experiences like Kosterin's. More seriously, the *Times* never questioned Duranty about why he barely used first-hand accounts of regular Russians and why, if a differing viewpoint about the famine and the situation in Russia was appearing all over the Western press, Duranty never presented the opinion of the other side.

The *Times* ran with a storyline that not only sat well with its owners but also won the paper a huge amount of acclaim, and a Pulitzer Prize along with it. But even once it had emerged from Walter Duranty's Russian dream spell, the *New York Times* still exhibited a crippling inability to address the massive failure of journalism perpetrated on its pages.

◆ ◆ ◆

Seventy years after the Duranty affair, the *New York Times*'s ownership and management was still unable to acknowledge the truth of the situation. After the 1986 publication of Robert Conquest's book on the real history of the Ukrainian Famine, the publication of S.J. Taylor's damning 1990 biography of Duranty, *Stalin's Apologist*, and, to top it all off, a series of highly critical articles about Duranty that rained down from the right wing, the far left, and everything in between, the *Times* saw it fit to hire a consultant to consider whether or not the Pulitzer Prize should be returned. It's not clear why the *New York Times* and its publisher could not make this ethical decision for themselves. However, the consultant, a professor of Russian and Ukrainian history, read Duranty's work and concluded that the Pulitzer Prize should be rescinded.[19] The *New York Times*'s own news report on the investigation by the specially hired consultant reported the professor's verdict on the Duranty affair:

That lack of balance and uncritical acceptance of the Soviet self-justification for its cruel and wasteful regime was a disservice to the American readers of the *New York Times* and the liberal values they subscribe to and to the historical experience of the peoples of the Russian and Soviet empires and their struggle for a better life.

For all invested in the question of the prize, including groups of Ukrainian-Americans who were appalled that the Pulitzer board would award a prize to someone who covered up the genocide of Ukrainians, the practical implications of all this was obvious: the *New York Times* should return the prize as quickly as possible.

The *Times*—more specifically, its then-publisher, Arthur Sulzberger Jr.—had a different take on the matter. According to the *Times*'s own reporting, Sulzberger wrote a cover letter to the consultant's report that was to be delivered to the board of the newspaper.[20] Sulzberger argued in his cover letter that the *Times* had for more than two years acknowledged the "slovenly" nature of Duranty's reporting on Russia but nonetheless insisted that the paper should *not* return the prize. Sulzberger's first rationalization as to why the *Times* should not return the Pulitzer was the outrageous (and frankly silly) excuse that the newspaper did not have Duranty's Pulitzer Prize and therefore could not return it. Sulzberger declined to say to where the prize, a gold coin, had disappeared.

Sulzberger's additional justifications for not returning the prize were even more ethically dubious than the first. Sulzberger told the board that giving it back would too closely resemble the "Stalinist practice to airbrush purged figures out of official records and histories." The logic is boggling and the ethics are appalling. But Sulzberger went on to provide another rationalization, this one again worse than the one before it. He wrote that if the newspaper were to give back the Pulitzer Prize, "the board would be setting a precedent for revisiting its judgments over many decades."

It seems that this last reason—editorial oversight and self-correction over time—would be the *best* possible motivation to return the prize. The managing editor of the *Times* at that point, Bill Keller, agreed with Sulzberger. His rationalization was identical to that of his boss: recognizing the reality of history and the reality of the *Times*'s huge failure by returning the prize would somehow amount to a Soviet-style "airbrushing" of history. Keller even used the same language as Sulzberger: "As someone who spent time in the Soviet Union while it still existed, the notion of airbrushing history kind of gives me the creeps."[21]

To the Ukrainian-Americans who initially called for the ill-gotten prize to be returned, it was the *Times*'s refusal to return the prize and the fact that the paper fought, despite the recommendation of its own hired consultant, against rectifying its journalistic failure, that represented the true airbrushing of history. It's difficult to see how such a justification for not returning a journalism prize could be advanced in anything resembling good faith by the owner of the country's most prestigious news outlet and one of his top editors. However, the excuse and its rationale were accepted by the *Times*'s corporate board, which chose not to accept the recommendation of their consultant to return the Duranty Pulitzer. Unfortunately, though, the *New York Times*'s faulty, skewed, and fallacious reporting on the Soviet Union did not end with the famine or the Pulitzer Prize they refused to return.

◆ ◆ ◆

The Ochs-Sulzberger family which still runs the *New York Times* today is a mainstay of the left-leaning, educated, and generally wealthy American intellectual elite that supported the Soviet "experiment" and its utopian aims from the beginning. The result of this infatuation with the Soviet experiment was very real and very painful—just not for Western idealists who enjoyed the material fruits of a free economy as they daydreamed about a Soviet secret garden. In *Utopia In Power*, Mikhail Heller and Aleksandr Nekrich summed up the dynamic between the actual unfolding history of the USSR and the Western media and intellectuals who romanticized and whitewashed it:

> A fire had indeed been raging in the Soviet Union. By 1930 it had devoured millions of people, but the West knew nothing about it—the West did not want to know...The Soviet Union's isolation from the rest of the world was possible only through the complicity of the West.[22]

Leftist Westerners who visited Russia came back with outrageously decep-
tive tales of Soviet abundance and bliss. The Irish playwright and noted
Fabian socialist George Bernard Shaw, who contributed to the *New York
Times* frequently (sometimes under headlines that referred to him in the
third person), visited Russia at the height of the famine yet still had the
temerity to declare that, "I have never eaten so well as during my trip to
the Soviet Union."[23] The *New York Times* reported on Shaw's 1931 trip
to Russia as it did with most of the other leftist intellectuals and celebrities who visited the country and came back with tales of a brand new
civilization. In Shaw's case, the *Times* covered a lecture by Shaw, saying,
"There was no limit to Mr. Shaw's enthusiasm over Russia as it bubbled
over to the 2,000 who packed the hall."[24] The article, of course, makes
no mention of what Shaw might have left out of his Edenic picture, such
as the extreme shortages (which even Duranty acknowledged) that had
taken hold of the country by the time of his visit. Other leftist intellectuals
echoed these claims, some of them more wildly and euphemistically
than even Shaw.

Ella Winter, a communist agent in the United States who was married
to the notorious correspondent Lincoln Steffens (of the infamously incor-
rect remark about Soviet Russia: "I have seen the future and it works")
compared Russia's economic "difficulties" to a woman's birth pains: "Is
a woman happy bearing the long-awaited child? They are giving birth
to a new world, a new world outlook, and in this process questions of
personal gratification become secondary."[25]

In Winter's view, "personal gratification" evidently meant having
enough food to survive. Winter had been in Russia during the famine
and probably saw conditions there for herself. But Winter was not in a
position to reveal the truth about the conditions in Russia for one very
important reason: the *Times* contributor was much more than a mere
Soviet apologist such as Shaw. Rather, Winter was an *official* Russian
propaganda agent whose mission was to advance a utopian view of Soviet
socialism regardless of the cost to the truth.

What the *Times* may or may not have known was that Winter was a
communist agent handled by the infamous Willi Münzenberg, the man

who helped direct global propaganda for the Communist International (or Comintern), which was founded to spread the communist revolution to all corners of the world. Münzenberg, Ella Winter's handler, has been called "the greatest propaganda chief the communist movement had produced."[26] He would later be tapped to head the Comintern's Agitation and Propaganda Department, more popularly known as Agitprop.[27]

Just as the socio-economic disaster of collectivization was taking hold in 1931, the New York Times ran a story by Winter that reported the Soviets were using "shock troops" to advance Russian industry. The headline of the article demands a double take: "Soviet 'Shock Troops' Speed Up Industry."[28] Shock troops were in fact used to "speed up industry," just not in the way Ella Winter represented it. The use of shock troops was part of the explicit politico-economic plan of the Soviet leadership under Stalin, who understood better than anyone the logic of force. But Winter's New York Times article on the use of brutality to get the Russian citizenry in line gives the story a velvet touch. Winter wrote that with "characteristic Russian realism," the shock troops were used to update and advance industry and that they were doing a good job of it. The article fails to mention how murder, exile, and imprisonment were the main tactics that the shock troops used to force collectivization of farms, brutalize the kulaks, and kill off unwilling peasants.

The Times published a number of other articles by and about Ella Winter, including an almost gushing review of her book, Red Virtue. Though the Times may not have known about Winter's position as an agent and spy for Münzenberg, it does not change the fact that the paper published blatantly pro-communist propaganda as news reports during the early critical years of the rise of the Soviet Union.

The success of Winter publishing successive propaganda pieces in the pages of America's greatest newspaper must have been dizzying for her propaganda masters. As an Agitprop chief and leader one of the main communist power bases outside of Russia, Willi Münzenberg's aim was to gain pro-socialist influence through propaganda. Insofar as Ella Winter, one of the many "Münzenberg Men" who were women, regularly published news articles on Soviet Russia in America's most prominent newspaper, Münzenberg's project was a staggering success.

But Winter was not the only agent run by Münzenberg. As a propaganda handler for authors and public intellectuals such as author Arthur Koestler, Münzenberg was able to spread communist propaganda across the United States. Koestler, who was published on occasion by the *New York Times*, later recalled that Münzenberg would storm into his apartment to check up on the progress of the work:

> He would pick up a few sheets of typescript, scan through them and shout at me: "Too weak. Too objective. Hit them! Hit them hard! Tell the world how they run over their prisoners with tanks, how they pour petrol over them and burn them alive. Make the world gasp with horror. Hammer it into their heads. Make them wake up..."[29]

Koestler once recalled that Münzenberg saw a piece of Nazi propaganda in a Berlin newspaper that claimed that the Red militia was passing out vouchers, each of which was good for the rape of a German woman. Münzenberg admiringly told Koestler, "That, Arturo, is propaganda."[30]

It might seem difficult to accept the idea that the *Times* neither caught Ella Winter nor apologized in retrospect for publishing her propaganda as news and analysis. After all, she was not a nameless communist soldier—she was a highly successful agent run directly by the leaders of global Agitprop in the 1930s. But, unlike Walter Duranty and some of the other well-known propagandists and apologists who wrote for the paper, it is unlikely that the *Times* management of today even knows the name Ella Winter. A glance at Winter's obituary in the *New York Times* in 1980 further underscores the point. The obituary makes no mention of Winter's sordid political background but writes about her simply as an "interpreter" of Russia's economic changes and an "observer" who monitored the political events of Russia at the time.[31] This idea, that Winter was a neutral observer, points to the somewhat disturbing fact that the *Times*'s ownership and management was in ideological lockstep with a Soviet propaganda operative.

George Bernard Shaw, Ella Winter and, maybe more than any single person, Walter Duranty, were opinion makers when it came to the question of Soviet Russia. In an article for the Hoover Institution's *Hoover Digest,* Robert Conquest explains that prior to 1933, American public opinion (including the predominant intellectual opinion) regarding the new socialist government was still largely undecided. Conquest notes that the famine, which was the hinge on which the pendulum of American public opinion would swing, was reported correctly by many. "The terror-famine early that year, in which millions died, had been widely and accurately reported in much of the Western press."[32] The American public was presented with two competing, diametrically opposed views of the famine—on the one hand that it was very real and on the other that it did not exist. In the end, according to Conquest, Duranty's version of events was vindicated when it won the Pulitzer Prize. The official celebration of Duranty's journalism led others to trumpet his "dispassionate, interpretive reporting of the news from Russia," as the Pulitzer committee put it. Thus, the pro-Soviet swing of the pendulum in American circles of power began in earnest.

The death blow dealt to the anti-Soviet and anti-Stalin camps of American government came not long afterward. Despite assurances by the *Times*'s article about Duranty's 1932 meeting with Roosevelt that "it is highly unlikely that [Roosevelt's] advisers would advocate formal recognition" of the USSR, that recognition came just a year after Roosevelt became president. And it was the *New York Times*'s Russia man who, yet again, was ushering events along.

A *Time* magazine article from January 8, 1934 gave a replay of the American recognition of the USSR and Duranty's involvement:

> When Foreign Minister Litvinoff was grooming Soviet Russia for recognition, New York Times Correspondent Duranty crossed the Atlantic at his side. Instead of returning to Moscow via Rome with Comrade Litvinoff, Mr. Duranty sailed back with the new U.S. Ambassador to Russia.

The previous November, the America-Russia Chamber of Commerce hosted a 1,500-person banquet at the Waldorf-Astoria in New York to commemorate America's recognition of the Soviet Union. The Soviet

Foreign Minister, the guest of honor, gave a short account of his easy negotiations with President Roosevelt, saying that "There were no long labors, no anxiety."[33] The banquet continued with introductions and speeches by a who's who of politicians, businessmen, and media elite. However, according to a *New York Times* article on the event, only one man was noted for receiving a standing ovation from the 1,500 people in attendance: Walter Duranty.

And though Duranty had by that point successfully covered up politically-motivated genocide committed by the Soviet regime, achieved international fame, met with future presidents and current foreign ministers, and was applauded by a room full of America's greatest power players, his crowning achievement was still yet to come.

◆ ◆ ◆

In January 1934, Joseph Stalin gave a rare and unusual order. The Soviet dictator personally sent for a reporter to interview him. What was even more strange was the fact that the reporter worked for an American newspaper. That reporter, of course, was Walter Duranty.

According to Duranty's own account, Stalin told the correspondent, "You have done a good job in your reporting the USSR, though you are not a Marxist, because you try to tell the truth about our country and to understand it and to explain it to your readers."[34] This was flattery from a dictator ruthless enough to sweep away millions of lives in pursuit of an ideology. For most, but especially for a news organization, flattery from a political monster would not make for a proud moment. For the *New York Times*, Duranty's interview with Stalin was a triumph.

With all this in mind, it is not Walter Duranty who presents us with an enigma. Reporters are people and sometimes fall victim to their human flaws. The real puzzle in the Duranty affair is how the mechanisms of journalism, which exist specifically to prevent the distortions and lies Walter Duranty perpetrated, failed so badly. The real mystery is how and why the *New York Times* not only published Duranty's reporting (and the reporting of people like Ella Winter) but refused to either take responsibility for the failure or develop new means of protecting against this kind of breakdown.

One very strong clue to this lies in a conversation that Walter Duranty had with a State Department official named A.W. Kliefoth at the United States Embassy in Berlin on June 4, 1931. Kliefoth recorded the conversation in an official memorandum, which is archived at the United States National Archives. Duranty had stopped by the embassy to renew his passport but ended up doing much more than that. He made a shattering confession, telling the embassy official that, "'in agreement with the *New York Times* and the Soviet authorities,' his official dispatches always reflect the official opinion of the Soviet government and not his own.'"[35]

That is a staggering admission—and one the State Department official considered so important to the American government that he entered Duranty's words, quoted verbatim, into the official State Department record.[36] That the *Times*—according to their own correspondent, and arguably the most famous, accomplished, and beloved journalist in the United States—was coordinating with the Soviet authorities is a scandal much bigger in scope and seriousness than the one generally associated with Duranty, that he covered up the famine or, by Sulzberger's account, was merely "slovenly" in his reporting. Rather, this confession amounts to one of the greatest instances of journalistic malfeasance on record, at the *Times* or anywhere else.

Duranty's personal history should not be discounted here. It is possible that Duranty simply lied, as he had lied before. However, Duranty's confession to the State Department officer is validated by one key fact: Duranty's reporting did indeed accurately reflect the official Soviet position on famine. But this was much bigger than one single reporter. As we have seen, the *New York Times* regularly carried "news reports" and analyses written by communist agents and Soviet sympathizers. If the *Times*'s leadership felt the pro-Soviet reporting was inaccurate or misleading, they certainly never did anything about it.

Further, the confession itself was by no means out of character for Duranty, who had offered up similarly self-damning confessions on other occasions. The journalist Eugene Lyons, who was the first American correspondent to get an interview with Stalin (though he got the interview by hanging outside of Stalin's office for days on end and was not ceremoniously invited, as Duranty had been), recounted in his book *Assignment in Utopia* that he once had dinner with his wife Billy, the *New York Times* correspondent Anne O'Hare McCormick, and Walter Duranty. When the conversation turned to the famine and its toll, Duranty offered an estimate on the number of people who had been killed. Duranty's own estimate far outstripped any other estimate at that time. The other journalists, who were familiar with Duranty's famine-denying stories in the *New York Times*, were shocked. Anne O'Hare McCormick asked incredulously if Duranty had meant what he said literally. According to Lyons, Duranty, in response to Lyons's interjection on Duranty's behalf that the reporter had not meant it literally, shot back, "'Hell, I don't...I'm being conservative,' he replied, and as if by way of consolation he added his famous truism: 'But they're only Russians.'"[37]

Lyons later wrote in a memorandum to the prominent journalist Malcolm Muggeridge that the number Duranty mentioned that evening was seven million deaths due to starvation. An estimate, Duranty informed the journalists with whom he was dining, he had formulated on the basis of visits to the affected areas he had made between 1932 and 1933.

The Making of a Messiah:
"And There Was Fidel Castro"

I n 1957, the *New York Times* brought Fidel Castro back from the dead. Only a year earlier, news reports about Castro's death had been circling around the press. News agency UPI published a story based on a Cuban government report that claimed Castro had been killed and his rebellion put down. The world had no reason to doubt the report, and Castro, who had been doggedly hunted by the army of Cuban dictator Fulgencio Batista, had little desire to risk his life by emerging from his mountain hideout.

But one determined *New York Times* reporter would change the fate of the guerilla leader—and the country where he was struggling to bring about a revolution. The reporter's name was Herbert Matthews. By the late 1950s, Matthews was a well-regarded middle-aged *Times* reporter with a good deal of experience under his belt. A dapper man with a taste for adventure and a political romantic, Matthews had befriended the likes of Hemingway in Spain during the Spanish Civil War and later went onto to write about Italy's conquest of Ethiopia—then known as Abyssinia—in the 1930s.

Despite Matthews's colorful background, it was an act of journalistic integrity and intrepidness for the *Times* reporter, then nearing sixty, to trek into the Sierra Maestra mountains in search of the rebel leader in 1957. The forested Sierra Maestras were so unforgiving and difficult to navigate that Batista's army had been unable to quash the rebellion of a few dozen under-supplied and poorly trained men simply because the army could neither find nor get to the rebel hideouts. Matthews also had no idea how he would be received by Castro, who was at that time an unknown quantity, even though the rebel leader had sent a man into Havana to find a journalist who could prove to the world he was still alive.

The meeting between Matthews and Castro originated with an unlikely source. Ruby Hart Phillips was the *New York Times*'s pre-revolution Cuba correspondent who had taken over the position from her husband, who had died in Cuba. As the years wore on, Phillips came to passionately disagree with almost everything Matthews wrote about Cuba. Former *New York Times* correspondent Anthony DePalma wrote in his book, *The Man Who Invented Fidel*, that the two *Times* reporters would often cover the same event in Cuba and come to opposite conclusions in their respective articles. But in 1957, neither Ruby Hart Phillips nor Herbert Matthews knew enough about the other to dislike each other. So when Phillips heard that Matthews, who had been a correspondent for the *Times* in the Abyssinian War and the Spanish Civil War, was visiting Cuba with his wife Nancie, she proposed that Matthews should go and find Castro in the jungle mountains. By his own account, Matthews "jumped" at the opportunity.[1]

"Fidel Castro and his 26 of July movement are the flaming symbol of this opposition to the regime," Matthews wrote in his first Castro article for the *Times*. "The program is vague and couched in generalities, but it amounts to a new deal for Cuba, radical, democratic and therefore anti-Communist."[2] Matthews took a huge journalistic leap in drawing the conclusion that Castro was democratic and anti-communist. In 1957, virtually nothing was known about Fidel Castro and his 26th of July Movement. Still, Matthews made the leap without hesitating. The *Times*'s Cuba man went on to describe Castro's childhood and background and cataloged almost every romanticized minute of his journey to the rebels' mountain hideaway. For almost three full columns of type, Matthews wrote about the government roadblocks he passed, an all-night drive across the Cuban countryside, using his wife as "camouflage" (as he put it), meeting up with one of Castro's scouts, talking in whispers in the jungle, and eventually encountering Castro himself. "The personality of the man is overpowering," Matthews swooned. "It was easy to see that his men adored him and also to see why he has caught the imagination of the youth of Cuba all over the island. Here was an educated, dedicated fanatic, a man of ideals, of courage and of remarkable qualities of leadership."

Matthews went on to speak about some of Castro's men before closing by directly quoting Castro in the final column of the article. "Above all," he quoted Castro as saying, "we are fighting for a democratic Cuba and an end to the dictatorship." Then, "to show that he deals fairly" with his soldiers, Matthews wrote, one of the rebels brought out a fat roll of money. Matthews quoted Castro as saying that while Batista's soldiers were paid just $72 a month, Cuba would pay its men $100 a month when he would become Cuba's leader.

The next day, Matthews penned another Castro article, which reiterated the same themes of his first article. He enthusiastically repeated his claim that Castro was a democratic reformer, even a liberator, who wanted to wrest power from the Batista dictatorship in order to hand it over to the people of Cuba. Castro and his men, Matthews wrote without even attempting to hide his admiration for the young rebel, "are giving their lives for an ideal and for their hopes of living in a clean, democratic Cuba."[3]

The last statement was key. Since his very first article, Matthews had championed the idea that Castro was pro-democracy and therefore "anti-communist." This question of the revolution's attitude toward communism was everything to everyone in 1957, a time when the United States and the USSR were locked in tension at the very height of the Cold War. To the Soviet Union, Castro's revolution looked like a potential opportunity to expand the borders of communism right up to the shores of America. To the people of Cuba, the question of Castro's link to communism concerned the kind of country they would have and the lives they would lead under this new "liberator." And, most consequentially of all—especially where reporting of the *New York Times* was concerned—to the United States,

Castro's embrace or rejection of communism would determine the specific policy America would adopt toward the island nation just ninety miles off its southern coast.

The Cuban missile crisis could not have made the point any more sharply. The crisis represented the realization of every fear Washington policymakers and politicians harbored in the days before the Cuban revolutionary government took form. Even Richard Nixon, who then served as vice president under Eisenhower and was known to be one of the most ruthless "communist hunters" in Washington, voiced not just the importance of figuring out whether Castro was pro- or anti-communist but also the incredible difficulty of it. When the Cuban revolutionary made his first United States visit as Cuba's head of state, then-Vice President Nixon met with him in order to get a grasp on the communism issue. Nixon wrote a secret memo after the meeting with Castro to brief President Eisenhower, the secretary of state, and the head of the CIA on who—or, rather, what—Fidel Castro was.

Nixon found Castro to be so evasive on the topic of communism that he was barely able to make heads or tails of Castro's comments. However, when the discussion turned to the kind of totalitarian government Castro would actually put in place in Cuba, the would-be dictator was frank. According to Nixon, when Castro was asked why he did not hold free elections now that Batista's regime was overthrown, his response was, "The people of Cuba don't want free elections—they produce bad government."[4] Castro's response on the topic of fair trials for those who'd opposed his rebellion used the same cynical invocation of "the people of Cuba" and what they supposedly wanted or did not want. Castro, according to Nixon, said, "The people of Cuba don't want them to have fair trials. They want them shot as quickly as possible."

Castro's words, at least according to Nixon, turned out to be frighteningly accurate. Castro wasted no time in installing a brutal totalitarian government in Cuba. Just six months after the meeting with Nixon, Castro made a move that could only have been more pro-communist if it had been accompanied by a public reading from Marx's famous manifesto: He ordered the arrest of one of his top lieutenants, Hubert Matos, after Matos publicly stated that there were too many communists in the government. It was only a week after Matos's arrest that Castro declared a full suspension of habeas corpus in Cuba, giving the revolutionary government the power to arrest anyone at any time for any reason. What made the arrest—and subsequent sentencing of Matos to twenty years of imprisonment for treason—so astonishing was not just the cause of the arrest (Matos's public claim that there were too many communists in an allegedly non-communist government) but that Matos was one of Castro's most trusted allies during the revolution.

Ten years later, Herbert Matthews, in his 1966 biography of Castro, was still calling the arrest of Matos a "logical" response to Castro's fears that Matos was receiving "encouragement" from the Americans. Even in 1966, four years after the Cuban missile crisis and at a time that Castro's pro-communist position was concretely established, Matthews wrote that in the late 1950s, "Castro was then working out his policy of 'unity,' which was neither pro- nor anti-Communist."[5]

Ruby Hart Phillips wrote the initial story for the *Times* on the arrest of Matos, which provided a straightforward account of what had happened. A little more than a week later, in October 1959, the *Times* ran another piece by Phillips on the suspension of habeas corpus, which touched on the pattern of Castro arresting his own supporters and revolutionaries and either throwing them in prison or having them shot. Phillips's piece also noted that 450 Batista men had been summarily executed after the revolution. Ironically, the *Times* management ended up removing Ruby Hart Phillips, who was critical of the new regime, and replaced her with Herbert Matthews as the main Cuba correspondent. The paper's top editors and publisher made the decision because they thought Matthews's skills as a correspondent vastly outstripped Phillips's skills and also because Matthews and the *Times*'s higher-ups found Phillips too sympathetic to the Batista regime.[6]

In the years leading up to the revolution, Phillips had fashioned herself as an expert on the economic situation in Cuba. In some cases, she called Batista's Cuba "prosperous" and wrote that the regime was making substantial strides in fixing the major problems of the economy. All in all, she presented a fairly pleasant picture of daily life in Cuba, one in sharp contrast to the Cuba that Castro was trying to portray, which was a Cuba of rampant illiteracy, horrific poverty, and widespread disease.

Castro had to paint this image of vast social injustice in order to fuel his revolution. However, the facts on the ground in Cuba agreed more with Phillips's version of Cuba than with Matthews's. Contrary to the myth of a Cuba comprising a large oppressed class of agricultural peasants, the Cuban population was mostly urban prior to the revolution, with fifty-seven percent of people living in cities and only forty-three percent in rural areas. Cuba's standard of living was the fourth highest in Latin America, and it ranked fifth in manufacturing. Cuban citizens on average had access to more goods and technology than most of their Latin-American counterparts, with one in five owning a radio (second to only Argentina) and 1 in 39 owning a car (compared to 1 in 60 in Argentina, 1 in 91 in Mexico, and 1 in 158 in Brazil).[7] Importantly, the trend was on the side of Cuban progress. Cuban ownership of sugar production, the island's most important crop, which comprised eighty percent of all exports, had increased drastically, cutting American ownership of the crop from eighty percent in the 1930s to just thirty-five percent in the days before the revolution.

There is no doubt that the Batista government had ruled in an authoritarian manner, with tight censorship and restriction on anything that resembled political openness, especially during flare-ups of the rebellion. But given Castro's subsequent rule, his immediate suspension of habeas corpus, the huge number of political prisoners taken, the brutal repression of homosexuality, and the total control of the press and public gatherings by the state, it is clear Castro's aim was anything but increasing transparency or liberty.

As Castro's repression took hold, the one big question left unanswered in 1959 was not whether Cuba would be free—it clearly was not—but whether it would become communist. In choosing Herbert Matthews over Ruby Phillips as the main Cuba correspondent, the *New York Times* took its first important step in covering Cuba in a way that would be favorable to Castro. One sentence from the Nixon memo aptly summed up Castro's likely intentional ambiguity on the question of communism in Cuba: "Castro is incredibly naïve about communism or is under communist discipline."[8] Nixon, who found nothing naïve about Castro, evidently got it right when framing his dichotomy. Despite successive waves of evidence to the contrary, Matthews and the *New York Times* did not.

◆ ◆ ◆

Nixon's memo was one that involved the highest levels of American power. It was sent by the vice president of the United States to the president, secretary of state, and head of the CIA, on the topic of the most geographically critical potential threat of the time. And yet, once again, the *New York Times* had a hand in the events. It might seem strange that Fidel Castro, enemy of America and devoted communist, would visit the United States and sit down with, of all people, Richard Nixon, just weeks after the Cuban revolution. But the unofficial visit had its roots in an institution that saw such a strange visit in a more natural light.

In 1959, the American Society of Newspaper Editors faced what they saw as a serious problem: the group had not yet booked a keynote speaker for its annual convention.[9] The leaders of a few major newspapers, including the *New Orleans Times-Picayune*, the *Chicago Tribune,* and *Newsday*, met at the upscale 21 restaurant in New York to brainstorm possibilities for a speaker. Castro's name came up. The beard, the military fatigues, the glasses, and the tropical revolution seemed like too great of a "get" to pass up. But there was one more person who had to sign off on the idea before they could go forward.

The editors at 21 called their colleague Turner Catledge, the fiery executive editor of the *New York Times*, who was bedridden with a flare-up of gout. When Catledge heard the idea to bring the newly empowered Castro to the United States in order to speak at the American Society of Newspaper Editors convention, he thought the idea was "'wild" but nevertheless liked it.[10] Four months later, Castro was standing before a crowd at the American Society of Newspaper Editors conference, where he told the group of media elite that he fully a supported a free press (just, apparently, not in his own country) as it was the "first enemy of dictatorship." Castro, whose tour was organized by a major American PR firm, flexed his publicity muscles in the United States, appearing on *Meet the Press*, laying wreaths at the tombs of Lincoln and Jefferson, and greeting thousands of cheering and screaming supporters every step of the way. The trip was a major success for Castro. For the Cuban people, it was an enormous failure.

When the newspaper editors at 21 cooked up the idea of a Castro visit and then called the *New York Times*'s Turner Catledge to get his final approval, they did not consider the possible consequences of inviting a revolutionary dictator to their convention. By taking it upon themselves to bring the new leader of Cuba to the United States, and by Castro accepting the invitation, they eliminated the possibility of Castro's first visit to the United States being an official one.[11] The organization of the visit had not gone through diplomatic channels so the State Department was not able to construct an agenda and schedule meetings with American government officials who could have cemented official ties between Cuba's new provisional government and the American government during that crucial first visit.[12]

Part of the problem was that the Castro visit, organized by Catledge and the other newspaper editors as an exciting way to fill an empty keynote speaker slot, was extremely premature. Just after Castro took power in January 1959, he began a wave of political executions that caused concern at the State Department. With this context, the State Department wanted time to see what Castro would do next before organizing an official visit that could prove damaging and embarrassing to the United States if Castro turned out to preside over a bloody wave of political reprisals. The newly placed US ambassador to Cuba, Philip Bonsal, later lamented that an official visit could have resulted in bilateral ties between the two countries, "But the time for such visits was still distant when the editors, so far as I know without consulting any responsible American official, issued their invitation."[13] Bonsal noted that if Castro's first visit to the United States had been organized by the State Department and been conducted according to government protocol, a later visit by President Eisenhower to Castro's

Cuba would have been possible. However, the *Times*'s executive editor, Catledge, and his fellow editors sank the possibility of early bilateral ties with Cuba by pulling off their Cuban publicity stunt.

◆ ◆ ◆

Herbert Matthews had launched Castro onto the world stage in 1957. The *Times* correspondent's focus on the perilous but romantic journey into the mountains occupied almost four full columns of his first 1957 Castro story. Instead of investigative reporting on the Cuban rebel group or a careful and critical analysis of the group's origins and intentions, Matthews and the *New York Times* printed romantic stories of the rebels and their youthful vision of a liberated and democratic Cuba. Matthews's flowery descriptions of Castro's movement as a movement of the people, of the youth, of all economic classes, and, most importantly, of democracy, traveled around the world.

As was the case with Walter Duranty, Matthews's report would have meant very little had he not worked for the *New York Times*. The reach of the newspaper, its budget, and its ability to organize, in the blink of an eye, an event like Castro's 1959 visit to the United States carried Matthews's reporting along a mighty river of journalistic power and influence. Also like Walter Duranty, Matthew was an erudite, educated, and experienced journalist. Like Duranty, he spoke multiple languages (including Spanish), and had similarly gained his first major experience in journalism by covering an important war in Europe for the paper. But unlike Walter Duranty, who was self-admittedly a cynical manipulator of facts and people, Herbert Matthews strove to live up to his own standards of journalistic integrity and ethics.

Reporting from Ethiopia during the Abyssinian War, he developed a theory of journalistic ethics that called for a reporter to openly acknowledge and report personal feelings on the subject he was reporting on. In Ethiopia, Matthews pursued this theory to a fault. The war had been ignited by Mussolini's 1935 invasion of the African country as part of the fascist dictator's plan to reestablish a Roman Empire that extended far into the Mediterranean Basin and Africa. The endeavor was an outright colonial war. Matthews covered the war for the *Times* and openly supported the Italian invaders. Despite his view on the war (which from today's anti-colonial perspective is questionable at best), Matthews was considered a skilled correspondent. He was on the ground during the bloody war, known for the Italians' illegal use of mustard gas,[14] sending in eyewitness accounts of important battles. But Matthews, then in his mid-thirties, was romantic—so much so that his romantic energy rivaled that of his friend and travel partner, Ernest Hemingway, who also covered the subsequent Spanish Civil War alongside Matthews.

In Ethiopia, Matthews developed his romantic sense and exercised his considerable talent for description:

> Stepping out of my tent under the over-full moon while the camp was fast asleep, except for the sentries whose fires twinkled along the crests of the surrounding hills, I was conscious only of the extraordinary beauty of the scene. A sense of timelessness of what I saw came over me. Caesar's legions had made just such marches in conquering Gaul, and set up just such camps with sentry fires gleaming around them. There was the same moon, the same urge to conquest, the same thrill of adventure—life and death and history in the making, whether it be De Bello Gallico, or just a hasty narrative for one day's newspaper.[15]

Despite this romantic tendency, Matthews had an ability to look back on his past experience with a certain amount of honesty. He wrote in his book, *Education of a Correspondent*, about his time reporting on the war between Ethiopia and Italy: "I was not concerned then with moral or ethical problems. They grew with time and experience and thought, as the wars took a political shape and the wanton, wicked, vicious quality of the suffering imposed on others, seared its way into my heart."[16]

Unfortunately, Matthews's romantic side won out. He could not resist the lure of living history and witnessing the continuity with antiquity that Mussolini's Italian fascists presented by invading Africa. And he was not bashful about his bias: "The right or wrong of it did not interest me greatly...If you start from the premise that a lot of rascals are having a fight, it is not unnatural to want to see the victory of the rascal you like, and I liked the Italians during that scrimmage more than I did the British or the Abyssinians."[17]

By the time Matthews went to Spain to cover the Spanish Civil War, he had fully developed his ethical theory that not only allowed journalists to have personal preferences but required it. To Matthews, the human element was inescapable and so no attempt should be made by journalists to avoid it. He felt that revealing everything would inform and provide the reader with enough context to sweep aside parts of the story that might be considered subjective. In terms of its intentions, the theory is not a bad one, especially when put next to Duranty's mercenary view of journalism or Guido Enderis's only half-hidden collaboration with an enemy of the United States. But in the already romanticized conflicts that Matthews came to cover, and most crucially the Cuban revolution, the theory would prove to be his undoing.

◆ ◆ ◆

The self-serving aspects of Matthews's theory and approach seem to have grown bigger and started to occupy a more substantive part of his work as time went on. More destructively, Matthews seemed to become not more aware of his bias but less so, to the point that his bias, so enabled by his approach to ethics, became justified implicitly. Meeting Ernest Hemingway in the most romanticized of all the twentieth century's wars, the Spanish Civil War, probably did not help. Hemingway was in Spain to cover the war not because he was a reporter or a soldier but because he was inspired. He saw in Spain a chance to partake in a modern French Revolution, to help free the oppressed people of a Western country and, maybe more than anything, to have a real adventure. Hemingway linked up with Matthews and a group of other foreign correspondents, including Martha Gellhorn of *Collier's* (whom Hemingway later married), Sefton Delmer, and Antoine de Saint-Exupéry, who would pen his famous book *The Little Prince* just a few years later. It was a romantic and inspired group, to say the least.

In a situation like this one, a personality like Matthews's could not resist taking on a preference or, in the language of journalism, bias. "In those years," Matthews wrote of his time in Spain, "we lived our best and what has come after and what there is to come can never carry us to those heights."[18] But while Hemingway was playing journalist-soldier (he once fired off a random round of machine-gun bullets, which, in the words of a British sculptor who was there, "provoked a mortar bombardment for which he did not stay"),[19] Matthews made a serious attempt at achieving the best kind of journalism he could. His open-bias approach to journalism took full hold in Spain. He wrote, "I would always opt for honest, open bias. A newspaperman should work with his heart as well as his mind."[20]

When Matthews arrived in Cuba in 1957, a seasoned journalist in his late fifties, his view on bias and his penchant for historical romance had not really changed. What had changed was his position at the *New York Times*. The dapper Matthews, who looked a little gallant and even a little ridiculous in his three-piece suits and checkered vests as he sat next to the cigar-chomping Castro, had befriended his boss, Arthur Hays Sulzberger. In the years between the Spanish Civil War and the Cuban revolution, Sulzberger had taken unusual steps to advance Matthews on both a personal and professional level. At one point in their relationship, Sulzberger went so far as to approve a loan from the newspaper to the correspondent (to the dismay of the paper's accountants) so Matthews could buy a house in London.

But Sulzberger also gave Matthews a big professional leg up by making the correspondent a member of the paper's editorial board—a violation of *New York Times* policy, since Matthews was a reporter—and by bestowing on him the title of associate editor, something Matthews had lobbied for despite the opposition of other members of the editorial board. Matthews had also gained the favor of Sulzberger's wife, Iphigene, matriarch of the Ochs-Sulzberger family, who eventually became godmother to Matthews's son.

After a twenty-year-long professional relationship that had morphed into a very personal one, the *New York Times* had clearly invested heavily in Herbert Matthews. While Matthews cannot be blamed for his choices as a journalist in the sense that Walter Duranty can be blamed (and partly because the Cuban revolution was on a much smaller scale than the Russian Revolution), the *New York Times*, as an institution of journalism, can be.

Just three days after the January 1, 1959 revolution, the *New York Times* ran a story by Matthews. The headline proudly proclaimed, "Cuba: First Step to a New Era."[21] The article was a celebration of the downfall of the Batista government, a lament of previous American policy, a defense of Cuban anti-Americanism and, most palpably, a show of support for the supposedly democratic liberation that Castro had ushered in. The article is so filled with enthusiastic over-exaggeration that even if it had been remotely correct, factually speaking, it would still constitute a journalistic embarrassment. After a quick criticism of Batista—who, according to Matthews, was "rich beyond the wildest dreams of the biggest US businessman"—Matthews informed readers that Castro was the undisputed hero of the Cuban youth. Matthews wrote:

> The whole youth of Cuba was behind Fidel, as he is universally called throughout Latin America. Thousands of girls and boys gave their lives, thousands suffered abominable torture at the hands of the police and army, and thousands spent varying terms in prison. But Fidel never lacked recruits.

Matthews had apparently forgotten the times that he had personally witnessed the lack of recruits with which Fidel, as Matthews called him, struggled. The rest of the article is an explanation of Cuban anti-Americanism, which Matthews found so self-evident he did not think it necessary to quote a single source. Only in the final paragraph did he move away from the topic of Cuba's anti-American sentiments and turn back to the positivity of Castro's revolution: "What the Cuban Republic has lacked thus far is honest, efficient government. Those who fought against General Batista believed that they fought for liberty, democracy and decent government."

Weeks later, the *Times* ran a March 8 article by Matthews with the headline, "Now Castro Faces the Harder Fight."[22] The article went far beyond the January article's pro-Castro predictions that were made on the basis of essentially nothing and uses language and themes that seem to have been lifted out of a Gabriel Garcia Marquez novel. The article begins with a needless rehashing of Matthews's adventurous trip to the Cuban interior, which occupies the space of the entire first paragraph and is even more breathless than the original account of the trip:

> The dawn of February 17, 1957, in a sunless jungle grove of Cuba's Sierra Maestra was a bare lightening of the gloom and wetness. A week of cloak-and-dagger negotiations in Havana, an all night drive to the eastern end of the island, the tricky penetration of an army cordon at the foot of the mountains the next evening, the long slippery climb in the dark after midnight, the two hours of welcome sleep on the ground in the rebel outpost—all this had now led to the anticipated moment.

After having set the scene, Matthews went on to introduce his main character with the mystique of natural metaphor: "A swift crackling of branches and leaves, a sweeping commotion as if a sudden gust of wind had hit us, and there was Fidel Castro."

There was Fidel Castro. Matthew knew how to write (even if his prose was at times a bit purple), which is no surprise, considering, as he once said, that he had spent his whole life preparing for a literary career, an impulse that had driven him away from journalism in his twenties. His subtle use of biblical styling ("There was Fidel"), his ability to set a scene while carrying a story, his tendency to seamlessly pluck cliché terms ("cloak-and-dagger negotiations") from the imagination and drop them into a narrative, all could have made him a talented novelist. There is something praiseworthy in his ability to sweep up a reader and carry him away. The problem with Matthews, in the Cuba articles of 1959 as with the rest of his journalistic writing, is that he swept himself up and carried himself away—and usually to ridiculous conclusions.

It is this, and not his tendency to over-stylize, that ultimately proved fatal to the accuracy of Matthews's reporting. A number of critics of the journalist, including Anthony DePalma, excused Matthews's early insistence that Castro was not a communist, arguing that it was really his blind unwavering belief in Castro's democratic idealism that led to the failure of the *Times*'s coverage of Cuba. Matthews seemed to even identify himself with Castro through what he saw as their shared idealism. His March 8 article illustrates this well: "Fidel Castro is an essentially simple young man faced with a task of extraordinary complexity. The process he is now going through is one of trying to put into effect the ideals for which he always fought...He freed Cuba and now he has to conquer himself."

Matthews went on in the article to point out that Castro had no experience in government or administration. He called Castro an "uninformed, untried, inexperienced young man" who defies categorization. However, the article subtly provided a very definite categorization of the "young idealist." In the forty or so paragraphs, spread over multiple pages, Matthews quoted only one person: Castro. He allows Castro to speak for himself and, unsurprisingly, the results are pro-Castro. In a thin effort to ground the article's intentions, Matthews claimed that "all of Cuba" was behind Castro. Matthews never bothered to seek out one of the many thousand pro-Batista or anti-Castro Cubans that would have provided much-need counterbalance.

In the course of subsequent articles, Matthews repeated most of these claims and further drove home an insidious and dangerous claim that was being championed by the international left at the time. This claim, that Castro ran a "direct democracy," was a rhetorical contortion that succeeded in covering up the fact that Castro's regime was as anti-democratic as was possible: it was totalitarian. The intellectual posturing behind the term "direct democracy" amounted to the bizarre claim that Castro was so much "with the people," and was so directly a representative of the people, that his one-man rule was actually a rule by the people themselves. That is, Castro literally *was* democracy. Therefore, elections would be a foolish and unnecessary formality since "all of Cuba" wanted him in power. But the point of an election is to find out if a claim like this is actually true. This seems like a simple, almost tautological statement from today's standpoint, but the apologists for socialism-turned-totalitarianism constituted a powerful force in the 1950s and 1960s.

One incident, which could be called the Lukewarm Lemonade Incident, involved the international left's intellectual leader, Jean-Paul Sartre, and illustrates the "direct democracy" fallacy perfectly. In *Castro's Revolution*, Theodore Draper relates how Sartre and Simone de Beauvoir (perhaps the next most important member of the international left at that time) were visiting Cuba after the revolution to gather material on the topic for magazine articles they were planning to write.[23] The two leading pro-communist intellectuals were, of course, greeted by Fidel himself. As Castro led them on an "inspection tour" of Veradero Beach, they came across a lemonade vendor. Castro offered de Beauvoir and Sartre some lemonade, but after he took a sip from his own cup he put it down and said that the drink was lukewarm. The vendor replied that her fridge was broken. When Castro asked if she had reported the problem to her supervisor, she said that of course she had. The supervisor had tried to get someone to do the repair, but the waitress shrugged, "You know how it is."[24] To most, the leader of a modern country being unable to get a cold drink because of a lack of repairmen would be an indication of something gone drastically wrong. Sartre, however, spun the story differently, writing that "It was the first time that I understood—still somewhat vaguely—what I called the other day 'direct democracy.' Between the waitress and Castro, an immediate secret understanding [*connivence*] was established."

Yet Sartre himself witnessed how the "immediate secret understanding" boiled down to nothing more than a threat of violence if things were not done the way the dictator wanted them done. According to Sartre, after Castro tried ineffectually to fix the fridge himself, he turned to the vendor and said, "Tell your superiors that if they don't get busy on their problems, they will have problems with me."

It is impossible to imagine an American senator, a Canadian parliamentarian, a Spanish minister, a French president, or any other representative of a legitimate democracy publicly threatening a lemonade vendor with "problems" if a fridge did not get fixed. But to Jean-Paul Sartre, this incident represented the pinnacle of democracy, a democracy so pure it did not even require the mechanisms of democracy.

If Matthews had not pioneered this view of Cuban "democracy," he certainly reinforced it. The problem was that Matthews was not writing in a socialist intellectual journal but in the *New York Times*. In a July 16, 1959 article entitled, "Castro Has a One-Man Rule and It Is Called Non-Red," Matthews reported that "in the midst of the first great social revolution in Latin America since the Mexican revolution, [Castro's] popularity has not diminished appreciably."[25] Needless to say, Matthews cited no poll and nor did he quote a single Cuban citizen on the topic. Yet, he made his own substantial contribution to the "direct democracy" myth about Castro: "No one in Cuba has any doubts that in a fair election, he would win overwhelmingly."

Draper called this phenomenon the "awkward problem" of Castro's apologists. He wrote, "Their argument ran: (a) Castro could win any election overwhelmingly, and therefore, (b) elections were unnecessary, and anyway, (c) all previous elections were crooked."[26] This line was exactly Castro's, as Nixon had related it to President Eisenhower in the 1959 memo about him. Later that year, the *New York Times* continued its coverage of the revolution. A number of other reporters and correspondents joined the reporting team, including Tad Szulc, the veteran *New York Times* Latin America correspondent who had gained a reputation within the newspaper for excellent reporting and for having an uncanny tendency to attract news. Despite a momentary changing of the guard on the *Times*'s Cuba coverage, Szulc ran with the *New York Times*'s line on Cuba. His reports echoed Matthews's stories about a Cuba that was on the verge of a "profound" social revolution, and though there were serious abuses and a general abrogation of human rights and civil freedom, there was always a convenient "but" waiting to justify them.

Szulc's first *Times* article in a series of four focusing on Cuba's progress during the first year of Castro's rule was entitled, "A Year of Castro Rule in Cuba: Leftists Speeding Vast Reforms."[27] The December 17 article began with a strange contradiction, which embodied the *Times*'s apologetic attitude toward Cuba in the early years. In the second paragraph of the article, Szulc wrote:

Unlike the other recent Latin American revolutions that, by and large, were confined to the elimination of dictatorships, the Cuban revolution addressed itself as well to the task of implanting sweeping economic and social changes at the expense of restoration of democratic institutions, battered by the Batista dictatorship.

According to Szulc, in order for Cuba to get past its previous dictatorship and institute economic and social reform, the country had to be, once again, a dictatorship. This view of a perpetual revolution led by a benevolent dictator was precisely the one that Lenin and Stalin had advanced (each for different reasons). However, Szulc, even if he tried to spin the Cuba stories and add a gloss of romance, did acknowledge the reality on the ground to a much greater degree than Matthews had.

By the time Szulc had been brought in to write on Cuba, Herbert Matthews was on the way out. His coverage of Cuba had taken a too stringently pro-Castro line for too long, even for *Times*, and people were starting to notice. A letter to the editor that was printed in the *Times* in July, 1959, just when Tad Szulc was beginning to take over coverage on the island, provides a good example of the criticism the paper was starting to receive. The writer, one H.T. Ossorne of Edgartown, Massachusetts, began his letter by saying, "Castro is dangerous for the same reason that Hitler was: He thinks he has a 'mission.' (The psychiatrists call it a 'Messiah complex.') His resemblance to Hitler is frightening." The writer says that though he was inclined to agree with Matthews that Castro probably was not communist, he considered Castro a "force for evil." Aptly, he noted that Cuba needs help in the form of investment, but, he wrote in his concluding sentence, "Who would invest in Cuba today?"

The letter writer's use of the psychiatric concept of a Messiah complex is particularly interesting when looking at some of Matthews's articles, which painted the dictator as a savior who appeared out of the jungle mist. However, the letter writer's criticisms are even more interesting following a closer look at Tad Szulc's Cuba reporting.

◆ ◆ ◆

Although Szulc was brought in to replace Matthews in an effort to do some damage control for the *Times*'s image when it came to Cuba, his articles were only slightly less adulatory and moderately more balanced. As part of his series on the continuing revolution, Szulc wrote an April 24, 1960 article, "Cuba: Profile of a Revolution," in which he acknowledged: "Cubans are caught in a mounting turbulence of hope and hatred, enthusiasm and suspicion, faith and fear, fanaticism and gratitude, hard work and conspiracy, total adulation for Premier Castro and his present version of the revolution, and total rejection."[28] Much of the rest of the article continued to present the dichotomies of Cuba and even quoted anti-Castro Cubans at length. But through all of this, Szulc carried the Castro-as-Messiah line Castro had manufactured and which Matthews had delivered to the outside world. In a bit of poetic editorializing that bordered on the bizarre, Szulc threw away all the tensions of a Cuba that was both good and bad, full of hope and despair, by referring to Castro and his men not as rebels or fighters or young politicos but as "young bearded revolutionary prophets." Even Matthews had not gone as far as calling Castro a prophet (at least not explicitly).

After Castro overthrew the Batista government, the United States State Department scrambled to get people and offices ready to deal with the new revolutionary government. On the basis of his 1957 interview with Castro, one of the only interviews with the rebel leader that had been conducted by an American prior to the January 1, 1959 revolution, Matthews was selected by the State Department to brief Ambassador Earl E.T. Smith on Castro. The State Department did not rely on one journalist to brief an ambassador, and Ambassador Smith noted that the briefing was a usual "course" of briefings that consisted of weeks of meetings with "a number" of different experts and officials. (Smith was quickly replaced by Philip Bonsal, who was the last American ambassador to Cuba.) But the fact that Matthews was selected for the briefing session indicates the significance of his reporting had gained in the early days of the revolution.

By September 1960, controversy concerning Matthews's pro-Castro influence was bubbling to the surface in Washington. Two Democratic senators, Senator James O. Eastland and Senator Thomas J. Dodd (father of former Connecticut Senator Chris Dodd) publicly charged that lower levels of government, particularly within the State Department, and segments of the American press had been "instrumental in Fidel Castro's rise to power in Cuba."[29] Unsurprisingly, Matthews was one of those accused by Senators Eastland and Dodd of creating pro-Castro sway in Washington. In testimony for a subcommittee of the Senate Judiciary Committee, two former ambassadors to Cuba, Earl E.T. Smith and Arthur Gardner, testified concerning the influence Matthews wielded. According to the *New York Times*'s report, Gardner testified:

> Three front page articles in *the* New York Times in early 1957, written my [sic] the editorialist Herbert Matthews, served to inflate Castro to world stature and world recognition. Until that time, Castro had been just another bandit in the Oriente Mountains of Cuba, with a handful of followers who had terrorized the campesinos, that is, the peasants, throughout the countryside.

> After the Matthews articles, which followed an exclusive interview by the *Times* editorial writer in Castro's mountain hideout and which likened him to Abraham Lincoln, he was able to get followers and funds in Cuba and in the United States. From that time on, arms, money and soldiers of fortune abounded. Much of the American press began to picture Castro as a political Robin Hood.

By that point, the State Department and even the *New York Times* had fully realized and admitted (though never publicly) the extent to which Matthews's articles, propelled to worldwide prominence by their repeated front-page placement in the *Times*, had transformed an inexperienced and ill-equipped middle-class student-turned-rebel into a Cuban dictator. The State Department, along with other parts of the United States government, had grown increasingly dismayed by the role the *Times* had played in the affair. But, as is often the case with congressional testimony, by the time the senators were testifying on the topic, it was too late. The tragedy of the story, though, is that the *Times*'s hand in bungling relations between Cuba and the United States did not end with the removal of Herbert Matthews from reporting on Cuba.

The final chapter in the story of the *New York Times*'s influence in the early years of the Castro revolution and Cuba involves, of course, the failed Bay of Pigs attack. In 1961, Tad Szulc once again came across a piece of news that many of his fellow journalists would have sold their grandmothers for. Szulc's vast network of Latin American and United States government contacts led him to a story that the United States was planning an ultra-secret operation to back Cuban exiles who would invade the island and overthrow Castro. Szulc conducted an impressive investigation, getting to enough high-level sources to even obtain an extremely accurate prediction for the date of the invasion. (Szulc thought it would happen on April 18; it actually took place on April 17.) He wrote his story and had it on Turner Catledge's desk on April 6. Catledge wanted to run the story, and he wanted to run it with the kind of prominence that a story of such importance deserved.[30] However, given the super-secret nature of the operation, Catledge thought he should check a few aspects of the story with the *Times*'s acting publisher, Orvil Dryfoos, who had married Arthur Hays Sulzberger's daughter Marian and eventually ascended to the throne of the paper, taking over operations and then officially becoming publisher on April 25. Dryfoos had misgivings about the story. He ended up speaking to President Kennedy about the piece to get a better idea on how to proceed. Meanwhile, Catledge was consulting with other top people at the *Times* on what to do. His decision, as Peter Wyden notes in his book, *Bay of Pigs,* was in line with his personal motto: "When in doubt, print it."

Catledge was determined to print it big. He wanted to run the story under an enormous four-column headline. Two of Catledge's top editors, the assistant managing editor on duty, Theodor Bernstein, and the news editor, Lewis Jordan, were not happy about shifting around the columns. They, to Catledge's dismay, went over their boss's head to speak with Dryfoos. But Dryfoos had already decided to err on the side of caution. The *Times*'s controlling family had been close to the Kennedys since JFK's father Joe Kennedy had wisely cultivated relationships with the owning families of some of the country's top newspapers, the *New York Times* being the most prominent among them. Joe Kennedy foresaw that handing down high-level media contacts to his sons John and Bobby would one day pay important political dividends. And he was right.

It seemed that a genuine concern for national security coupled with the relationship between the president and the publisher of the paper would win out. Dryfoos ordered the story to be downplayed, and what would have been a massive headline with a warning of an "imminent" invasion of Cuba became a moderate headline that read, "Anti-Castro Forces Trained to Fight at Florida Bases." Szulc and Catledge were disgusted by the decision.[31]

The invasion went forward and was an unmitigated disaster. Militarily, it failed completely. Members of the now famous Brigade 2506 who were not killed were captured. Almost worse than this was the public embarrassment regarding the episode. The Kennedy administration was humiliated, and the failure, under the banner of the invasion's infamous name, precluded any later action against Cuba's totalitarian regime.

Two weeks after the invasion, a humbled Kennedy made a bitter confession to Turner Catledge: "Maybe if you had printed more about the operation, you would have saved us from a colossal mistake." Similarly, JFK lamented to Dryfoos more than a year later that "I wish you had run everything on Cuba...I am just sorry you didn't tell it at the time."[32]

Blame for the Bay of Pigs episode rests squarely on the shoulders of Kennedy and his administration. But considering that for years, the *Times* pushed to prominence almost all of Herbert Matthews's romantic, borderline fictional stories about Castro and then just when it had a credible, fully sourced story about Cuba, it decided *not* to run it, it's hard to avoid the conclusion that the *Times* had failed in its own duty. Propelling Castro into the international limelight, where he could reach out to the world for money and support, and then downplaying a major story of endless significance, the *New York Times* botched its coverage of Cuba. And each step of the way, as responsible reporters and editors at the paper objected to the bungling, the paper's ownership stepped in to set them straight.

◆◆◆

When Fidel Castro made his first visit to the US in 1959 at the invitation of the American Society of Newspaper Editors, the trip was a celebration of the newly anointed dictator. In New York, crowds thronged the streets, lining up to catch a glimpse of Castro, who was escorted around town by a guard of New York Police Department detectives.[33] It was Castro's first visit to the United States as Cuba's head of state, and as such, it was a momentous event for the revolutionary dictator. Castro spent a week in the US, where the papers covered Castro's every move (including the self-inflicted trouble he had in finding a place to stay in Manhattan). The Cuban dictator's speech at the United Nations, which characteristically ran over its time length and completely knocked the United Nation's scheduling out of place, was also covered, as was the presence of large pro- and anti-Castro crowds in New York, and the police department's difficulty in managing security.

What did not get covered were the details of the meeting between Castro and the *New York Times* publisher Arthur Hays Sulzberger, correspondent Herbert Matthews, and a few of the newspaper's top editors.

Castro had not come to New York just to bask in the glory: the newly installed Cuban leader was so grateful for what the *Times* had done for him that he felt it incumbent to show his appreciation—and to do so in person. On April 21, 1959, Castro strode into the *New York Times* building, where he was greeted by a few very important people.[34] One of them was Arthur Hays Sulzberger, the publisher of the newspaper and head of the Ochs-Sulzberger family. Another distinguished member of the welcoming group was Herbert Matthews.

Castro was savvy when it came to the media and no doubt understood the reach and influence of the *New York Times*, making it likely that the gratitude he expressed was as much about currying favor for the future as it was about expressing genuine appreciation for coverage in the past. Still, Castro had much to be thankful for when it came to Herbert Matthews, Arthur Hays Sulzberger, and the *New York Times*'s reporting on the newly empowered Cuban dictator. And, indeed, according to Anthony DePalma, one of Castro's most trusted allies, Ernesto "Ché" Guevara, attested to the fact that "Matthews's work was more important to the rebels than a victory on the battlefield."[35]

For its part, the *New York Times* seemed equally aware of this debt of gratitude—even if it was less than eager to share this fact. An article that appeared in the *Times* on April 22, 1959 reported that a meeting had indeed taken place between Castro and *Times* management. But it left out one important detail: the newly installed ruler of Cuba had "profusely" thanked Sulzberger, Matthews, and the *New York Times* editors for their role in bringing about the Cuban revolution.[36]

Whispering Conspiratorially:
"Unrest Grows in Vietnam"

The *New York Times*'s correspondent in Vietnam in the early years of the war was a young, brash, and brainy reporter named David Halberstam. Still in his twenties when he arrived in Vietnam, Halberstam had acquired a decent amount of experience as a correspondent covering the civil rights movement in the South and war in the Congo. Before these few years of reporting, however, his only newspaper experience had been as a reporter and later managing editor of Harvard's student newspaper. Halberstam was considered headstrong and sometimes arrogant, even by friends and colleagues.[1] Only three assignments and four years after joining the *New York Times*, Halberstam thought enough of himself as a journalist to refuse an assignment from his editor, Arthur Gelb. In fact, Halberstam did not just refuse the assignment—he even crumpled up the paper on which the assignment was written and handed it back to his boss, remarking, "I've just won the Pulitzer, and you're sending me to Buffalo?"[2]

Halberstam's self-assurance was not something he picked up in Vietnam or realized when he received the Pulitzer Prize for his reporting there. On the contrary, he arrived with his ego and self-confidence in hand. It was these two qualities, in addition to his intelligence and skill as a journalist, that positioned him to become America's first big

Vietnam reporter. He quickly became a journalist-celebrity (which may explain how his bloated, rambling prose made it past the red pens of his book and magazine editors).

Halberstam made his position on Vietnam known from the very start, and given that he was public about these opinions from the first months of his time "in country," he expressed his views as quickly as he formed them. Richard Holbrooke, the former United States ambassador and assistant secretary of state, arrived in Vietnam in 1963 as a junior diplomat and quickly made contact with Halberstam. "Halberstam was only 29," Holbrooke later recalled, "but he was already the dominant figure among an influential group of journalists who reported what they observed even when it contradicted the official version of the war put out by the military."[3]

In an article written after Halberstam's death in 2007, Holbrooke told the story of his first meeting with the Times's Vietnam correspondent and his close friend, Neil Sheehan of United Press International (UPI), who would later take Halberstam's place as Vietnam correspondent for the Times.[4] "They were tall and intense and noisily exuberant," Holbrooke wrote. "They knew they were covering the biggest story in the world, with very few competitors. They knew the official version was wrong, and they were going to get the truth."

During the conversation, discussion turned to the different people and forces involved in Vietnam, specifically who the journalists thought could be relied on for information, and who was unreliable and disliked. "At that time they still supported the war. They wanted those who were lying to the public, both the corrupt South Vietnamese government and American military commanders, to be held accountable," Holbrooke recounted. "They especially despised the senior commander, World War II veteran, Paul Harkins, and after giving me some advice—'Don't trust anything those bastards tell you'—David [Halberstam] and Neil [Sheehan] spent most of the night denouncing Harkins."

That same night, as the hours fell away, Halberstam and his soon-to-be successor, Sheehan, got more and more drunk on wine. At one point, the two journalists "conducted a mock trial of the four-star general [Harkins]" for what they called "incompetence and dereliction of duty."

"In his rumbling, powerful voice, David pronounced Harkins 'guilty' of each charge, after which Neil loudly carried out the 'sentence': execution by imaginary firing squad against the back wall of the restaurant."[5]

That night, the reporters imagined themselves to be judge, jury and even executioner of the forces in Vietnam that they opposed, despite the fact that they had been in the Southeast Asian country for little more than a year. Even though the mock trial and sentencing were made in fun, the drunken joking of two twenty-something journalists, the ersatz events turned out to be a surprisingly accurate reflection of how things would later turn out: Harkins would be stripped of his position just a year later and the "corrupt South Vietnamese government" that Halberstam and Sheehan railed against would be overthrown in 1963, its leaders unceremoniously executed in the back of a truck.

When President Kennedy learned about the coup and the execution of the South Vietnamese Government's leader, Ngo Dinh Diem (Diem for short), and his brother, Ngo Dinh Nhu, he was crushed. "I was present with the president when together we received information of that coup. I'd never seen him more upset," said Kennedy's secretary of defense, Robert McNamara, in Errol Morris's documentary, *The Fog of War*.[6]

"President Kennedy and I had tremendous problems with Diem but my God," McNamara continued, "he was the authority, he was head of state and he was overthrown by a military coup. And Kennedy knew and I knew that to some degree the U.S. government was responsible for that."

Parts of the United States government did have a major hand in the coup. But Kennedy did not. For him and McNamara (who would go down, in part, as a warmongering "SECDEF" who could not stop a war he helped start), a stable South Vietnamese government was the only path to the removal of American troops from Vietnam and the end to the war, at least as far as the United States was concerned.

"October 2. I had returned from Vietnam," McNamara said about his high-level 1962 visit to Vietnam to try to assess the situation there. "At that time, we had 16,000 military advisers. I recommended to President Kennedy and the security council that we establish a plan and objective that we remove all of them in two years."[7]

It was a drastic plan, but by that point it had become clear to Kennedy that America could not win that war and that its best option was to get America troops, known euphemistically as "military advisers," out of Vietnam. The only way to do so, according to McNamara, was to pull the troops out as soon as possible. White House tapes recorded McNamara telling Kennedy that "We need a way of out of Viet and this is a way to do it."[8] For the first time since American participation in the ill-fated war, the United States had a plan. It may not have been a plan that some of the military's planners would have approved of with any enthusiasm, but it was a plan.

"Kennedy," McNamara recounts in the Morris documentary, "announced that we were going to pull out all of our military advisers by '65. We were going to take 1,000 out by the end of '63 and we did." Everything was on track to extricate the United States from the quagmire it had stepped into. But then disaster struck: Diem was overthrown and killed. While Kennedy was deeply troubled by the fact that, as chief executive, he bore some responsibility, even if indirectly, for the murder of a head of state (and a fellow Catholic), what was equally if not more disturbing was the fact that he knew the United States was now trapped in a long and dark tunnel of war. Just when he and McNamara had managed to create a bit of light at the end of that tunnel with plans for troop removal from Vietnam, the light was snuffed out with the death of Diem.

What happened between Holbrooke's first meeting with Halberstam and Sheehan in May 1963, when the reporters expressed their disgust with Diem's government and the need for him to be overthrown, and the October coup of that same year was not all that complicated (at least not by the standards of a coup occurring in the midst of a major war). All it took was the arrival of a Boston Brahmin diplomat named Henry Cabot Lodge Jr., a group of repressed but politically motivated Buddhists, a core of power-hungry South Vietnamese generals, and two young *New York Times* journalists eager to put their stamp on events, in order to create a sea change in Vietnam.

◆ ◆ ◆

In the days before the coup, Richard Holbrooke noted that Halberstam and Sheehan were not just in the know about the coup but acted, in the days before it, as if they were a part of the conspiracy. Holbrooke wrote, "In late October 1963, in a fever pitch of excitement, David and Neil took me to lunch, and, whispering conspiratorially, told me that a coup against the Saigon government would begin right there and then. Every few minutes one of them would run outside to look for troops marching on the presidential palace. When lunch ended without a coup, Neil left for a brief vacation in Tokyo and David stayed on. The coup happened a week later, exactly the way they had predicted, and David won a Pulitzer for his work that year."[9]

The involvement of Halberstam and Sheehan in the coup d'état was not just direct—it was also explicit. The journalists themselves, if not boasting, spoke confidently about their role in overthrowing the Diem government in their later articles and books. The two (especially Halberstam) had trained their sights on the Diem government, which they regarded as brutal and authoritarian, and went to great, and ultimately very effective, lengths to weaken the regime.

One of Halberstam's earlier *Times* articles, "Diem Regime Under Fire" of July 7, 1963, presented a narrative of boiling discontent with the Diem government both on behalf of "the people of Vietnam" and the American government.[10] Halberstam wrote that according to "some observers"—whose names, positions, and even nationalities are never identified in the story—relations between the United States and the Diem government were not just bad but were "more nearly impossible." The whole problem, which Halberstam explained in a single sentence, was not that the Americans were angry with the Diem government or that the Diem government felt insulted by the Americans. The problem was a case of "each being horribly miscast for the other." The basic idea that Halberstam was trying to articulate was that America was a democracy and the non-communist South Vietnam government was not. He explained that the South Vietnamese embraced a "mandarin" view that demanded the people treat their president as a representative of God.

Whether or not this accurately reflects Vietnamese political belief is beyond the scope of this book, just as it was beyond the scope of a single *New York Times* news article written for readers who could not identify Vietnam on a map. But there is a more important question underlying Halberstam's involvement in the Diem coup and the subsequent disaster of the war: what made Halberstam think that any subsequent Vietnamese government would relinquish this approach to governance and do a better job fighting the war against the communists? It was a question Halberstam neither answered nor addressed.

The *Times* man in Vietnam went on in his July 1963 article to inform readers—in a manner eerily similar to Herbert Matthews's statements about the beliefs of *all* the people of Cuba regarding Castro—that "while the anti-Communist stand of the Diem government, by itself, is enough for the Americans, it is not enough for the people of Vietnam. For them, a government must be more than against Communists…"

Many other reporters would have found it appropriate to provide a quote of one of the many Vietnamese people who may have harbored this view. But Halberstam did not. In fact, the three-column, almost forty-paragraph article, one of the first major articles Halberstam wrote against the Diem government, did not include a single identified source. Rather, "one cynic," "some observers," "one American officer," "old hands," "one American," and another "one American," "some Americans," "many Vietnamese," and finally "many Americans" were the only sources Halberstam cited in the entire article. In no case did Halberstam speak about who these "many Americans" were or what they were doing in Vietnam, nor did he make transparent the identities and ideologies of the "many Vietnamese" or, still less, of the mysterious "some observers" or sagacious "old hands."

Instead, Halberstam spoke with the authority of the passive voice, mounting all of his seemingly factual claims on linguistic platforms. He wrote that certain kinds of activities "are looked down upon as cheap politicking." He similarly claimed that "the Americans are viewed with considerable suspicion." He went on with endless claims, all in the passive voice, for which he never provided a speaker or the person doing the "looking down upon" or viewing the Americans with suspicion.

Armed only with the passive voice and unnamed sources as his tools, Halberstam attempted to establish three very big and very important claims in the article. The first was that, by that time, the American government no longer supported the Diem government. The second claim was that the Vietnamese people never really supported the Diem government in the first place. And the third claim Halberstam tried to make was that many parts of the Diem government neither wanted the support of the American government nor believed in the Diem government itself. Of course, the overarching idea of the analysis (the article was in no way a news report, as it reported no news) was blatantly anti-Diem.

A day after the July 7 anti-Diem piece, Halberstam's view on the Diem government was confirmed, but only in a personal way for Halberstam and fellow journalists. Halberstam and a group of reporters, including Neil Sheehan and Malcolm Browne of the Associated Press, were covering a Buddhist demonstration against the government when the police began to push the journalists, knocked one of them down, and broke one or two cameras. Halberstam cried conspiracy. In the eyes of the journalists, they were now the focus of the Diem government's brutal repression. The journalists' reaction to the incident reveals the extent to which they dramatized the scuffle on the basis of their view of the Diem government. Instead of filing a report with the chargé d'affaires at the United States embassy in Saigon, Halberstam, Sheehan, Browne, and Peter Kalischer (of CBS), in a move that aptly represents the involvement the journalists would later take in government affairs in Vietnam, sent a cable directly to the president of the United States, who was vacationing at Hyaniss Port at the time. In a somewhat strange move, it was Halberstam himself who reported and wrote the article (referring to himself in the third person while his name was on the byline) and noted, a few times, that the journalists had sent a cable to the president's family compound about the issue.[11]

After the incident, Halberstam's articles on the Diem government's repression of the Buddhists became fiercer and more frequent, eventually bordering on the obsessive. An August 14 article reported the story of a seventeen-year-old Buddhist who burned himself to death to protest "religious persecution" by Diem and his government.[12] The narrative claimed that the Diem's government's harshness against the Buddhists was creating a "religious crisis" in the country that was splitting the population from the government. A little more than a week later, on August 25, Halberstam continued the narrative with the most shocking and damaging story yet. In an article entitled, "Repressions Are Seen Creating Sharp Divisions in Vietnam," Halberstam carried the anti-Diem narrative along on the basis of the same "some observers" and "many Americans" who served as the sources of his earlier anti-Diem stories.[13] The article, written the day the new American ambassador Henry Cabot Lodge arrived in Vietnam, reported that the Diem government's attacks on Buddhist pagodas of the previous week had brought the country to a "political watershed."

Halberstam had covered the raid of the previous week vigorously but, unfortunately, falsely. In one of the most important raid stories, "Anti-US Feeling Rises in Vietnam as Unrest Grows," of August 24, Halberstam reported that under the direction of Diem's brother, Ngo Dinh Nu, government troops had raided a pagoda in the city of Hue and massacred thirty Buddhist monks.[14] Importantly, Halberstam was careful to tie the raid *not* to the military, which Halberstam knew was the only power structure in South Vietnam capable of overthrowing Diem, but to the Diem government itself, which, in Halberstam's view, was disposable.

The reports of the brutality of the government attacks that occurred at the pagoda sparked such a great public response that the United Nations launched a commission to investigate the deaths of the thirty monks . However, the story was not just flawed. It was completely false. Historian Mark Moyar details in his book *Triumph Forsaken* that by the time the United Nations commission arrived in Vietnam to conduct its inquiry, further investigation revealed the actual number of Buddhist deaths was *at most* two.[15] When the United Nations team conducted its investigation, two of the people interviewed about the events of that day turned out to be two of the Buddhists Halberstam had reported were dead. But reports of their demise were clearly premature, as these Buddhists were, in fact, living, breathing, healthy, and unharmed. The United Nation's investigation further found that, in fact, *no* Buddhists had been killed that day. But the public relations damage of Halberstam's claims of a massacre had already been done. It was a major win for the political motivations of the Buddhists, the conspiring generals in Diem's military, and the *Times* journalist who was eager to see Vietnam rid of Diem.

Nevertheless, Halberstam repeated the claim that Ngo Dinh Nhu was planning and leading the raids on Buddhist pagodas that had resulted in the fictitious deaths. However, it was an August 23 *Times* report that ran under the headline, "Plan Said to Be Nhu's," which went after the claim most aggressively.[16] Halberstam cites only "highly reliable sources," never naming or identifying a single one of them, to make the claim that it had been Diem's unstable brother, Nhu, who had been exercising this brutality against the Buddhists. In the article, Halberstam went to pains in order to prove that Diem was no longer in control. "The sources in Saigon now feel that the situation is that Mr. Diem remains President but that the Nhus have gained so much power that they may be more important than the President," Halberstam wrote. But Halberstam's thinly sourced speculations went even further. "These sources said that the Nhus acted to crush the Buddhists, to teach the Americans...a lesson, and to warn all dissident elements in the population."

The other important piece of news that Halberstam included in the story was the arrival of Ambassador Henry Cabot Lodge Jr. Halberstam discussed the arrival of the diplomat, his wife, and two special assistants and that the diplomatic mission received passes from the government that would exempt them from curfews. Then, without any segue or any visible reason for stating it, Halberstam wrote, "Mr. Nhu and his wife are regarded as being somewhat anti-American."

In Halberstam's view, the two seemingly unrelated facts—Lodge's arrival in Vietnam as the new ambassador and the spurious claim that the Nhus had effectively taken over the government—were connected, and this would prove to be disastrously correct in the coming months. Shortly after Lodge arrived in Vietnam, he called three journalists to his residence:

Malcolm Browne, Neil Sheehan, and David Halberstam, three of the four journalists who had angrily cabled President Kennedy about their scuffle with South Vietnamese police. The new ambassador told the journalists that he wanted their advice on the situation in Vietnam. Sheehan, in his book, *A Bright Shining Lie*, wrote, "I told [Ambassador Lodge], in sum, that the Ngo Dinhs were so mad and hated that they were incapable of governing, that the Viet Cong were gaining rapidly in the countryside, and that if Diem and his family stayed in power the war was certain to be lost."[17] According to Sheehan, who took over from Halberstam as the *Times* Vietnam correspondent in 1964, all three journalists reported roughly the same anti-Diem line—exactly the one that Halberstam and Sheehan loudly proclaimed in their drunken dinner with Richard Holbrooke only months earlier. Sheehan wrote:

> We did not realize that our dispatches had been arming Averell Harriman, who had moved up to become undersecretary of state for political affairs, and Roger Hilsman, who had replaced Harriman in the Far Eastern affairs post at State, in their attempt to persuade Kennedy to authorize the overthrow of Diem and his family. We would have been still more encouraged had we known how much our reporting…had contributed to the judgment of this man [Henry Cabot Lodge Jr.] who was to take the power of the United States into his hands in Vietnam in the late summer and fall of 1963 and wield it as he saw fit.[18]

In the view of the two *New York Times* correspondents, Sheehan and Halberstam, the overthrow of Diem was not just a good possibility—it was the only possibility. As two of the top journalists in Vietnam, they were able to make a convincing case to Lodge, not in their short lunch conversation with the diplomat but through their false reporting of Buddhist massacres and widespread discontent among the people of South Vietnam.

The use of unnamed sources may have been one of the most damning decisions Halberstam and Sheehan made. One of the secret sources the two (along with a number of other journalists in their circles) relied upon most heavily was a Vietnamese man named Pham Xuan An. An worked as a stringer for Reuters and a correspondent for *Time* magazine and freely fed hot information to his fellow journalists. According to Morley Safer, who covered Vietnam for CBS, An was "among the best-connected journalists in the country." But there was a reason for this: An was a communist spy and, because of this, he had access to the top levels of the communist North Vietnam government. The information he fed the *Times*'s Sheehan and Halberstam was propaganda for the other side, which served both the journalists and the communists equally well. In fact, An's information gave Halberstam the ability to scoop so many big stories that even after learning of An's role as a spy who had used his colleagues as tools for the communist propaganda machine, Halberstam still maintained that he had no hard feelings. "I still think fondly of An," he said. "I never felt betrayed by An."[19]

Halberstam's insistence that he had not been betrayed by An is probably based on two factors. The first is that if Halberstam considered himself betrayed, it would mean that his role as a journalist, as someone who reported the truth, had also been compromised and the credibility of his reports tainted. In making this claim, Halberstam was suggesting that if the person who stood to be most damaged by An (i.e. Halberstam himself) did not feel betrayed, the journalistic impact of An's actions were little more than negligible. But the second—and by far more important—factor is that both Halberstam and Sheehan believed their views about the Diem government to be in line with those of President Kennedy and Secretary of Defense McNamara. Ambassador Lodge had been convinced (at least in part by the two journalists) that a coup d'état was both a necessity and an inevitability. Lodge, according to Sheehan, had set to the task of convincing his boss, President Kennedy, of the same idea. Sheehan wrote in *A Bright Shining Lie* that "Kennedy ended by deferring to Lodge's judgment...Kennedy asked only that Lodge guarantee him a successful coup, that he not be forced to endure the disgrace of another Bay of Pigs."

So, in the end, Halberstam and Sheehan reasoned, even if they had written stories sourced by a communist agent, and even if the facts were not exactly correct, the basic idea and the political attitudes behind them were accurate, a notion that was corroborated (in Halberstam and Sheehan's view) by Kennedy's support for the coup. The president had not been tricked, since he had approved the coup—or so they thought. In their minds, Halberstam and Sheehan's ideas about Vietnam and the Diem government not only ultimately received the approval of the president but resulted directly in Kennedy's decision to proceed with an overthrow.

In the source notes for his book, Sheehan wrote that he relied on "particularly the secret cable traffic between Lodge and President Kennedy" to establish the fact that Lodge had actually managed to convince Kennedy to approve the coup. However, according to McNamara's account at the beginning of the chapter, Kennedy was not only crestfallen but shocked to learn about the coup in Vietnam. The reason for this is simple: after weeks of deliberation and meetings with his highest level advisers, Kennedy concluded that a coup was not the way to go and that the South Vietnamese generals who were plotting it were more volatile than Diem and offered no evidence or indication that they would run the war any better than Diem.

Halberstam and Sheehan were unaware of this crucial fact, even years later when they authored books on Vietnam. On September 25, 1973, the *New York Times* ran a story about E. Howard Hunt, the White House "plumber" who, as a CIA agent under President Nixon, worked to fix White House "leaks," one of which was Nixon's Watergate scandal. The September 25 story reported that in testimony to the Senate Watergate Committee, Hunt revealed that he "had fabricated State Department cables to show a link between President Kennedy and the assassination of the President of South Vietnam, Ngo Dinh Diem, a Roman Catholic, to estrange Catholic voters from the Democratic party." The cables were taken from Hunt's safe in June 1972, the *Times*'s report said, and handed over to the acting director of the FBI at the time, L. Patrick Gray. Mr. Gray confirmed that he had burned the cables.[20]

Like many of the *Times* reporters' important anti-Diem stories on Vietnam, the evidence the two relied on to prove that Kennedy had both wanted and authorized the overthrow of the Diem government had been faked. But even in books, articles, and interviews *after* the *New York Times*'s story about Hunt's fabrication of the State Department cables, the *Times* reporters stuck to their chosen narrative about the entire affair.

Whether they did so because it was convenient for them and their careers or because they actually still believed what they had reported is unclear.

◆ ◆ ◆

Kennedy did not have the hand in the Diem overthrow that Halberstam and Sheehan thought and *wanted* him to have. Since the two were journalists on the ground in Vietnam, tasked with the job of reporting facts (at least, theoretically), and not with making or intervening in government policy, they could not have known that Kennedy and McNamara were actually planning a complete pull out from Vietnam that would begin in 1963. Accordingly, they did not know that the withdrawal plan required a stable and intact South Vietnamese government if it were to be put into action. It was with this context that news of the coup and the deaths of Diem and his brother shattered Kennedy and McNamara, who, prior to the coup, had finally found some hope in the bleak Vietnam situation. Both the president and his secretary of defense understood that the overthrow of the government, perpetrated with the assistance of parts of the CIA and State Department, and based on the false, unsourced, and spectacular claims of the *New York Times* reporters, meant one thing: the war would go on. And for another twelve years, at the expense of untold millions of dollars and, far more tragically, hundreds of thousands of lives, it did.

The White Taffeta Gown:
"People Who Happen to Be Jewish"

Of all the major failures of the *New York Times*, its coverage of the Holocaust is the most bitter and difficult to digest. There are many dimensions and many reasons for why the *Times* chose to cover the events the way it did. Unlike other stories the *Times* got wrong, covered up, or lied about, there is no central character, no Walter Duranty to blame, no Guido Enderis to condemn, no Herbert Matthews to pity. There is only a newspaper, its owners and managers, and their disastrous decisions regarding the most important story in modern journalism.

It was not until after the systematic mass slaughter of Europe's Jews that the event was given the name "Holocaust," which means "a complete burning." But even during the war, the genocide of the Jewish people committed by Hitler was recognized as something different than the war itself. It was then, and is now, thought of as a "war within a war," a war fought not to gain territory, amass power, resources, or prestige. Rather, its aim was to erase an entire people from the face of the earth.

Genocide had been committed before the Holocaust, but never had it been so ruthlessly effective. The numbers are still staggering and seem to grow more abstract as time goes on and investigation of the horror deepens. Six million Jews in a few short years. One third of the world's

Jewish population was obliterated in six years. Not only was the speed and efficacy of the killing on a previously unseen order, but the nature of the brutality was so gruesome that even hardened eyewitnesses had difficulty believing that what they saw in the concentration camps was real. Former First World War reporters who witnessed the horrific use of gas on the battlefield, who had covered massacres and blood-soaked battles, found themselves reduced to tears and nausea at the sight of the human skeletons covered in "obscene" rags, wandering among massive piles and pits of the bodies of individuals who only months before were each other's neighbors, friends and family members.

The ability for people to believe in the reality of what was occurring in Europe beyond the front was further impaired precisely because it all happened in the era of the United Nations. The First World War had been widely considered the end of global warfare, and the establishment of the League of Nations and its successor body, the United Nations, were believed to be signs of a new kind of interaction among the world's nations. With mass communication, an international forum, and, most of all, the dire lessons of recent history, there was a general consensus that things would finally be different.

And they *were* different: they were worse. The tragedies of the Holocaust are endless, but one stands out among them in the historical record. As the Jews were being culled as casually as a virus-infected stock of fowl, they comforted themselves with the thought that their brothers outside of Europe and the Good Samaritans of the nations, particularly in America, were learning of their plight and were moving to help them. But for the most part, this was not true. The *New York Times* was only one of many newspapers that failed in its duty, not just to the Jews interned in death camps, but also to the newly established concepts of international justice and to their own journalistic standards of unwavering truth-telling.

Many papers missed the story, downplayed the story, cheek-turned away from the story. But the *Times* was different than these many newspapers. First, it was the most prominent of the American newspapers of that time, to the extent that the Associated Press ran a daily news summary of what the *Times* printed each day, since what the *Times* considered "news" was subsequently covered by the mainstream of American journalism. Second, the *Times* had a reach that most other newspapers did not have. It had correspondents in every corner of the world who (as we have seen) had enough influence to broker the recognition of nations and create or conceal stories of large-scale famine and widespread murder. By the 1940s, the *Times* syndicated stories to 525 newspapers around the country, was read by powerbrokers and policymakers of the time, including the United States secretary of state and members of the Supreme Court. Even the pope, at that time Pius XII, was a "careful reader of the foreign press in general and the *New York Times* in particular."[1] The paper, in other words, did not merely cover the news—it created it.

Lastly, the *New York Times* was owned and run by a Jewish family, the Ochs-Sulzbergers. It does not go without saying that because the family was Jewish the *Times* had a moral obligation to give coverage of the Holocaust due prominence and attention. A strong case can be made that there was an obligation. But that is not the one that is being made here. Rather, looking at the history of the ownership and their relationship with their ethnic-religious background, it becomes disturbingly evident that the owners of the *New York Times* actually *downplayed* and, for all practical purposes, obscured the story of the Holocaust *because* they were Jewish. This is the tragic irony of the *Times*'s Holocaust coverage, which, like a stain that cannot be removed, is now part of the fabric of the newspaper itself.

◆ ◆ ◆

On June 27, 1942, the *New York Times* ran a story that declared in its headline, "More Executed in Yugoslavia, Czechoslovakia & Poland—Jews' Toll 700,000."[2] The headline was roughly accurate—historical records reveal that by that point, the Nazis had slaughtered not just 700,000 but almost 1,000,000 Jewish people from those countries. This first wave of massacre in the Nazi Final Solution program represents more than ten times more murders than all of those committed in the Bosnian genocide. Just an early, relatively small round in the killing of the Jews of Europe, it equals the total number of people killed in the entirety of the Rwandan genocide.

Furthermore, the deaths of the Jews did not happen overnight—they were the culmination of a lengthy process that began when the Nazis stripped Jews of their property and citizenship and started to herd them to detention centers and early concentration camps. The Nazis had set the ball rolling toward genocide as early as 1935, when the Reich openly and unabashedly made Jews into second-class citizens with the Nuremberg Laws. It banned Jews from the 1936 Olympics and oversaw Kristallnacht, or "Night of the Broken Glass," when thousands of Jewish stores and homes were ransacked and burned in 1938. Then came the multiples rounds of deportations in which Jews were simply told to leave Germany and Austria, and then packed up and shipped off, also as early as 1938. All of these atrocities were known by newspapers around the world, which had reported on the Germans' increasing crimes against the Jews. There was little reason to doubt that the Nazis were taking another step along their path toward racial extermination.

Still, the *New York Times* did not see it fit to dedicate an entire article to the revelation that 700,000 Jews had recently been murdered by the Nazis. Rather, the editors of the paper ran the information as a sub-story that was given about two inches of the famous gray paper—about the length of your little finger—amounting to a mere seventy-four words. The article was buried on page five.

Strangely, what little the editors at the *Times* did choose to run about the 700,000 murders accurately reflected the seriousness of the situation. The blurb about the genocide quoted a BBC broadcast based on a ground-shattering report, the Bund report, on the situation regarding the Jews of Europe. The quotation remarked on the huge death toll: "To accomplish this, probably the greatest mass slaughter in history, every death-dealing method was employed—machine gun, gas chambers, concentration camps, whipping, torture instruments, and starvation."

The words "the greatest mass slaughter in history" stand out. The *Times* printed these words and acknowledged that the Nazis, who had provoked a world war and were ravaging Europe, had committed one of the greatest crimes in history. It also put its finger on the variety of devices used to kill the Jews, from new technologies like gas chambers to the simplest methods of brutality such as starvation and whipping. Yet the story ran as it did, with less space and attention in the paper than what is routinely given to an off-Broadway theater review.

The article is a disturbing symbol of the *New York Times*'s reporting on the Holocaust: the newspaper had detailed information about the slaughter, found the sources of the information reliable enough to print, and yet, relegated the story to a two-inch blurb on page five under a tiny headline. The source of the story's information was a report written by the Jewish Labor Bund of Poland in May 1942, which tallied the number of deaths from known and confirmed Nazi massacres in and around Poland.[3] Members of the Jewish Labor Bund succeeded in getting the report to the Polish government, which was exiled in London. The Bund report concluded that the Nazis were pursuing the "physical extermination of the Jewish people on Polish soil" and confirmed that Hitler was pursuing a policy that was expressed by the Nazi maxim that no matter how the war ends for Germany, the Jews will be wiped out.

The *Times* had actually quoted Nazi propaganda minister Joseph Goebbels's citation of this "no matter what, the Jews will perish" policy in an article that ran long before the June 1942 article on the Bund report. Already by late 1941, Nazi determination to wipe out the Jews and the implementation of the process, which came to be known as the Final Solution, was appearing in the *New York Times*'s own reporting. In a November 14, 1941 article entitled, "Goebbels Spurs Abuse for Jews," the *Times* (in an article reprinted from United Press) reported, "Dr. Goebbels promulgated a new ten-point charter for the Nazi campaign against the Jews. He exhorted all Germans to harbor no sympathy for the Jews in connection with the government's measures against them."[4] The article quotes Goebbels as saying that the emerging fate of the Jews "is indeed hard, but more than deserved." It continues to quote the top-ranking Nazi, who said, "In this historical showdown every Jew is our enemy, regardless of whether he is vegetating in a Polish ghetto or delays his parasitic existence in Berlin or Hamburg, or blows the war trumpets in Washington or New York." The article concluded with Goebbels's own conclusion—that it was Germany's determination to "finally finish" the Jews.

Among the articles that graced the front page of the *Times* on that day, November 14, 1941, was a story about coal mining tests. Another article that made the hallowed front page was an article entitled, "Frankness Urged on Tokyo Leaders." A further front-page story was about American police officers who had been demoted for infractions. There was also a report about *one* man from Iceland who had been killed. The article that quoted Goebbels's use of Final Solution language did not make the cut. The report on the Nazi war against the world's Jews was printed on page eleven.

The unfolding story of Nazi persecution and murder of Europe's Jews was furthered by a March 1942 article that reported that a representative of the American Jewish Joint Distribution Company named S.B. Jacobson had come back from the Balkans, where he had been working during the years preceding the Nazi declaration of war on America. Jacobson, according to the *Times* article, "gave an eyewitness account of the barbarities affecting the lives of tens of thousands of Jews in the Balkans." Jacobson spoke about the situation of Balkan Jews.[5] "They have had a taste of all the measures which the Nazis inflict on the Jews who fall within their grasp," Jacobson said at a press conference, describing how 18,500 Jews (including women and children) were packed into cattle cars and shipped off and that the Gestapo killed at least fifty percent of them when they arrived at the destination. He also went on to say that "Internment camps and forced labor camps exist in Hungary for thousands of Jews. Those who are still at liberty suffer in other ways."

Jacobson also made a point to note that Jews in other countries in Europe were suffering still harsher fates, if that was possible to believe. The story had all the trappings of front-page piece: it was of a global scale, told of unthinkable horrors committed by a wartime enemy of the United States, and came from a highly reliable source. As an eyewitness to the Nazi horrors, Jacobson stood to open the eyes of Americans who were mostly still ignorant about the situation in Europe. Despite all this, editors at the *New York Times* found it appropriate to give the massively important story nine short paragraphs relegated to page seven.

At that time, accounts like the one based on the Bund report and that of S.B. Jacobson were bubbling to the surface of the Jewish American press. Jewish readers in the United States began to pay more attention to the catastrophe unfolding in Europe, and it was not long before their collective anger and grief found an outlet in some form of action. In *The Abandonment of the Jews*, historian David Wyman explains that a few Jewish American groups, including the American Jewish Congress, B'nai Brith, and the Jewish Labor Committee joined forces to organize a New York demonstration in protest of the situation.[6] The demonstration, which took place on July 21, 1942, turned out to be huge. At least 20,000 people gathered in Madison Square Garden, and an estimated 10,000 more ringed the area around it. President Roosevelt sent a message to be read, and New York notables like Mayor La Guardia turned out to protest.

The rally represented one of the early—and one of the strikingly few—instances where a Holocaust story would make the front page of the *New York Times*. The article was 2,783 words long, but in all those words the *Times* report did not make a single mention of the fact that Jews were being mass slaughtered as part of a Nazi racial extermination campaign. In fact, the article took a tone of optimism and led with a quote from Roosevelt's statement that "The American people will hold the Nazis to strict accountability," and offered details on how the rally was organized.[7] The article provided no background on the situation in Europe and did not reprint information from earlier reports, such as the statistic of the 700,000 murdered Jews, which the paper had only lightly touched on in its June article about the Bund report. Rather, the first paragraph spoke of Roosevelt's statement; the second paragraph talked of the Jewish organizations involved in the rally; the third "revealed" the large number of Jews fighting for the Allies in Palestine, and the fourth laundry listed some of the rally's notable attendees. The remainder of the article mostly comprised statements made by speakers and politicians at the event. But even the statements made by Roosevelt and Churchill (which accounted for a large part of the article) said nothing of what was happening in Europe—they spoke only of what would not be allowed to happen. In Roosevelt's words: "The Nazis will not succeed in exterminating their victims any more than they will succeed in enslaving mankind." Churchill's message spoke mainly of Jewish fighters in Palestine.

No mention was made in 2,783 words that genocide was being carried out against the Jews in a campaign that was specifically being waged against them and was independent of the broader war. It was as if the editors and publisher of the *New York Times* had not actually read their earlier reports about the genocide-level massacre and mass deportation of Europe's Jews. (Given that the vast majority of these reports were buried as afterthoughts in the final paragraphs of articles on page five, seven, and eleven, maybe they had not.)

Around the time that the Gray Lady was publishing its early, between-the-pages accounts of the Nazis' war against the Jews, Arthur Hays Sulzberger, the publisher of the paper at that time, was going about life as a major newspaper publisher during wartime. In May 1941, Sulzberger gave a speech at the University of the South on the topic of government censorship during war. Sulzberger expressed his support for a certain amount of domestic censorship in war, saying:

> I believe that we can have military censorship and still preserve a large measure of our freedom…I am not at all certain, however, that if we attempt to preserve our freedom by closing our eyes to our responsibilities—by turning away our heads from those who suffer because of that loss of freedom from which we would suffer were we in their place—I cannot believe that under such circumstances we could preserve and keep alive those spiritual values that must be alive when all this nightmare is over.[8]

In light of how Sulzberger's newspaper covered the Holocaust, sweeping stories of the deaths of 1,000,000 of his own people under the rug of mundane stories like tests on coal and the deaths of individual Icelanders, the statement is devastatingly hypocritical.

Less than two months later, Sulzberger was at another prominent function the *New York Times* found newsworthy: the marriage of his daughter. The nuptials were a full blown affair, and accordingly, the *Times* devoted 880 words to the event—more than eight times the amount of space that it gave to the findings of the Bund report, which reported the 700,000-person massacre. The wedding article celebrated the marriage of Sulzberger's daughter Marian to Orvil Dryfoos, who would become publisher of the

New York Times in 1961 after being fast-tracked through top positions at the paper.

> The gown of the bride was of white taffeta, made with a fitted bodice and a full bouffant skirt, on which were taffeta bows scattered here and there. The bodice was fitted with short puffed sleeves and embellished with a little net yoke and revers of heirloom rose point lace that outlined the V-neck.[9]

The article continued on about the bride's dress and then detailed the members of the bridal procession and what each of them wore, going into almost the same level of detailed that was used to describe the bridal gown, noting that "they all wore blue organdie frocks, with a panel of white organdie down the front of their bouffant skirts."

The same day of the Sulzberger wedding, July 8, 1941, an event of a different type took place. One of the first waves of killings in what would come to be known as the Ponary executions or Ponary massacres was perpetrated by the Nazis in Poland, just outside of Vilnius.[10] Polish Jews were brought to the Ponary train station outside of the resort town, where many of them had vacationed before the war. They were made to strip and give up any valuable possessions. They were then lined up in groups of ten around an open pit and shot with such efficiency that it was no stretch to murder a thousand Jews a day at the Ponary station. The Nazi executioners, some of them armed civilians, did not bother to see if the victims were actually dead before throwing a thin layer of dirt over them. The Nazis carried out the execution of more than 70,000 Jews, and 100,000 people in total, at and around Ponary station. The method used on that first day of execution would be the one adopted and then perfected for the remainder of the Ponary executions, which continued for another four years.

In May 1941, Arthur Hays Sulzberger had spoken words to affirm that he and the American journalism establishment could not "turn our heads away from those who suffer." He spoke of a need to confront the horrors of other people's suffering in order to keep alive "spiritual values" to be once again embraced "when all this nightmare is over." And yet, less than two months after the lofty speech at the University of the South, he attended his daughter's white-taffeta wedding on the same day that his fellow Jews, who had not had the good luck to be born in America, were being lined up around a pit and, standing naked and terrified with their families, shot dead.

Whether or not Sulzberger's attendance of his daughter's wedding at a time of such darkness was right or wrong is essentially a personal judgment for each reader to consider. There is also a question of what Sulzberger meant by "all this nightmare" as he sat in his office in the *New York Times* building on Times Square or celebrated at a lavish party for his daughter's wedding.

The Sulzberger wedding, complete with the bride's "gown of white taffeta…with a full bouffant skirt," took place as the Ponary massacres had begun to unfold. But only one of those two stories made it into the next day's issue of the *New York Times*—and it was not the bloodshed at Ponary that was covered. In fact, in all of its coverage of the war, the *Times* mentioned the Ponary massacres only once, in only one article out of thousands upon thousands of articles about the war but also about coal, police demerits, sporting events, and, of course, elite New York weddings. With this in mind, the questions of what Arthur Hays Sulzberger thought or how he acted as an individual become painfully irrelevant. The only question that remains is not whether Sulzberger failed as publisher of America's most prominent newspaper. The failure is clear and unquestionable. The real question we have to ask is how badly the *Times* failed, what effect this failure had, and why it occurred.

◆ ◆ ◆

Arthur Hays Sulzberger came to age as the publisher and leading figure of the owning family of the *New York Times* during a dark period for Jews in America. In the 1930s and 1940s, there were no equal opportunity laws, no diversity oversight councils, and very few public outcries against racism. By the 1940s, anti-Semitism in the United States had reached a historic peak, and a sentiment that had been seething beneath the surface in the decades prior suddenly exploded into a full-blown atmosphere of hatred. Mass movements opposed America's entrance into the Second World War on the basis that it was a "Jews' war" and that getting involved would be a catastrophic blunder for America and a boon for international Jewry. (There were also cries that the war was another "British war" made at a time when the Nazis were shouting that the British were "white Jews.") Consequently, once America did get into the war—an action Roosevelt knew was necessary years before Pearl Harbor, as conquest of America was one of the final phases of the Nazis' larger plan—domestic hatred for Jewish people found expression in the lie that Americans were fighting for the Jews while Jews stayed at home and relaxed.

David Wyman cites a common anti-Semitic song from that period that was printed as widely as it was sung:

From the shores of Coney Island
Looking out into the sea
Stands a kosher air-raid warden,
Wearing V for victory,
who chants:
Let those Christian saps, go fight the Japs,
In the uniforms we've made.
So it's onward into battle,
Let us send the Christian slobs
When the war is done and Victory won
All us Jews will have their Jobs.[11]

Another common anti-Semitic piece Wyman cites notes the important "firsts" of the war:

First American killed in Pearl Harbor – John J. Hennessy
First American to sink a Jap ship – Colin P. Kelly
First American to sink a Jap ship with torpedo – John P. Buckley
Greatest American air hero – "Butch" O'Hare
First American killed at Guadacanal – John J. O'Brien
First American to get four new tires – Abraham Lipshitz.

(The piece neglects to mention, Wyman notes,[12] a few important facts, such as when the first American to sink a "Jap ship," Colin P. Kelly, was killed on a mission, a bombardier named Meyer Levin, a Jew, was on the same mission and died for the same country as Kelly.)

Wyman cites the Great Depression as one of the major triggers of American anti-Semitism. Once again, Jews were scapegoats in the New World exactly as they had been in the Old World. The 1930s saw a drastic rise in anti-Semitic hatred, and by 1942, "sociologist David Riesman was describing it as 'slightly below the boiling point.'"[13]New York, today a bastion of Jewish culture, was in 1941 one of the cities hit hardest by anti-Semitism of the period. Wyman writes of roving bands of teenagers who abused Jewish residents of New York on a daily basis, desecrating every single synagogue in some areas of the city. Further, New York's commissioner of investigation conducted a report that found that in seventy percent of anti-Semitic incidents, the police exhibited "laxity and inaction."[14]

This was the environment in which Arthur Hays Sulzberger, as publisher of the *Times*, inherited his position at the newspaper. But it was in a very similar environment that his father-in-law Adolph Ochs, a German Jew, organized a financial deal that would allow him to salvage the *New York Times*, which enjoyed a solid reputation but had floundered financially after the reign of its first owner, Henry Raymond. Ochs knew that in order to right the paper, he would have to ensure it operated as a sound business. As a metropolitan newspaper in a city rife with anti-Semitism, any appearance that the *Times* was a "Jewish newspaper" or that it had an inclination to take on Jewish issues or stances would prove fatal. Under Ochs, the paper openly opposed the nomination of Louis Brandeis, who would become the first Jewish Supreme Court Justice, to the Court. In editorials, the paper did not mention Brandeis's Jewishness as a reason for opposition but rather spoke vaguely of his "radical" tendencies. Even after admitting, "of his ability and of his experience, there can be no question," and noting, "A former Chief Justice of the court to which Mr. Brandeis had been nominated declared that he was one of the ablest of all the counsel that appeared before that tribunal [the Supreme Court],"[15] one of the main editorials on the subject spoke only of the idea that the Supreme Court must be a "conservative body" and that "to supplant conservatism by radicalism" would produce disaster. But the author of the editorial never made an effort to explain why Brandeis should be considered a "radical" who would engage in what the editorial made out to be a severe form of judicial activism rather than uphold the Constitution.

Like Adolph Ochs, Arthur Hays Sulzberger was an American Jew of German background. Only a few decades before Ochs bought the *Times*, German Jewry had seized upon the freedoms of the Jewish emancipation in Germany, where, for the first time in history, they were treated as somewhat equal to Christians. With their newfound freedom, the Jews of Germany did not turn to an open practice of their religion, as their forefathers had yearned to do during the time (up until the late eighteenth century), when Berlin charged Jews a pig tax in order enter the gates of the city.[16] Rather, many of the Jews of Germany advanced what became known as the *haskalah* or Jewish Enlightenment, whose fundamental belief was that Jews could assimilate the ideas and beliefs of the German culture around them and become Germans of Jewish ancestry instead of Jews living in Germany. They also began to change their religion. Until this period, German Jews were among the most devout in Europe, largely because of the extreme isolation they suffered under Prussian rule. A new form of Judaism was developed in Germany during this time, which came to be called Conservative Judaism. It spoke of the intention and spirit of the religion in favor of the obedience and ritual that Judaism had previously embodied. Jews found that they could practice Judaism in a way that was more similar to the way their German neighbors and business partners practiced Christianity.

This worked for a little while. But soon massive numbers of German Jews, including some of the top Jewish minds and artists of that century, converted to Christianity, forgot Yiddish (or let it fall into disuse), and began to take up German language and life. They joined the German army in the First World War and fought alongside their German brethren. And many immigrated to America along with thousands of other "regular Germans" who did so at the time. But, of course, it did not last.

Even Germans whose Jewish grandparents had converted to Christianity during the *haskalah* were identified (thanks to the meticulous German record-keeping systems) and slaughtered as Jews during the Holocaust.

The German Jews who came to the United States before the Holocaust continued the tradition of the *haskalah*. Instead of forming the small tightly knit Jewish communities that many Polish and Russian Jews cultivated, on the whole, the German Jews of America opted for active assimilation. On the basis of this approach, the Conservative sect of Judaism developed by Jews in Germany emerged in America as Reform Judaism, which became increasingly universalistic and, with coming-of-age ceremonies called "confirmations" (instead of bar or bat mitzvahs) and a preaching of universal love, moved closer to a Christian model of a faith, or a form of worship that a person of any national or ethnic background could choose to practice, in place of the traditional Jewish model of membership in a religious nation.

Arthur Hays Sulzberger fit this pattern of German Jewish assimilation perhaps even better than his father-in-law, Adolph Ochs. One of Sulzberger's central beliefs regarding Judaism was that it is neither a race nor a people. For him, it was only—and nothing more than—a faith. This was a very new idea in the history of Judaism, and it conflicted with the traditional core biblical and historical perspective of Jews as a people, namely, the "Chosen People."

In an article entitled, "A Tragic 'Fight in the Family,'" journalism scholar Laurel Leff explained the beliefs of Arthur Sulzberger and his wife Iphigene, daughter of Adolph Ochs.[17] According to Leff, Arthur and Iphigene were adherents to a particular form of Reform Judaism called Classical Reform Judaism. The sub-sect was developed largely by Adolph Ochs's father-in-law, Isaac M. Wise, who was adamant on the point that Judaism was only a faith and not a race, ethnicity, or people. This belief made the term "Jew" an empty one—or at least, that was its goal. Since believers in Classical Reform Judaism reduced the category of Jew to someone who worships in a Jewish way but is no different than any other person, labeling someone a Jew said nothing about who or what they were—it only said something about what they did during prayer time. One of the greatest goods, according to Classical Reform Judaism, was social assimilation of the Jews, and the greatest misdeed was anything that would publicly separate one person from another, even—or especially—if it was on account of a ritual rooted in deep belief, such as the wearing of a skullcap.

Sulzberger strove to run his life and his newspaper according to this view of his religion. When it came to the increasingly critical issue of Zionism, the paper deferred to the belief of its religious leaders. Leff cites a resolution adopted by the Union of American Hebrew Congregations, a hub of the Classical Reform Movement, that illustrates Sulzberger's opinion regarding a Jewish state. The resolution stated, "America is our Zion. Here in the home of religious liberty, we have aided in founding of this new Zion, the fruition of the beginning laid in the old."[18]

The anti-Semitism that was running rampant in New York at that time would, on the surface, provide Sulzberger and the Classical Reform Jews with a serious problem. If America was Zion, then why were Jews being persecuted on the streets at record levels while the police remained passive? It was not a new conundrum for Classical Reform Jews who, in previous decades, read the reports of death and destruction committed against the Jews in Poland and Russia in waves of vicious pogroms. Members of the movement found a convenient way of explaining away (without actually explaining) the violence against Jews. They considered the massacres and anti-Semitic violence to be "lapses" in an otherwise peaceful situation and considered them a "small price" to pay for being "servants of the Lord."

Sulzberger saw the situation in New York in a similar way. To him, it was the Jew's responsibility to downplay his Jewishness, to not rock the social boat by creating or displaying any Jewish differences that might create animosity in the larger culture around him. As owner and top executive of a major newspaper, Sulzberger took this belief to its logical conclusion. Almost unbelievably, in cases where editors or reporters had names that sounded too Jewish, Leff notes, the names were abbreviated. Thus, Abraham Rosenthal, one of the paper's most celebrated editors, became A.M. Rosenthal. But far more egregious than the abbreviation of Jewish names (something that could be interpreted as a tendency to be overly subtle) was Sulzberger's policy of holding back Jewish staff members from rising to higher positions explicitly because they were Jewish. One such case was that of Arthur Krock, an extremely gifted newsman who over the course of his career won four Pulitzer Prizes (three of them for the *Times*) and had so many contacts in Washington that he came to be known as the "Dean of Washington Newsmen." Despite Krock's illustrious career, Sulzberger prevented the journalist rising to a position as editor of the editorial page. According to a later *New York Times* article, Sulzberger worried that "he would be criticized if he appointed a Jew as editor, since the ownership was in the hands of Jews."[19] Ironically, this was a watered down version of the racial prejudice Jews were forced to live under in Nazi Germany, only in this case it took place in America and was put in place not by an "Aryan" non-Jew but a Jew of German extraction.

Gay Talese, one of the *Times*'s most illustrious reporters, known as much for his elegant dress as for his elegant prose, wrote about the Ochs-Sulzberger family's relationship with their Jewishness in his book *The Kingdom and the Power*:

> The *New York Times* does not wish to be thought of as a "Jewish news-paper," which indeed it is not, and it will bend over backwards to prove this point, forcing itself at times into unnatural positions, contorted by compromise, balancing both sides, careful not to offend, wishing to be accepted and respected for what it is—a good citizen's newspaper, law-abiding and loyal, solidly in support of the best interest of the nation in peace and war.[20]

All this amounted to a "genteel anti-Semitism" that gripped the *Times*, in the words of the niece of Theodore Bernstein, another exceptional *Times* editor who suspected his rise to the very top position at the paper was prevented by his Jewishness.[21]

Sulzberger's beliefs about Judaism started to cause him to make increasingly extreme decisions at his newspaper, including a bizarre and somewhat shocking decision to keep the word "Jew" out of the newspaper altogether, except when it was absolutely unavoidable. Leff writes that Sulzberger explained at one point that he had made "a great deal of effort" to ensure that "the word Jew" would no longer be "the common denominator for any activities in which people who happen to be Jews participate."

By any standard or definition, the Holocaust was an activity "in which people who happen to be Jews" participated, even if they participated unwillingly. From where Sulzberger's newspaper stood, the war against the Jews, the Nazi plan to exterminate Jews, the forced marches of Jews, the resistances movements of the Jews were not and could not be about "Jews." But since Hitler identified his main target for annihilation as Jews, and since almost all of these people identified themselves as Jews, the paper's decision to leave out the word "Jew" meant it had to engage in an astounding act of historical revision that, unlike most such cases, was undertaken as the events were unfolding. This process of contemporaneous historical revision has another, much simpler name: denial.

Sulzberger rationalized that to identify the Jews as a race, ethnicity, or even just a "people" would be to play into Hitler's hands, to agree with the genocidal madman and validate his effort of extermination. But a judgment like this one is irreparably confused. It assumed that if the premise "the Jews are a race" were true, then Hitler's targeting of the Jews as a separate race would also be based in truth. Why Sulzberger thought that this would make Hitler's effort at genocide seem more justified rather than make it seem more evil and immoral cannot be explained by any amount of psychobiography. What can be said is that Sulzberger's transference of his convoluted personal religious beliefs onto his newspaper—and its staff who "chafed" at the position and the moratorium on the word "Jew"—made the situation worse, since by that point, what was unfolding in Nazi Germany was no longer a secret. The top echelons of American government knew from a very early period about what was happening in Nazi-occupied Europe. The United States and Britain ran a large spy network in Europe and brought back information about the Nazi plan. Roosevelt was also supplied with detailed documentation about the extermination plan and concentration camps by Jewish leaders who sought to press him to act. On one such occasion, which took place December 8, 1942, a group of Jewish leaders led by Rabbi Stephen Wise secured a meeting with President Roosevelt and presented him with a twenty page brief that documented the situation for the Jews in Europe. Wise was also a German Jew and a leading member of the Reform (but not Classical Reform) movement in America and had worked with prominent American Jews like Louis Brandeis and Felix Frankfurter to push for equal rights for all citizens of the United States, regardless of race, religion, or gender. The report showed that two million Jews had already been murdered in Europe and another five million faced death. Roosevelt responded that he knew of the situation all too well. One of the Jewish leaders at the meeting noted Roosevelt's response:

> The government of the United States is very well acquainted with most of the facts you are now bringing to our attention. Unfortunately we have received confirmation from many sources. Representatives of the United States government in Switzerland and other neutral countries have given us proof that confirms the horrors discussed by you.[22]

Roosevelt authorized the group to co-author a statement with the White House that warned the Nazi perpetrators of the Holocaust that they would be prosecuted as war criminals after the war. The group held a press conference after the meeting to announce Roosevelt's determination to try Nazis for crimes committed against the Jews. The press conference focused on the numbers of two million murdered Jews and five million more at risk. Many newspapers covered the press conference and the information provided by the report to Roosevelt, the *New York Times* among them.

But the *Times* took a different approach to the story than the one taken by many of these papers. While most reasonable observers would consider a top-level meeting with the president of the United States about the genocidal murder of two million people (with another five million on the way to the gas chambers) to be front-page news, the *New York Times* did not. In fact, quite the opposite: The *Times* buried the story on page twenty.

At this point, a critical question arises: Even if the story of the Holocaust had been adequately covered by America's leading newspaper, what difference would it have made? We might reason that, by 1942, the Nazis had control of large parts of Europe, and America was already fighting the war. The Holocaust would stop when the war was won. However, this is an oversimplification. At no point had the Nazis rounded up all of the Jews of Europe and then proceeded to grind them through its machine of extermination. Many Jewish people were still located in countries not yet occupied by the Nazis. But it was clear that they soon would be. Roosevelt, who had monitored the situation in Germany from very early in the lead-up to the war, had eased immigration restrictions for immigrants from Europe. He saw the persecution of the Jews increasing, and in 1938, he pushed to offer the full amount of possible visas for immigrants from Europe. It was an important gesture, and a move in the right direction. But given that only 40,000 total visas for Europe immigrants were available per year, its effects could only have been nominal.

At that moment, American wariness of immigrants had reached a high point, along with record levels of anti-Semitism, since the devastating rates of unemployment during the Great Depression had triggered extreme xeno-phobia and anti-Semitism. But as the country emerged from the Depression, the levels of xenophobia and anti-Semitism did not subside. Instead, war fears continued to stoke the trend. As the United States ramped up for war, the number of visas was cut and a clamp-down on immigration all but ceased refugee immigration or asylum into the United States.[23] At the same time, Britain took similar action and instituted its infamous White Paper of 1939, which, as if to make a cruel political joke, slashed the number of immigrants allowed into British Mandatory Palestine (part of which is modern-day Israel), the last haven of refuge for Jews fleeing Hitler, to 10,000 people per year. This development came less than a year after Hitler's Anschluss annexation of Austria, which put another 100,000 European Jews directly at risk of murder in Hitler's concentration camps. Under this new immigration policy, it would have taken ten years to provide refuge to the Jews of Austria alone. As the war against the Jews marched on, the nations of the world, including the United States, closed their doors with greater stringency.

Far from establishing itself as a pro-immigration champion as it has today, the New York Times was, at best, silent on the issue. Early in the war, France's Vichy government, perhaps on account of its ability to see what was coming to the Jews of France, pleaded with the United States to accept thousands of refugees, "particularly Jews," who faced death in Nazi Europe.[24] The State Department flatly refused the plea, saying that it would have been impossibly chaotic to admit that many refugees.

On January 9, 1941, the *Times* ran a news story—not an editorial—supporting the State Department's refusal to accept refugees. The article, "U.S. Refuses French Plea to Take Refugees; Reich Curb Called Bar to Orderly Emigration," laid out virtually every possible defense of the decision to refuse the refugees as they had been laid out by the State Department, noting that "no orderly procedure could be followed" to allow them in; that the principles of an "intergovernmental committee on refugees" had to be respected; that the State Department was "disposed" to help "to the full extent of existing laws and regulations"; and that even if State had been able to help, according to the intergovernmental committee, no distribution of refugees could be made on "grounds of race, nationality, or religion."

What the *Times* article on the refugees of France never once offers is context: that the hundreds of thousands of Jews whom France was begging the United States to accept faced certain torture and death at the hands of the Nazis. In its 500-plus words, it mentions the word "Jews" only twice.

Over the next few years, the *Times* would continue to back the government's anti-immigration policy. In some cases, as when it supported admitting refugees on a very limited basis, such as accepting a number of German children or a pitifully small number of entrances from Europe, the paper was quick to point out that it did not support the admittance of particular groups of refugees, such as Jews. A January 12, 1941 editorial, "The Refugee Problem," pressed just this point.[25] The line was the one advanced in accordance with Arthur Sulzberger's religious beliefs: that Jews were not a separate ethnic group but only a social group among many other social groups who were being persecuted by Hitler. Sulzberger reasoned that it would be unfair to admit Jews in significant numbers to the United States while not admitting other European refugees who had as much right as the Jews to entrance.

Sulzberger was right to think that all groups equally deserved asylum and protection from persecution. However, it was the Jews who needed it in a way that no other European group did. While political prisoners of Europe, who were sometimes sent to concentration camps, might die or fall victim to Nazi persecution, for the Jews death was virtually certain. Socialists caught in Nazi-occupied countries had a very real chance of being captured and murdered. But as Italians, Belgians, communists, or Christians, they also had a very real chance of being accepted into one of the countries in Europe sympathetic to members of that particular group. For the Jews, there was literally nowhere to go and no one to turn to—except America. But American public opinion at that time was not with these persecuted Jews, the name of whom the country's biggest paper, and one of its few Jewish-owned major newspapers, would utter on only rare occasion.

By 1944, the number of murdered Jews made the gruesome number of 700,000, which the *Times* noted in its two-inch, seventy-four-word summary of the Bund report, seemed like a pittance. Four million people had been murdered—as Jews and because they were Jews, whether or not the *New York Times* chose to acknowledge the fact. By 1945, the number had grown again, and the newspaper remained cold and adamant on the question of allowing the final few living Jews of Europe to take refuge in the United States. Only then, Leff explains, did the *Times* approve of a government decision to allow in some refugees. The number was a thousand souls. However, by 1945, when the Holocaust against the Jews was a well-known and well-accepted fact, the position of the newspaper resembled the position of the most stridently anti-immigration newspapers of today.

A prominent *Times* editorial of January 27, 1945 began with a contemptuous statement about accepting the hunted refugees from Nazi Europe: "The fact that a person is a refugee does not make him a hero or a saint. It does prove that he does not like tyranny or cannot get on with it, points which are in his favor."[26] The editorial laid out his hardline case against accepting refugees in three paragraphs and ended with a chilling statement that, in part, helps explain the *Times*'s lack of concern for the massacred Jews of Europe: "The days of mass immigration are no doubt over, so far as this country is concerned. Selective immigration of persons who have something to give the United States as well as something to ask from it is another matter. It should continue, within proper quota limits, after the refugee crisis is over."[27]

◆ ◆ ◆

The Allies overran the Nazis in the spring of 1945. Part of the victory meant liberating the concentration camps where Jews had been burned, starved, gassed, shot, and beaten to death for six years. The *Times* covered the liberation of one of the horrific camps in a May 8, 1945 article, "Oswiecim Killings Placed at 4,000,000."[28] The report told of the endless horrors perpetrated at that particular camp, from the "public baths" where victims were gassed to the pits where "excess bodies burned over huge fires." The article mentioned the Nazi practice of selling the bones of its victims, which were turned into superphosphates and the "loads of women's hair...sold for industrial purposes." It went on to discuss the concentration camps' crematoria, which could "consume" 10,000 bodies every twenty-four hours, and it mentioned the worse fate of those who were not killed but were turned into "human guinea pigs kept alive for experimentation" or were put into hard labor and worked to death. And the article told of the biggest and most shocking aspect of the Oscwiecim camp: 4,000,000 people had been slaughtered there in a few short years. But one critical element was, once again, left out of the *Times* report.

Oswiecim was the Polish name for the place. The Germans called it Auschwitz. Today, it is the most infamous of the Nazi death camps where between one and three million people were murdered. Even though ninety percent of those victims were Jews, the reporter never once mentioned the word "Jew" in the article. Looking at the identity of the reporter, it is not hard to understand why: He was C.L. Sulzberger, the nephew of the newspaper's publisher, Arthur Hays Sulzberger.

More disturbing than all of this, however, was that the *Times*'s treatment of the Bund report, which told of the confirmed deaths of 700,000 Jews in Poland, would come full circle to end a disgraceful and endlessly damaging period of reporting at the *New York Times*. When the *Times* originally printed news of the Bund report in 1942, it gave it less than a hundred words and buried the article on page seven.

At the end of the war, in C.L. Sulzberger's Oswiecim article, the *Times* reported on the most gruesome symbol of the Holocaust of the Jews and never mentioned the word "Jew." But despite the epic nature of the story and the prominent identity of its author, the *New York Times* decided to downplay—one more time—the story of the Holocaust and placed the story on page twelve.

◆ ◆ ◆

In the six years of the war, the *New York Times* printed Holocaust-related stories on its front page exactly six times. Never once in the more than 18,000 *Times* issues during the war was a Holocaust story a lead article for the day. And, accordingly, never once has the *New York Times* officially apologized for the way that it covered—or did not cover—the Holocaust. Arthur Hays Sulzberger and the Ochs-Sulzberger family are entitled as individuals to their views on their religion and to practice it however they see fit. But in doing so, they violated the very standards of journalism that Sulzberger himself preached at numerous lectures around the country during the war. The paper failed his call for journalists to not turn their faces away from the sight of other people's suffering. But worse, the *New York Times* failed in this task intentionally, willfully, and for the specific reason that the tens of millions of Jews who suffered and the six million who perished in Europe had something in common with the people who ran the newspaper—and this was something that the *New York Times*'s controlling owners somehow found unacceptable.

Little Boy, Fat Lie:
"We're on the Way to Bomb Japan"

Common sense speaks to us about lightning not striking twice in the same place or at the same time. After a close look at the *Times*'s coverage of the Holocaust, it is hard to believe that the newspaper could make the same mistake of covering up the victimization of an entire population a second time. The *New York Times*, however, managed to defy common sense yet again in 1945.

Just as the paper was publishing redacted stories about the liberation of concentration camps, stories that took from the Jewish victims their very last possession—their identities—the *Times* was whitewashing another war, stripping another group of victims of the truth of their situation and, essentially, covering up another Holocaust. The second group of victims was, it is true, smaller in number and their horrors less drawn out, at least on the surface. But the ramifications of what the *New York Times* helped to cover up still echo through the corridors of history.

◆ ◆ ◆

On August 6, 1945 a mild-mannered, brainy navy captain named William Sterling Parsons was crammed into the bomb bay of a B-29 bomber. Parsons was tinkering with a mechanism that over the previous months he had helped design, build, repair, and perfect to an extent that no one else had. After the bomber took flight, Parsons began the very precarious task of inserting a detonator into a metal cylinder that would arm the device. The jostling of the plane made the task so difficult that Parson's superior, a general named Leslie Groves, insisted that it was better to put the civilian population near the air base at risk by arming the device on the ground than to perform the dangerous operation in the air, where civilians were out of range. But Parsons knew what he was doing well enough to defy the general's advice. He knew every nut and bolt, every crevice, every piece, every shard of metal. So much labor had been put into the device by Parsons and his small army of engineers that they had given the thing a name. They called it Little Boy. It was the first non-test atomic bomb in history.[1]

Parsons was up to his task. He armed the bomb despite the turbulence of the plane. At 7:25 a.m., the crew of the Enola Gay received a coded message that the skies over Hiroshima were clear. And so, it was determined that the Japanese city of more than 300,000 people would be the first to feel the wrath of a nuclear weapon. The bomb was dropped. The crew of the Enola Gay saw a bright flash and watched as an erupting cylinder gave way to a furious mushroom cloud that rose higher and higher into the air. They saw the cap of the mushroom split off and rise to the heavens and then watched as another cap grew out of the still rising purple cylinder. What they did not see was the effects that this weapon and its seemingly organic clouds of smoke had on the ground beneath them.

Two days after the Hiroshima bomb, the New York Times ran a story about a squadron of B-29 bombers that had hit an industrial area in Japan called Yawata.[2] Alongside the front-page story, the Times ran photos of William Parsons, the pilot of the Enola Gay, a man named Colonel Paul Tibbets, and the crew's bombardier. As tactical commander of the mission and chief of the Ordnance Division of the bomb project, Parsons was one of the most important people in the development and use of the world's first nuclear weapon, and far more significant than either of the other two men pictured. However, in the August 8 issue of the New York Times, the paper ran a photo of the wrong William Parsons.

As embarrassing as the photo gaffe might have been for the *Times*, it came nowhere near the magnitude of the central failure of the Gray Lady in reporting on the nuclear bombing of Japan. Just as Walter Duranty had gained unprecedented access to Stalin, Herbert Matthews got coveted interviews with Fidel Castro, and David Halberstam had private meetings with the American ambassador to Vietnam, the *New York Times* was able to put its man in the key position once again, this time to report on the development and deployment of the world's most awesome and terrifying weapon.

The reporter's name was William L. Laurence. He was born in Lithuania as Leid Siew (he was Jewish, but, characteristically, the *Times* made no mention of this in its lengthy 1977 obituary of him). Laurence was by all standards a brilliant man, studying at Harvard College, Harvard Law School, and Boston University not long after arriving in the United States as an immigrant. By 1926, Laurence was writing for a New York newspaper, the *World*, and four years later, he got his science beat at the *New York Times*, where he demonstrated the incredible gift of being able to recognize a lurking story, crystallize it, and tug the narratives and particulars out in a way that regular readers of the *Times* found not just understandable and interesting but often fascinating.

In 1937, just six years after joining the paper, Laurence was awarded his first Pulitzer Prize, which he (along with four other reporters) received for coverage of the Harvard Tercentenary Conference of Arts and Sciences.[3] The prize was among the paper's first ten Pulitzers, awarded just five years after the one given to Walter Duranty. But much more important than any Pulitzer Prize was Laurence's incredible prescience in early *Times* articles dealing with the mysteries of the atom and the power that scientists speculated it might hold. Already in 1929, in a June 29 article, "The Quest of Science for an Atomic Energy," Laurence had pegged the key points of the atomic issue and the potentials of nuclear power.[4] In those early days, years before most scientists ever dreamed of nuclear power, Laurence was writing about that possibility in clear, easy-to-understand prose. "Suppose, scientists asked, we could speed up the process [of nuclear decay]," he wrote prophetically, "then a small amount of radium could liberate as much energy as Niagara Falls."

Laurence ingeniously compared the exploration of the atom and the possibility of manipulating it to the fabled "Philosopher's Stone," which alchemists of previous centuries believed could turn common metals into gold. He went on to lay out how a drop of water could provide enough energy to feed a 200-horse-power engine for a year and outlined the beliefs of scientists like British chemist Francis William Aston and physicists Sir Ernest Rutherford and Sir Arthur Stanley Eddington about the potentials of nuclear energy. He made special use of Eddington's famous metaphor that compared the secret of nuclear energy to a "locked cupboard" to which mankind did not have the key.

Laurence's exploration of the topic and his willingness to consider the possibility of human mastery of the atom were visionary. Others had identified the possibility of deriving energy from manipulating the atom and its core particles, but they were the few early sages of the atom. Among them was the science-fiction writer H.G. Wells who predicted the use of atomic energy and nuclear weapons in his 1913 novel, *The World Set Free.* (Amazingly, Wells also accurately predicted the year, 1933, that the chain reaction process needed for nuclear power would be discovered.) And the Hungarian physicist, Leo Szilard, had begun a personal crusade in the early 1930s to catalyze the top minds in science to explore the possibility of nuclear power since he understood, very acutely, that if Hitler were to unlock the secret first, the world would be doomed.

But these were the exceptions to the rule. Even Rutherford, whom Laurence quoted in his 1929 article as saying, "The human race may trace its development from the development of a method of utilizing atomic energy," rebuffed Leo Szilard's talk of liberating the energy of the atom in a scalable way as "moonshine."[5] The distinguished Italian physicist Enrico Fermi, who was later involved in developing the first early nuclear reactors, responded to Szilard's push to do research on a possible nuclear "chain reaction" with a simple, but informative, exclamation: "Nuts!"[6]

In the following years, Laurence stayed on top of the developments in atomic research. The year 1933 proved to be staggering for the field, and for science in general, as researchers found that bombarding gold and platinum atoms with a "deuton" (now known as deuteron), or a coupled proton and neutron, produced enormous amounts of energy. By Laurence's account, the gold and platinum nuclei that the deuton was smashed against proved so hard—"So hard are their inner fortifications"—that the deuton bounced back and split into component parts. The amount of energy released was 7,500,000 electron volts—enough energy to send a ship across the Atlantic and back. Five days later, on June 29, Laurence penned a story about a new "Jove" or lightning bolt hurler that had been announced by Massachusetts Institute of Technology. The particle accelerator, it was announced, could launch protons and neutrons with an energy of up to 10,000,000 volts.

Laurence continued to cover every important step in nuclear research, rarely (if ever) missing a beat. The 1930s presented the *Times*'s science writer with a storm of staggering breakthroughs and achievements of a magnitude and frequency that is probably unrivaled in the history of science. For Laurence, as for anyone involved in science or even remotely interested in the topic, witnessing that decade was like watching the secret hand of the universe opening up finger by finger to reveal a palm full of physical truth. Between articles on cancer, controversy over the genetic theory of heredity, studies on hormones, and the activities of Einstein and other members of the scientific elite, Laurence created an opus of articles on atoms, their nuclei, and the unbelievably vast stores of energy locked in the bonds between infinitesimally small particles. Just a year after the unveiling of the ten million-volt accelerator, Laurence covered the announcement at a Berkeley symposium of two new accelerators in the works, one of twenty million volts and another of thirty million volts. Laurence called the accelerators "atom artillery" and "atomic siege-guns," since they shot atomic particles together, and noted that the competing atomic research teams had created "what may be described as a friendly 'atomic armament race.'" We know today that it was those events which led to the actual atomic armament race of just a few years later.[7]

In April of 1935, Laurence's articles rose to a crescendo. On April 25, Laurence wrote that scientists, including the nuclear researcher Ernest

O. Lawrence, had managed to split the deuteron, the bound proton and neutron that lies at the core of a hydrogen-2 atom, in order to penetrate the nucleus of copper.[8] Two days later, on April 27, 1935, the *Times* ran a piece by Laurence, "Energy Multiplied 200,000,000 Times."[9] Columbia physicists, taking a methodological cue from the Italian Fermi, attempted to bombard the nucleus of a lithium element with a "slow neutron," a neutron that was shot through paraffin to slow its speed, instead of one moving incredibly fast. The results were a watershed. According to Laurence, the research team found that the slow speed of the neutron gave it deadly accuracy in penetrating the nucleus of the atom. The splitting of the atom's nucleus unleashed 5,000,000 volts, which was a lot by any measure but an enormous amount compared to the amount of energy put into the nucleus's splitting. The result was that the energy given off in the splitting of the nucleus was 200 million times greater than the energy put into it. Just as importantly, the researchers realized that they could replicate the process with just about any atom. They found that when they shot a slow neutron at an atomic nucleus, the nucleus expanded by a huge factor. In boron's case, it grew by 800 times, with cadmium 10,000 times, making the target for the bombarding neutron larger by a staggering factor and consequently the firing of the neutron more accurate by the same factor. Ernest Rutherford, who in 1933 told Leo Szilard that the prospect of unlocking nuclear power in the foreseeable future was "moonshine," now admitted that the key to the nuclear cupboard had been found.

One year later, Ernest O. Lawrence and colleagues at University of California realized the alchemists' dream about which Laurence had written metaphorically years before—and made gold. They did so by bombarding platinum with deuterons, unleashing massive stores of energy. On May 2, 1936, Laurence wrote that scientists discovered a "cosmic force" forty times greater than electricity in the heart of atoms.[10] On April 23, 1939, the paper ran a story covering scientists' finding of a particle that held a trillion volts (though it came from cosmic, not experimental, sources).[11]

Each article in Laurence's almost endless series on atomic advances was important, if not world-changing, but one of them stood out among all the others. On May 5, 1940, Laurence penned a story that was similar to all the other atom-smashing, energy-releasing articles he'd written throughout the 1930s.[12] However, the May 5 story held one small but ultimately explosive detail: instead of cadmium, copper, or platinum, it was an isotope of uranium called uranium-235 that scientists had managed to isolate. Laurence picked the story up from an obscure physics journal called the *Physical Review*. He translated the technical findings into practical terms, noting that a pound of U-235 could power an ocean liner indefinitely and would equal the energy output of thirty million pounds of gasoline and fifty million pounds of coal. With this discovery, the stage had finally been set. Researchers had mastered the process of fission, had perfected the methods, and had now had found the right material to produce an explosion of energy that for all practical purposes had no end.

Only a few people in the world were paying as much attention to this matter as William L. Laurence. A few of these people were Leo Szilard and his physics colleagues, many of whom were actively engaged in the research. When Szilard witnessed uranium-235 undergo fission and emit two neutrons instead of one, providing the basis for the necessary chain reaction of nuclear energy, he knew that science was standing at the event horizon of a terrible power. He instantly enlisted all those around him to get to the United States government in order to inform the unwitting politicians about the potential of the energy and the potential of the technology falling into Nazi hands. The fact that Laurence was able to publish his May 5 story at all was an indication of how far ahead of the government, and basically everyone else, the research scientists (and Laurence) were. The *Saturday Post* picked up Laurence's May 5 article for the September 1940 issue of the magazine. It took the United States government four months to catch up with the story and what it meant, but finally, military censors came swooping in and put the September *Saturday Post* issue in "quarantine" on account of the information presented in Laurence's story. The censors requested that all remaining copies of the article be withheld and any specific requests for that issue be reported to the military.[13] Someone in the government had figured out, months after Laurence and the scientists he wrote about had, what the spate of atom stories and the crowning article on uranium-235 meant for the world.

After Laurence's uranium article of May 1940, his writing on nuclear research slowed to a trickle. Between 1940 and 1945, as the United States government began to wake up to the implications of nuclear research and findings, Laurence did little more than one article a year on the subject of nuclear research. This was in large part due to a clamp down on the publication of nuclear-related research that began in 1940 with the decision by the National Research Council to censor publications containing sensitive information regarding uranium and nuclear energy. As a result, after 1940, Laurence was back to the more mundane aspects of his job as a science writer. He wrote stories about research on the measles, the effects of vitamin A on whooping cough, the effects of vitamin B complex on gray hair, the benefits of mushrooms for hypertension, a number of stories on cancer (including a 1940 story that cited a correlation between cigarette smoking and lung cancer), and other bread-and-butter stories of any other science writer at any other newspaper.

In the summer of 1945, all that changed when the atom bomb was dropped. On August 7, 1945, the *Times* ran the story on the front page under the headline, "New Age Ushered."[14] The article commented on President Truman's morning announcement from which it was evident, the article remarked, that "one of the scientific landmarks of the century had been passed, and that the age of 'atomic energy,' which can be a tremendous force for the advancement of civilization as well as for destruction, was at hand." That same day, the paper ran an editorial, "Science and the Bomb," invoking the now-cliché observation that nuclear energy could prove a massive force for both progress and destruction. The piece went on for a few paragraphs to give a brief scientific background on nuclear research, but the conclusion the article came to was definitive:

> The potentialities of this first harnessing of atomic energy are unlimited. The main point to be kept in mind is that this world is driven by energy and that out of this war has come the first invention which has made it possible to use, unfortunately for destruction, the energy in stuff that rated only a little higher than dirt.[15]

The following day, the *Times* ran a story on the nuclear plant at Oak Ridge, where most of the fission work was done.[16] The story repeated the words of the colonel who dealt with reporters, saying the people at Oak Ridge had done a "magnificent job" and that the plant had maintained safety records better than those of most industrial plants. However, among all the early stories of the bomb and atomic research, there was no reporting from William Laurence, the journalist who almost singlehandedly had championed nuclear energy in the 1930s.

There was, however, a small August 7 story not by William Laurence but *about* him. The headline of the article read, "War Department Called Times Reporter to Explain Intricacies to Public."[17] The story, just five paragraphs long, told readers that Laurence, the "unassuming *New York Times* reporter," was the man behind the "bales of War Department 'handouts' designed to enlighten laymen on the working of the atomic bomb that was used for the first time over Japan." Although the *Times* article was subtle about it, its admission was shocking: its science writer, William Laurence, had been working for the United States Department of War on its ultra-secret nuclear bomb program.

Finally, on September 9, 1945, William Laurence broke his months-long silence. The first line of the story was jaw-dropping: "We are on the way to bomb the mainland of Japan." Any regular reader of Laurence's stories could only have been left wondering what the "unassuming" science writer of the *New York Times*, who had spent more time in the past five years writing about fungus and cancer than nuclear technology, could have meant by saying "we" were on the way to bomb Japan.[18] Laurence was not writing figuratively, as if the United States were collectively on the way to bomb Japan. He meant the statement literally: at the time he wrote the sentence, William Laurence was sitting in one of the three B-29 Superfortress bombers on a mission to drop the second atomic bomb in history. Laurence went on to say, "We have several chosen targets. One of these is the great industrial and shipping center of Nagasaki."

Gradually, the story of what the *Times* science report was doing on a B-29 bomber on its way to drop a super-secret mega-weapon began to unravel. Laurence wrote that he was one of only a few people "privileged" to see final assembly of the bomb and the loading of Fat Man, the bomb's nickname, onto the plane. Like others who had been in close contact with the bomb project, Laurence had been infected with the sense of awe and power that projected aesthetic and even organic traits onto the weapon in their eyes. Laurence was not at all shy about his reverence for the bomb, saying, "It is a thing of beauty to behold, this 'gadget'" and hailed its creation as the "most concentrated intellectual effort in history." Laurence continued to write about the loading of the bomb and the crew of the three B-29s, including the names, ranks, and even home addresses of most of them. He described the long wait for the mission to begin, the rise of the plane into a storm, the appearance of a glaze of electric blue light (static electricity) on the plane's propellers, which one of the crewmen told him is called "St. Elmo's Fire." In a more personal moment in the article, he described a chat between himself and a twenty-year-old radio operator on board the bomber. Laurence had remarked, "It's a long way from Hoopeston, Illinois," and the sergeant replied, "Yup." The sergeant asked Laurence if he thought this second atomic bomb would end the war, and Laurence replied that he thought it would, and if did not, then the next one or two bombs would, explaining, "It's power is such that no nation can withstand it for very long."

Laurence explained to the reader that it was not his personal opinion that led him to that conclusion, it was something that the people all around him had expressed, and that anyone who had seen the "man-made fireball in action" as he had, would know it to be true. The reporter did not leave the reader hanging concerning the last point. He revealed that in addition to being the only non-military, non-scientist on board one of the two atomic bomb runs, he had also been the *only* journalist to witness the first testing of the atomic bomb in New Mexico.

Laurence carried on, flexing his impressive ability to paint a picture with words without wandering (as Herbert Matthews had often done) onto a tangent of irrelevant dreamy prose. He wrote,

Beyond these vast mountains of white clouds ahead of me there lies Japan, the land of our enemy. In about four hours from now one of its cities, making weapons of war for use against us, will be wiped off the map by the greatest weapon ever made by man. In one tenth of a millionth of a second, a fraction of time immeasurable by any clock, a whirlwind from the sky will pulverize thousands of its buildings and tens of thousands of its inhabitants.

The Great Artiste, the bomber in which Laurence was flying, started to climb to its bombing altitude and eventually met with the lead ship, the Bockscar, which carried the bomb. They reached the Japanese coast, and everyone on board, including Laurence, began strapping on parachutes. After flying over the mainland for a while, they noticed that it was Nagasaki among the list of target cities that presented clear skies. After avoiding a few rounds of flak fire, the planes got ready for the fatal moment.

With arc welders' glasses over their eyes, William Laurence and the crew of the B-29 waited for the moment. Then they saw a "black object" fall out of the Bockscar's bomb bay. Someone yelled, "There she goes!" and as the pilot of Laurence's plane swung the B-29 out of range, they saw a bright flash that flooded their cabin with intense light. Moments later the blast wave struck the airplane, and then four more blasts hit the B-29 in succession. The men on Laurence's plane witnessed what he described as a

> …giant pillar of purple fire, 10,000 feet high, shooting skyward with enormous speed…Awe struck, we watched it shoot upward like a meteor coming from the earth instead of from outer space, becoming ever more alive as it climbed skyward through the white clouds. It was a living thing, a new species of being, born right before our incredulous eyes.

Laurence described the mushroom cloud that burst out of the fiery pillar that broke off and floated to the sky. He told of another mushroom cloud that emerged in place of the first. And finally, "As the mushroom floated off into the blue it changed its shape into a flower like form, its giant petal curving downward, creamy white outside, rose colored inside." Laurence wrote that the blast cloud kept its rose-colored flower form when they last turned to look at it.

On the ground, things were certainly not as rosy as they seemed from the sky. The bomb had laid waste to everything within a one kilometer radius of ground zero. Plants, animals, and, of course, humans within that immediate radius were instantly killed and, in many cases, vaporized. Wooden structures and debris were blown away as if they were dust. Some concrete structures remained but were destroyed. Beyond the one kilometer radius, some of the people and animals present died instantly, but others did not. Most wooden structures were destroyed, and fire consumed the wooden buildings that were not immediately destroyed. Humans and animals suffered injury from flying debris and severe burn wounds from the intense heat of the radiation three to four kilometers from the hypocenter of the bomb.[19]

The official line of the American government and, in particular, the War Department, was that *all* the damage was caused by the force of the blast. The bomb, the government sought to convince people, was just like a conventional bomb, only much bigger and more powerful. However, the official line was not consistent with what a few intrepid and determined journalists found on the ground. One of these journalists was an Australian correspondent named Wilfred Burchett. Burchett managed to get to Nagasaki during the first week of September, nearly a month after the bombing, through a difficult journey by train and, of all things, rowboat. When he arrived at the devastated city, he found something beyond belief. According to an article in the Yale Global Online, Burchett sat down on a concrete block in the midst of a sea of destruction and began tapping out his story on his portable typewriter. He opened his article with the following:

> In Hiroshima, thirty days after the first atomic bomb destroyed the city and shook the world, people are still dying, mysteriously and horribly—people who were uninjured in the cataclysm from an unknown something which I can only describe as an atomic plague.[20]

Burchett spoke with Japanese doctors around the area and found that they were reporting what eventually came to be known as radiation sickness. He quoted one of the doctors as saying,

At first we treated burns as we would any others, but patients just wasted away and died. Then people without a mark on them, including some not even here when the Bomb exploded, fell sick and died. For no apparent reason their health began to fail. They lost their appetite, their hair began to fall out, bluish spots appeared on their bodies and bleeding started from the nose, mouth and eyes...And in every case the patient dies... there is nothing we can do about it.

The bomb was continuing to kill people who, weeks after the bombing and after Japan's surrender, were no longer enemies of the United States. The London *Daily Express* published Burchett's account on September 5 and the United States War Department, by this point in a state of paranoia compared with its early days of aloofness regarding nuclear research, swooped in to do damage control in the United States. The military censors wasted no time in confiscating the article of an American reporter named George Weller, who confirmed Burchett's report of an "atomic plague." Weller, who wrote for the *Chicago Daily News*, penned an article that told of "The atomic bomb's peculiar 'disease,' uncured because it is untreated and untreated because it is not diagnosed, is still snatching away lives here. Men, woman and children with no outward marks of injury are dying daily in hospitals."[21]

The War Department was intent on moving forward with research and development of its new "miracle weapon." It understood that its potential was limitless. (Think today not just of advanced nuclear warheads but of nuclear-powered submarines and aircraft carriers.) But it also understood it could not withstand a major opposing current in public opinion that would sweep the bomb funding away with mass disgust and fear of the true horrors of nuclear technology and radiation poisoning.

The government stepped in and, like any effective publicity apparatus, put to use its best-placed assets. In this case, it was William Laurence, the "unassuming *New York Times* reporter," who, it just so happened, was also on the War Department payroll.

Laurence wrote an article on September 8, three days after the publication of Burchett's radiation sickness article, which the *Times* published on September 12.[22] The headline read, "U.S. Bomb Site Belies Tokyo Tales," and the import of the article was that stories of radiation sickness around Hiroshima and Nagasaki amounted to nothing more than "Japanese propaganda." The *Times*'s science reporter, who understood the nuclear issues and repercussions as well as many of the top scientists, wrote that the New Mexico atomic bomb test site was proof that the Japanese were lying. He recounted how he and some other reporters visited the test site along with radiologists armed with Geiger counters and found the levels of radiation, two months after the test, to be insignificant. He mentioned, incidentally, that the reporters had to put white covering over their shoes so as not to pick up radiation still in the ground, but he made sure to state that the place was completely habitable and that the radiation levels were minimal. Further, Laurence wrote, "Japanese sources" (whom he did not name) were said to have admitted that the radiation levels on the ground near the bomb sites were much lower than tolerance level, and according to the head of the bomb program, General Leslie Groves, people could live there "forever."

For its part, the *New York Times* took full advantage of the unique proximity to the Manhattan Project that its reporter enjoyed. On September 12, the paper ran a story comparing Laurence's account of the bombing to the biblical account of the war between the Israelites and Canaanites.[23] Another account that Laurence's reporting called to mind, the *Times* article said, was that of Homer. The article labeled the epic poet as "the pioneer newspaper man" and noted that just as Homer had listed all the various nations who partook in battle, so had Laurence listed all the names of the crewmen, their hometowns, and addresses.

Two weeks later, the *Times* ran Laurence's retrospective account of the July test of the atomic bomb on its front page.[24] Laurence again wrote about a "dawn of a new day," calling the first bomb test a "great moment in history." Laurence told readers that as the engineers were preparing for that first test, the huge question on everyone minds and lips was, "Will it work?" But, Laurence wrote,

> With the mighty flash came a delayed roll of mighty thunder, heard just as the flash was seen for hundreds of miles. The roar echoed and reverberated from the distant hills and the Sierra Oscuro Range near by...The hills said 'yes' and the mountains chimed in 'yes'. It was as if

the earth had spoken and the suddenly iridescent clouds joined in one mighty affirmative answer. Atomic energy—yes.

The *Times* continued to keep the spotlight on its new star reporter. As it did with Walter Duranty and Herbert Matthews, the newspaper began writing stories on their own journalist's public appearances. In this case, the paper ran a story about a lecture Laurence gave on the topic and proudly noted that he was the man whom "the Government permitted to study the development of the bomb, as well as witness its first test in New Mexico."[25] It was a dramatic—and very innocent-looking—picture the *New York Times* was painting of William Laurence and his involvement with the development of the bomb. The newspaper, and Laurence himself, trumpeted the bomb and the journalist's "privileged" position as a witness to it but kept the story behind the story to an absolute minimum. The official line of the paper was simply that Laurence had been on a "detachment" (a military term, not a journalistic one) to help "enlighten" the laymen about the bomb, as the paper wrote in its August 7 article about the science writer. This was the largest, most expensive, most risk-fraught military development undertaking in history, and the *Times* made it seem as if Laurence simply stumbled into the secret laboratories and ultra-secure test sites. Of course, there was much more to the story.

◆ ◆ ◆

In William Laurence's 1977 obituary, the *Times* detailed that one day in spring 1945, the science writer simply did not show up to work.[26] The obituary claimed that only the managing editor of the paper knew where he was. Not quite. What had actually happened was that Laurence had been selected to participate in a painstakingly choreographed plan that took into account every aspect and detail of the bomb program. The plan's creator was General Leslie Groves, the director of the bomb development program. Groves worked tirelessly to make sure that everything would go according to plan and that all the plans were sound. Unlike many military planners, he believed the social response to the bomb was something that had to be considered and, to the mind of a military man, countered.

Journalist Amy Goodman, with her brother David Goodman, conducted an in-depth investigation on Laurence and the *Times*'s involvement with the bomb program. In *Exceptions to the Rulers,* they explain the arrangement between the paper and the War Department.[27] The cooperation began when General Groves visited the *New York Times* in the spring of 1945 and met with Arthur Hays Sulzberger and William Laurence.

It was no stretch for a military man working on a secret project to visit the *New York Times* for assistance. Sulzberger's nephew, C.L. Sulzberger, was known to have so many high-level intelligence and CIA connections that he had been accused, by reliable sources, of being an agent himself. Groves came with a proposition. The Manhattan Project knew it could handle the science and military security but it could not do an adequate job of publicity. The solution, as Goodman explained in a 2005 "Democracy Now" radio program, was elegantly simple: Laurence would go "on loan" to the government while staying on as a *Times* reporter.[28] It was a win-win situation. The War Department would get a talented reporter along with his outlet to the country's leading newspaper to help it spin the bomb's development and use. The *Times* would gain unprecedented access to not just a top-secret military program but a scientific project of unprecedented scope and proportions. As an enormous added bonus, the paper would get to place its reporter on an atomic bombing mission. (Laurence pushed to get on the bombing mission for Hiroshima but was unable to.) All Laurence would have to do is toe the government line in press releases, statements he wrote for President Truman and War Department Secretary Stimson and, most critically, in *New York Times* news articles. His job was to celebrate the power of nuclear energy, something he had already done with great expertise in his 1930s articles, and assure the public that the atom splitting represented a great new source of cheap energy—and nothing more. Only one party would lose out on the deal between the *New York Times* and the War Department: the American public, who still had little or no real understanding of what nuclear weapons meant for the world.

In a twist of irony that (after becoming familiar with the accounts in this book) it seems only the *New York Times* could pull off, another reporter at the Gray Lady participated in the very same cover up of radiation poisoning and sickness of Japanese civilians. His name: William H. Lawrence. Unlike the *Times* science reporter William L. Laurence, the *New York Times*'s correspondent William H. Lawrence was not on the government's payroll. And this small but hugely significant detail explains why he published a true account of what was happening on the ground in Japan after the bomb was dropped while his homonymous and more famous colleague published outright lies.

"The atomic bomb is still killing Japanese at a rate of 100 daily in flattened, rubble-strewn Hiroshima," Lawrence wrote an article on September 3, 1945.[29] He went on to report that as one of the first foreigners in the bombed city, he witnessed the massive destruction and spoke with doctors who found that they could do nothing for patients who were mysteriously dying of wounds that did not seem serious enough to treat.[30] The account Lawrence provided from the ground was completely opposite to the one that Laurence gave from the sky. The former Lawrence told of how, even to him, who had seen major wars around the world, the sight of the death and destruction of the atom bomb took his breath away. He witnessed the straggling survivors wandering around aimlessly. He spoke of a discussion he had with a Japanese doctor who remarked that the United States was now in the possession of a weapon that could end the life of every living thing on earth. And he also remarked that a member of the official United States scientific investigatory team told him the bomb definitely had the ability to wipe out a body's white blood cells.

One week later, Lawrence wrote another article.[31] This one flatly contradicted his article of one week earlier. Its headline made very clear the purpose of the story: "No Radioactivity in Hiroshima Ruin." The article focused on the military's pronouncements that Hiroshima was a military target (given that it was one of the largest military centers in Japan, this was true) and that its bombing was a military success. It quoted only one source, Brigadier General T.F. Farrell, who insisted the main cause of death was the blast and that only a minimal amount of harm occurred afterwards as a result of damaged "corpuscles." Lawrence made no mention of his findings on the ground or of his earlier discussion with Japanese doctors.

A *Times* editorial from the same day provides an explanation for Lawrence's about-face.[32] The editorial restated science writer Laurence's earlier article, which claimed the New Mexico A-bomb test results did not support Japanese claims of radiation sickness in Hiroshima and Nagasaki. The editorial went on to claim that although an American scientific team was still investigating conditions on the ground, "it is hardly to be expected that residual radioactivity will be detected."[33] The editorial authoritatively explained that Japanese claims about the destruction of red blood cells must be "dismissed as fiction" and that Japanese claims that white blood cells were damaged "may be considered skeptically." The *Times*'s editorial informed readers that the test in New Mexico, which the War Department controlled without any independent observation or monitoring, would "allay any lingering doubts."

This was the official line of the United States War Department and, by virtue of the deal that centered around William Laurence, also that of the *New York Times*. It was not just *Times* articles but newsmen on loan and editorials that were put into service of the War Department to support the government's propaganda claims. It is possible that the *Times* had been "misinformed." But the truth was that it not only refused to acknowledge the facts of the first-hand accounts of its own reporter, William H. Lawrence, but it chose not to investigate them further. The result of this approach to reporting was not just a theoretical blunder or the failure to meet some abstract journalistic standard. The *New York Times* participated in a government propaganda program, when it should have been providing reliable, independently sourced information to the public. William L. Laurence, the brilliant, incisive writer who understood nuclear issues before most government scientists did, was fully aware that radiation would pour out of a nuclear bomb. But Laurence made a choice in a different direction and trumpeted the beauty of the bomb—the "affirmative yes" to this terrifying new technology—in glittering terms. It would only take a few years before the effects of this failure of reporting would once again become deadly.

◆ ◆ ◆

The lack of accurate information about the effects of the atomic bomb on human bodies accomplished one critical thing: it allowed the United States government to press forward with research and funding of its nuclear program, including the weapons program. An important part of the research included the testing of more and more powerful nuclear weapons, first in the Bikini Atoll, in the Pacific Ocean, where entire sections of the atoll[34] were vaporized by bombs in 1946, and later on the Marshall Islands in 1954.

The Marshall Island tests studied the effects of a hydrogen bomb called Bravo, which was a thousand times more powerful than the bomb dropped on Hiroshima. During the Marshall Islands test, the government failed to evacuate more than a hundred islanders until fifty hours *after* the H-bomb was dropped. By that point, the bodies of the islanders had been suffused by radiation from the fallout of the massive bomb. The government failed a second time, according to a *Honolulu Weekly* article by Beverly Deepe Keever, to safeguard the lives of these people by transporting them back to the islands just three years later, when the islands were still massively unsafe for human habitation.[35]

The results, from today's perspective, are unsurprising. Women from the islands gave birth to babies that had thyroid problems so severe they could not survive. Other women gave birth to shapeless deformities. Ninety percent of the children under the age of twelve at the time of the test developed thyroid tumors. In short, the bomb tests ruined the lives of hundreds of people, damning them and their children to shockingly short lifespans and illness.[36] And the American public, still under the spell of the myth that nuclear weapons did not produce after-effects other than burns, a myth championed by the *New York Times* and its science reporter—who won a Pulitzer Prize for his bomb reporting—as they assisted the propaganda program of the United States War Department, barely batted an eye.

Mideast Martyr:
"A Young Symbol of Violence"

There is a name that was once known to every member of global Islamist jihad. This name was spoken by the lowest terrorist foot soldier just as it was passionately cried out, in their last few moments, by jihadist suicide bombers. The name adorned jihad-themed postage stamps in Jordan as well as streets in Cairo, Damascus, and Gaza. The name was taught to schoolchildren in textbooks and on TV as a reason to become a "child martyr" and take up the AK-47 or bomb vest. This name was called out by Osama bin Laden in his infamous videos. And the name was echoed by bin Laden's successor and former top lieutenant Al-Zawhiri, who spoke it with as much hatred as his jihadi commander. The name has been invoked to justify the beheading of an American journalist and the lynching of two Israeli citizens who made a wrong turn. The name emerged as the burning symbol of Islamist jihad. The name is Muhammad Al-Dura, and the story behind the name, we now know, represents one of the greatest, most insidious and damaging propaganda blitzes in recent memory.

On September 30, 2000, a number of Palestinians gathered at a junction near the village of Netzarim in the Gaza Strip to stage a protest.[1] There was little chance that this would be what is called a "peaceful protest" in the West. Only three days before, a bomb had killed an Israeli soldier near the village. Two days earlier, organized Palestinian mobs had turned out to riot in Jerusalem under the pretense that then-Israeli minister of transportation and, later, prime minister, Ariel Sharon, was visiting the Temple Mount—called the Noble Sanctuary by Muslims—in the heart of Jerusalem's Old City. The day of Sharon's visit marked the beginning of a long bloody wave of Palestinian terror and Israeli retaliation that lasted for more than four years.

On that last day of September, a man named Jamal Al-Dura and his son Muhammad were traveling through Gaza, according to Jamal to look for a used car. By the time they arrived at the Netzarim junction around mid-afternoon, the crowd of soon-to-be rioters had already gathered. The situation was looking ominous. The driver of the taxi the father and son were traveling in refused to cross the junction. Jamal made the decision to get out, cross the junction on foot and catch another taxi on the other side. This—the very beginning of the story—is where anything that resembles clarity ends.

Hours after the arrival of the father and son, a short video clip was being circulated around the media that would change the world and fan hatred in millions of hearts. The video, little more than fifty seconds long, showed Jamal and Muhammad Al-Dura crouching behind a cement barrel, taking cover from gunfire. Jamal pulls Muhammad closer to him with his right hand as his left shoulder is pinned against the concrete barrel they were using to shelter themselves from the bullets. Moments later a burst of gunfire appears to strike the wall behind them. The camera jostles violently as a puff of smoke or dust passes in front of the screen. When the camera refocuses on the father and son, Muhammad is lying limp across his father's lap, while Jamal's head bobbles as he sits upright against the wall, apparently wounded.

There were many camera crews on hand that day from many different news agencies, including Reuters, AP, and France 2. However, only France 2, a French state television channel, caught any real footage of the death of Muhammad Al-Dura. Hours after the incident, France 2 circulated a copy of the video—free of charge—to news agencies all over the world.

The video is chaotic and difficult to follow even though it was edited by France 2 to present a clearer narrative. A voice-over is heard along with the video as the action is explained and narrated by France 2 then-Jerusalem bureau chief, Charles Enderlin. Enderlin's voice provides structure to the chaos and explanation for the mystery of the chaotic action on camera. Charles Enderlin, however, did not witness the incident and was not even present at the scene that day.

In his absentee narration, Enderlin states that Jamal and Muhammad Al-Dura are the "the target of fire coming from the Israeli position."[2] Enderlin, of course, had neither witnessed the event nor had he conducted any sort of investigation by the time he made his accusation against the Israeli military of intentionally targeting and murdering an unarmed child (and attempting to murder his father). The charge was definitely a serious one, maybe the most serious one. To make matters worse, the video did not show what Enderlin was narrating. Rather, it showed the Al-Duras coming under fire from an unidentified position and then cut to spliced-in shots of the Israeli firing position with puffs of gunfire smoke coming from the slits in the concrete outpost. By any reasonable standard of journalistic ethics and norms, a charge of that seriousness and magnitude, in a region of that volatility, would demand a thorough investigation, especially given that the charge was based on a sketchy video narrated by someone who was not present at the scene. But when it came to its reporting, the *New York Times* punted.

The day after the incident, a *Times* report on the growing violence in Israel, Gaza and the West Bank mentioned the death of the boy. The headline of the story was, "Mideast Violence Continues to Rage; Death Toll Rises."[3] The reporter, William Orme Jr., wrote in the first few paragraphs that an ambulance driver and a twelve-year-old boy were killed. Orme went on to explain the death of the boy: "The boy was filmed by a foreign television crew as he cowered behind a cement block with his father, who shouted at the Israeli soldiers to hold their fire." The sentence, which connects the death of the child to the Israeli fire by noting the father's shouting at the Israeli soldiers, imputes the responsibility for the death very clearly. But just in case anyone missed the point, Orme went on to quote a source on the topic who said, "This is a killing in cold blood, an attack on an innocent child without any excuse." Orme identified the source of the quote as one "Mr. Aburdaineh," without giving any further qualification to the source other than the "Mr." in front of his name. Aburdaineh, it turns out, was a top Palestinian advisor to Palestine Liberation Organization (PLO) leader and Palestinian terror chief, Yasser Arafat. Orme did not seem to think it was worth mentioning that his only source on the incident was paid for his bias.

Orme further provided no counter-response from the Israeli (or any other) side. Instead of seeking out an Israeli comment on the incident, the *Times* reporter simply noted that there was not one, and went on to explain that Israelis "spent the day strolling to synagogues and family gatherings."

Orme's October 1 story about the boy triggered a flurry of subsequent *New York Times* stories about Muhammad Al-Dura. Only one day later, on October 2, Orme penned a story devoted in its entirety to the new "symbol" of martyrdom that had been created only two days earlier and had yet to be investigated by the Israeli military, the Palestinian Authority, independent non-governmental organizations, the United Nations, or even journalists such as himself.[4] The story ran under the headline, "A Young Symbol of Mideast Violence," began with a description of the boy, a "boisterous blue-jeaned Gaza fifth grader," and promptly asserted the boy had been shot dead. As for the source of the fire, Orme deferred to the boy's father, Jamal Al-Dura, who said that the Israelis had killed Muhammad. Orme also quoted Al-Dura's mother. But, in nearly 600 words, he provided no other quote and cited no other source. Rather than offer sources and facts, the story worked toward its headline, announcing in the fifth paragraph that the boy had become a symbol of "what angry Palestinians contend is their continued victimization by Israeli occupiers." In other words, two days after the incident, as far as the *New York Times* was concerned, the narrative had already been determined: the boy had been killed by Israeli fire, and he was now a "symbol" (a more hygienic substitute for the word "martyr") of the Israeli victimization of Palestinians.

This particular narrative of the *Times* regarding the Israelis and Palestinians had not just popped out of the Al-Dura story. Rather, the narrative had been long brewing, especially in the hands of William Orme and his *Times* bureau chief, Deborah Sontag. The coverage of the beginning of the Second Intifada (or "uprising") by the *Times*'s Jerusalem bureau makes this clear enough. On the same day Al-Dura was filmed in the crossfire of a gun battle, September 30, 2000, the *Times* published a story by Deborah Sontag, "Battle at Jerusalem Holy Site Leaves 4 Dead and 200 Hurt."[5] Sontag stated in the opening paragraph that violence had erupted in the contested Old City of Jerusalem. In the second paragraph, after giving a brief body count, Sontag plainly stated that the Palestinian rioting began when Ariel Sharon, "the rightist opposition leader," visited the Temple Mount, or what Sontag called the "Muslim compound."

The place that Sharon visited is Judaism's holiest site. It is the platform where the Second Temple is known to have stood and is in the vicinity of where the First Temple was located. Israel gained control of the Old City of Jerusalem and the Temple Mount (which had been closed to Jews during centuries of Muslim control) during the Six-Day War in 1967, after Jordan had annexed the area in the war it declared, along with Egypt, Syria, Saudi Arabia, Iraq and Lebanon, against Israel in 1948. However, in a move that many religious and secular Jews have criticized harshly, the Israeli defense minister at the time of the 1967 war, General Moshe Dayan, awarded control of the Temple Mount to the Waqf, or Muslim Authority, in a bid to increase chances for peace with Israel's Arab neighbors. Ariel Sharon's visit to the Temple Mount was, according to the general-turned-politician, not a bid to "reassert Jewish claims" to the site, as Sontag speculated, but a way of reminding both Jews and Muslims that Jews have as a right to visit the holy site, just as Muslims do. However, Sontag asserted only the claim coming from Arab-Muslim sources at the time. In her September 30 article, she quoted a leader of the Muslim Waqf who had said that he and other Palestinian leaders had warned the Israeli government not to allow Sharon's visit and that the visit and the police who protected Sharon on that day were a provocation. Sontag accepted and printed this claim, stating flatly that "That is the reason for the confrontations of today."

Along with the September 30 story about the beginning of the violence, the *Times* printed a dramatic photo that showed an Israeli soldier in riot gear approaching a bloodied young man who was stooping on the ground. In the photo, the Israeli soldier is holding a club in his hand and is shouting violently. The *Times*'s caption explained that the soldier was an Israeli, and the bloodied man, who looks as if he is about to be struck by the screaming, armed Israeli, is Palestinian. The caption also noted that the scene occurred on the Temple Mount. Although the caption made clear what was going on in the photo, it was entirely unnecessary, given that Deborah Sontag's article was a description of the larger situation that the photo embodied: an armed Israeli in riot gear was attacking an unarmed Palestinian worshipper.

There was only one problem with the dramatic photo. A few days after its publication, the *Times* received a letter from a Dr. Grossman of Chicago. Grossman wrote to inform the *Times* that "The Palestinian is actually my son, Tuvia Grossman from Chicago. He, and two of his friends, were pulled from their taxicab while traveling in Jerusalem, by a mob of Palestinian Arabs, and were severely beaten and stabbed."[6] Furthermore, Dr. Grossman noted, the incident could not have occurred on the Temple Mount. If any of the many editors whose hands the story passed through had bothered to check, they would have noticed that behind the soldier there was a gas station. Not surprisingly, there are no gas stations at one of the holiest sites in the world.

The *Times* printed a correction on October 4, which identified the "Palestinian" as Grossman.[7] It made no mention however of what was really going on in the scene. This sparked an outcry, and so, the *Times* returned to the subject a few days later printing another correction that mentioned that Tuvia was in an Arab neighborhood of Jerusalem.[8] The second correction admitted that the solider was waving a nightstick at the Palestinian mob to keep them away. But, again, the second correction did not provide the whole story, which is that Tuvia and a fellow Jewish student had been attacked by the mob who had beaten, stabbed and attempted to kill them. The soldier, made out as to be brutally beating an already injured Palestinian, was actually saving a Jewish civilian from a Palestinian lynch mob.

The story created an uproar. Given a photo that showed an unclear scene, assumptions had to be made in order to provide a narrative to explain the photo in the caption. The *Times*'s operating premises were unintentionally revealed by the caption that the paper chose to print. The newspaper-reading public following the story of the photo began to learn how the *Times* viewed the conflict, no matter what the actual facts on the ground might have been. The working assumptions revealed by the photo incident are reinforced by the *Times*'s explanation of how the Second Intifada began.

In article after article, William Orme and Deborah Sontag relied on unsourced phrases or statements to put the blame for the violence squarely on the shoulders of Ariel Sharon and his visit to Judaism's holiest site. In many of these cases, articles dealing (in some way) with Muhammad Al-Dura's death relied on the claim that Sharon was the cause of the violence to explain the events unfolding at the time.

A day after his October 2 Al-Dura article, Orme wrote a story about then United States Secretary of State Madeleine Albright putting pressure on the two sides to return to negotiations and either slow or stop the violence.[9] Midway into the story's introduction, Orme casually explained that "Since Thursday, when a defiant visit by Israel's right-wing opposition leader to the most sacred Islamic site in Jerusalem ignited Palestinian protests throughout the territories and in Israel itself, at least 48 people have been killed." After describing that most of the deaths occurred as Israeli police responded with bullets to Palestinians who were throwing rocks, Orme slipped in the mention of the Netzarim junction, where he said, two people were killed, "including a twelve-year-old boy who has been embraced by Palestinians as a symbol of the conflict." Whether or not in the space of three days Muhammad Al-Dura had actually been "embraced" by the whole Palestinian people as a "symbol of the conflict" is difficult to ascertain. Orme provided no justification of the claim in the article. But for the readers of the *New York Times*, the notion that Muhammad Al-Dura was now a "symbol of the conflict" was served up as hard-and-fast fact.

Just ten days later, the now famous (or infamous) *New York Times* reporter Judith Miller joined Orme and Sontag's chorus. She wrote in an October 13 article on the spread of the conflict to Lebanon about "Ariel Sharon's trip to holy sites in Jerusalem's Old City, [and] the violent protests that followed it..." [10] Of course, having mentioned Sharon's visit to the holy sites as the cause of the violence, Miller, like Orme and Sontag before her, was compelled to assert that the Israeli military had murdered a twelve-year-old boy. She wrote, "Arab television networks and newspapers have repeatedly shown photographs and film of Muhammad Dura, 12, and other Palestinian children being shot, as well as other victims of Israeli soldiers and military actions." Miller left no room for doubt: Israel had not only shot and killed the twelve-year-old but many other children had become "victims of Israeli soldiers and military actions." Who these other children are and under what circumstances they were killed, Miller decided to leave unspecified.

The *New York Times* and its correspondents in Israel kept up their flurry of Al-Dura claims throughout the month of October. Just one and two days after the incident at Netzarim junction, before there was time for any trend of opinion to solidify in the Arab world, the *Times* was declaring the creation of a symbol and mentioning that symbol in articles that had virtually nothing to do with the incident itself. Worse, however, is that the *Times*'s chosen narratives regarding the Second Intifada and Muhammad Al-Dura were patently false. In the first case, the Palestinian leadership made little secret (at least in the Arabic-speaking press) of what they had managed to pull off with regard to the intifada. Speaking to the Arab newspaper Al-Hayat, widely considered the Arab "paper of record," Palestinian terror leader Marwan Barghouti admitted that the PLO and various Palestinian terror group leaders had formulated an understanding that a major violent uprising would begin sometime in September.

"I knew that the end of September was the last period (of time) before the explosion," Barghouti told Al-Hayat. When Sharon's pending visit to the Temple Mount became known, Barghouti explained, the Palestinian leadership knew they had a perfect opportunity to strike, "but when Sharon reached the Al-Aqsa Mosque, this was the most appropriate moment for the outbreak of the intifada." Barghouti explained how he and other Palestinian terror leaders gathered after Sharon's visit and "discussed the manner of response and how it was possible to react in all the cities and not just in Jerusalem. We contacted all (the Palestinian) factions."[11]

As concern about the violence grew, United States Senator George Mitchell decided to commission an investigation into the causes and factors behind the Second Intifada. The Mitchell Report,[12] as it came to be known, flatly contradicted the claim that Sharon's visit to the Temple Mount triggered the intifada. "The Sharon visit did not cause the Al-Aqsa Intifada," the report stated. The Mitchell Commission, which was made up of the senator, European Union foreign policy chief, Javier Solana, a former NATO secretary general, former senator Warren Rudman, a former president of Turkey, and Norway's foreign minister at the time, released its report in April 2001. However, the release of the report had no effect on the *Times*'s subsequent claims that Sharon who had triggered the "cycle of violence" which, by 2001, was still in its earlier stages.

In fact, a major article written by Deborah Sontag in July 2001 was firmly based in the fallacy that Sharon had started the intifada. The July 26, 2001 article by Sontag was titled "Quest for Mideast Peace: How and Why It Failed."[13] The article ran nearly 6,000 words long and purported to be an in-depth look at the peace talks with President Clinton, then Israeli Prime Minister Ehud Barak, and PLO chairman Yasser Arafat. The opening of the article immediately presented the claim that despite conventional wisdom, it was not Arafat who had scrapped the peace talks at Camp David by walking away from the negotiating table. Sontag told the story of a meeting between Arafat and Ehud Barak in late summer of 2000, after the failed Camp David talks, at Barak's home in a quaint Israeli suburban village. According to the report, the private talks between the men were going so well that at one point Barak jumped up to call President Clinton in order to tell the American president that things were coming along so flawlessly that he was sure that the two men would be the ones to finally broker peace.

The private talks at Barak's home, Sontag wrote, were part of a months-long process of continuing diplomatic moves and meetings that were still carrying the peace process forward, and that Camp David had not actually failed, since it was only one step in a larger process. In late August and early September, according to Sontag, things were still going well between the two sides. They held meetings, there were what she called "field trips," complete with Palestinian officials joking about putting GPS devices in citizens' shoes, and even a super-secret final status agreement that was made by a Palestinian negotiator and an Israeli negotiator which was so sensitive it could not be shown to other people—including the other negotiators. In other words, according to Sontag, things—for the first time in the history of the region—were looking up. And then, Sontag wrote, Ariel Sharon decided to take a field trip of his own: "Mr. Sharon's coming visit to what Muslims call the Noble Sanctuary and Jews know as the Temple Mount. Mr. Arafat said in an interview that he huddled on the balcony with Mr. Barak and implored him to block Mr. Sharon's plans." Barak, Sontag wrote, was implacable, seeing the visit as an "internal" Israeli matter. "On the heels of very intricate grappling at Camp David," Sontag explained, "over the future status of the Old City's holy sites, Mr. Sharon's heavily guarded visit to the plaza outside Al-Aqsa Mosque to demonstrate Jewish sovereignty over the Temple Mount set off angry Palestinian demonstrations."

She then explained the "Palestinian demonstrations," which in actuality were a violent riot that included (but was not limited to) a hailstorm of stones raining down on Jewish worshipers at the Western Wall, which sits below the Temple Mount, resulting in the Israelis using "lethal force." From there, Sontag traced a line to the intifada: "The cycle of violence started, escalated, mutated and built to a peak," she hypothesized.

The article made waves, and people on both sides of the political isle started to weigh in. One of the more prominent responses was published in the *New Republic*. Its author, Mideast policy expert Robert Satloff, began the article by asking readers to imagine a *New York Times* article about the sinking of the Titanic that makes only a "passing reference" to an iceberg.[14] Satloff, who published many articles in the *New York Times* as well as in other top newspapers, compared Sontag's landmark July 2001 story to the imagined *Times* article about the Titanic, which pays no attention to the actual cause of the sinking. He writes that in almost 6,000 words of the article, an explanation of why peace between Israel and the Palestinians had mentioned the word "intifada" only once. Instead, Sontag strained to argue that all parties involved, and not just Arafat, caused the Camp David talks to fall apart and that diplomatic on-goings just after Camp David had brought the two sides closer than ever to a deal.

However, according to Satloff, "a close look at Sontag's story reveals lazy reporting, errors of omission, questionable shading, and an indifference to the basic fact that the Palestinian decision to wed diplomacy with violence, not American and Israeli miscues, damned the search for peace." Satloff goes on to explain the many serious (if not fatal) problems with the article. He notes that among the nearly forty people heavily involved in the talks, Sontag cited only eight from her own interviews. The rest of the quotations were provided through what could be called journalistic hearsay. Sontag quoted from her own interviews only one of the many American diplomats at Camp David and mysteriously chose to leave out material from interviews she conducted with four considerably important people at Camp David: President Clinton, Secretary of State Madeleine Albright, the national security advisor, and the special Middle East coordinator. What Sontag did with her Israeli sources, Satloff wrote, was "downright ideological." For one of her three Israeli sources, she relied on Yossi Beilin, an extreme left-wing politician. One other source was a former Labor minister, Shlomo Ben Ami, who subsequently said that Arafat was indeed responsible for the collapse of the talks and considered Arafat so unwilling to negotiate that he pursued a campaign to get the international community to impose a peace deal on the two sides. The last of the three Israelis quoted was Ehud Barak's chief of staff, Gilead Sher, who, she wrote, said that peace was entirely "doable." Sontag chose not to write, however, about a speech Sher gave three months before her article in which he said that by September 2000, Arafat had made it clear that he would not reach an agreement unless "all his demands were met."[15]

Sontag, Satloff noted, left out any interview or even mention of the substantial number of Israeli negotiators who had reached the conclusion, during Camp David, that peace with Arafat was impossible. When it came to the Palestinian side, Satloff went on to say, Sontag provided the tell-them-what-they-want-to-hear quotes of the top-three negotiators about how close they had come to achieving peace and how willing they were to complete the deal. But she failed to provide accounts of these men's statements in the Arab press, where one of them had endorsed the Algerian-Vietnamese model of talking and shooting at the same time. Another adviser had told journalist David Brooks a few weeks before Sontag's article that it was impossible "from now to 1,000 years" for the Palestinians to make concessions regarding the 1967 borders. And of course, Sontag left out the many statements by Arafat's advisers that the intifada was part of a larger strategic plan.

For Sontag, the intifada that was raging had little or nothing to do with the failure of peace. The Palestinian violation of the 1993 Oslo Accords, which stipulated that Israel would officially recognize the PLO in exchange for a cessation and foreswearing of PLO violence, goes unmentioned. Sontag never mentioned nor did she even hint at the Palestinian sacking, desecration, and takeover of Joseph's Tomb, the third holiest site in Judaism, in October 2000. For Sontag, the cycle of violence was one spun only by Israel.

William Orme's stories took a very similar, if not identical, perspective. On October 24, 2000, Orme published a *New York Times* story about the Israeli military's rocketing of the transmitters of the Palestinian radio station, Voice of Palestine.[16] The silencing of the radio station was part of an Israeli retaliation for the lynching of two Russian-born Israeli reservist soldiers, ten days earlier, who had made a wrong turn and ended up in Ramallah. The two were arrested by Palestinian police and, not long after, a mob gathered at the police station. The two men were beaten and trampled to death before their bodies were dragged down the main street of the city by cheering Palestinian crowds.

Orme covered the story about Voice of Palestine transmitters being rocketed in a way that was consistent with Sontag's approach to the Camp David talks. The article's second paragraph consisted entirely of an angry statement by one of the station's Palestinian hosts. The only other quote that Orme provided was an Israeli colonel responsible for monitoring Palestinian media. The colonel said, "They call us murderers," and remarked that Voice of Palestine perpetuates a narrative of Israeli soldiers targeting children.

Orme provided the Palestinian response in the form of the radio host remarking, "Every word the Israelis hear on Voice of Palestine they think is incitement." With this statement in mind, Orme went on to provide a sample of some of the incitement on the station, which he limited to a single quote by a Palestinian imam that had been broadcast on Voice of Palestine the day after the lynching. According to Orme, the imam had said only that "Whether Likud [Party] or Labor [Party], the Jews are the Jews."

What Orme chose to leave out of the quote, however, is revealing—and disturbing. The "Whether Likud or Labor" quote was only the first sentence of the entire quote by the imam. Orme redacted the rest of it. The remainder of the quote broadcast on Voice of Palestine, the day after the lynching of two men, is chilling:

> The Jews are the Jews. Whether Labor or Likud the Jews are Jews. They do not have any moderates or any advocates of peace. They are all liars. They must be butchered and must be killed...The Jews are like a spring as long as you step on it with your foot it doesn't move. But if you lift your foot from the spring, it hurts you and punishes you...It is forbidden to have mercy in your hearts for the Jews in any place and in any land. Make war on them any place that you find yourself. Any place that you meet them, kill them."[17]

Why Orme thought that of all this, only the first sentence about "Labor or Likud" should be included as a sample of what was said the day after two Jews were murdered in Ramallah, is anybody's guess. Deborah Sontag had written the initial October 14 *Times* story about the lynching.[18] After giving the basic facts of the story (complete with some typical shading about "Israeli military might"), a character by that point familiar to readers of the *New York Times* makes an appearance.

About halfway into the lynch story, Sontag wrote that the photo of one of the lynched soldiers with the head of his corpse drooping is "the Israeli counterpart of the Muhammad Al-Dura image." In case a reader of the *Times* had missed one of the half-dozen *Times* stories in which the name "Al-Dura" had already appeared by October 14, Sontag went on to remind readers that "Muhammad was the twelve-year-old shot dead by Israeli troops in a gun battle in Gaza, caught on film by a French cameraman, as the boy cowered behind his father and then slumped dead in his lap."

The problem, once again, is one of truth. It begins with the small truths: the so-called "French cameraman" (whose nationality was mentioned, in all probability, to demonstrate his objectivity) was not French. He was, in fact, a self-declared Palestinian nationalist who stated that he sees his work as part of the Palestinian national struggle. This was not an obscure or hidden fact. Interviews with the Palestinian cameraman abounded in the media and on the internet from the day of the Al-Dura incident until the day of Sontag's lynch story, making the cameraman's identity more than clear.

But the problems grew larger and larger until the much doted-upon story about the innocent twelve-year-old Palestinian boy "shot dead by Israeli troops" proved far more complicated than it was originally presented. Doubts about the death of Muhammad Al-Dura began to surface not long after the incident. People who had seen the France 2 video began asking questions. The Israeli fire was coming from Jamal Al-Dura's left side, which is why he crouched behind a cement barrel to his left and motioned to his left to the Israelis to stop firing. But on the video, the cement barrel does not appear to be seriously damaged at any point in the shooting. If the Israeli soldiers had indeed used machine guns to target the Al-Dura hiding by the barrier, the barrier would have sustained heavy damage.

More and more doubts began to arise. France 2 shot twenty-seven minutes of film that day, but only fifty-five *seconds* were released to the media. What did those other twenty-six minutes and five seconds show (or not show)? Furthermore, why was Charles Enderlin narrating the events on video when he, by his own admission, was not at the scene?

James Fallows in a June 2003 article for the *Atlantic*, "Who Shot Muhammad Al-Dura?" recounted the first full Israeli investigation of the shooting—a hasty investigation in the days after the shooting had concluded that the Israeli soldiers "probably" had killed the boy, despite the fact that there was no serious ballistic or forensic investigation at the time—was commissioned by an Israeli general.[19] Heading the investigation were an Israeli physicist and an engineer. The team managed to find the exact kind of concrete barrel that had been at the junction on the day since the original barrel bore a seal from the Israeli Bureau of Standards. They reconstructed the scene and found that the barrel was indeed an excellent place for the Al-Duras to shelter since it sat directly between them and the Israeli line of fire. The Israeli investigation team fired M-16s, which is what the Israeli soldiers that day were armed with, into the barrel from the distance that the soldiers were at on the day of the incident. They found that the barrel would had to have been hit on both sides for a bullet to penetrate. Later inspection of the actual barrel showed, however, that no bullets penetrated the two inches of cement.

The team then investigated the bullet marks on the wall behind the Al-Duras and concluded that those shots could not have come from the Israeli position. The marks that the bullets made came from guns that were positioned straight ahead of the wall and the Al-Duras, while the Israeli position was located to the extreme left of the Al-Duras (or to the right of the wall when looking at it head on). The team came to the conclusion and released its report, which stated that there was no way the bullets that killed Muhammad Al-Dura could possibly have come from the Israeli position.

Given that the report came from the Israeli military, it was not given much credence or attention. In fact, it is safe to say that the report made literally no difference when it came to what people believed. In the case of the Arab world, it probably only strengthened the belief that Israeli soldiers killed the boy. But the story did not end there. France 2 and its Jerusalem bureau chief Charles Enderlin would draw themselves into a legal battle that would eventually cast very grave doubts on their narrative of the incident and, where the public legal record is concerned, provide compelling evidence that Israeli fire had not killed Muhammad Al-Dura.

◆ ◆ ◆

Thousands of miles away from Israel, the director of a low-profile French media watch group called Media-Ratings was served with a summons to appear in court. The summons informed the non-governmental organization's director, Philippe Karsenty, that he was being charged with "impugning the honor or esteem of the national television company, France 2, and Charles Enderlin"—in other words, libel. What had the unassuming and relatively unknown Karsenty done to warrant the charge? He had written an article for his website entitled, "France 2: Arlette Chabot and Charles Enderlin Should Be Removed from Their Positions Immediately." At the time, Arlette Chabot, the other plaintiff in the 2006 case, was the editorial director at France 2.

Karsenty had done some of his own investigating and claimed to have found serious reasons to doubt France 2 and Charles Enderlin's version of the events under discussion. In an interview with Honest Reporting, Karsenty explained his claims: he said first that on the day the Al-Duras were supposedly going to a used car market, all the stores in Gaza were closed for the same reason that Muhammad was not in school: Arafat and the PLO had ordered everything to shut down in the wake of the violence at the Temple Mount. Karsenty also stated that during the filming of the shooting of the father and son crouched behind the barrel, someone flashes two fingers in front of the camera in a "take-two" fashion. "It doesn't make sense," Karsenty said, "You can see it. It's done in the way to show that a scene has just ended."

There was more to come. France 2's cameraman, Talal Abu-Rahman, claimed to have filmed for forty-five minutes, but in that period of filming, only one volley of gunfire is seen hitting the wall above the Al-Duras. Furthermore, the angle of the bullet strikes indicates the fire came from the Palestinian position, which was directly across from the Al-Duras. Finally, there is absolutely no footage of the Israeli firing position whatsoever. When asked about this glaring omission, cameraman Abu-Rahman explained that he did not have enough battery power to film the Israeli position—despite having filmed twenty-seven minutes of the scene, which included random and indecipherable shots of Palestinian men running in different directions.

Still, Karsenty lost the libel case. The court ordered him to pay a fine of 1,000 euros. In addition, he was ordered to pay a symbolic amount of one euro to Charles Enderlin and one euro to France 2, and an additional 3,000 euros to both for court costs. Karsenty appealed. He had been fighting the case alone since, at the time, the libel case was considered a French issue and the Israeli government refused to provide any evidence or assistance to support Karsenty's claims that Al-Dura had not been shot by the IDF. Meanwhile, the importance of the case had been growing. Journalists and scholars around the world were beginning to either notice the importance of the Al-Dura affair or, in the case of those who had followed it since the beginning, began to give it more and more attention.

When Karsenty's appeal case came to trial in mid-September 2007, the case had only gained in importance. The French media were uniformly opposed to Karsenty and supported their colleagues at France 2, almost without exception. The judge in the appeal case ordered France 2 to provide the full twenty-seven-minute "rushes" (raw video footage) that Abu-Rahman shot that day. Two months later, France 2 complied—but only partially. Nine of the twenty-seven original minutes were missing from the rushes that France 2 and Charles Enderlin provided. Enderlin justified the omission by claiming that the other nine minutes had been destroyed.

As part of the trial, an independent French ballistics expert and investigator was brought in to offer his own expert opinion on the matter. The expert, Jean-Claude Schlinger, is a professional ballistics and forensics expert who has worked for the French court system for more than twenty years and had no connection to Israel or any interest in the case. Schlinger conducted a lengthy ballistics and forensics investigation. In his official report, Schlinger wrote:

> If Jamal [the boy's father] and Mohammed Al-Dura were indeed struck by shots, then they could not have come from the Israeli position, from a technical point of view, but only from the direction of the Palestinian position.[20]

But the French ballistics expert went further. He wrote that in light of the context, it was reasonable to consider the possibility that the whole incident had been staged:

In view of the general context, and in light of many instances of staged incidents, there is no objective evidence that the child was killed and his father injured. It is very possible, therefore, that it is a case [in which the incident was] staged.

After inspecting evidence regarding Jamal Al-Dura's wounds, the French expert found that, "If the injuries are genuine, they could not have occurred at the time of the events that television channel France 2 reported."

France 2 and Charles Enderlin lost the case. But by this point, the libel case was of only secondary importance to the findings of the independent French expert who concluded that Muhammad Al-Dura could not possibly have been shot or killed by Israeli gunfire. Seven years after the incident that created a "symbol" of hatred and provided a nearly universal thirst for vengeance among the world's jihadists, an independent French expert had found not that it was simply *unlikely* or *improbable* that Israeli fire killed Al Dura but that it was *impossible*. The strange and inexplicable "anomalies" regarding the video, the fact that the famous fifty-five seconds were narrated by someone who had not been present during the incident (and that audiences were not made aware of this fact) and the Israeli investigation all foreshadowed what the independent French expert eventually concluded.

The question, then, is how the *New York Times*, which so emphatically insisted on the Palestinian narrative of the incident in the early days of the intifada, which proclaimed Al-Dura a symbol and which published stories from multiple writers who all maintained Israeli soldiers murdered an innocent boy, reacted to the findings. What, any *Times* reader who had followed the story would be compelled to ask, would the *New York Times* say? Would it print a retraction? Would it run a story about the French court's findings? Would it run a series about the progression of the case and what came to be known as the Al-Dura affair? The answer to all of those questions was "no." The *New York Times* did not publish a single story about the appeals case or its findings. It ran only a small blog post about it, which neglected to quote from the French expert's report or its findings. None of the reporters who wrote about Al-Dura in 2000 and in the following years bothered to return to the topic when the truth surfaced. There was neither a retraction, nor a correction, nor an editorial printed in the *Times*. It seemed that after the paper's initial frenzy of unsubstantiated Al-Dura reporting, it had nothing more to say on the topic.

◆ ◆ ◆

Throughout the Second Intifada and the Al-Dura affair, neither of the two prominent Israel correspondents for the *New York Times*, William Orme Jr. and bureau chief Deborah Sontag, thought it worthwhile to do a more in-depth investigation on the Al-Dura story. Only once, in November 2000, after the Israeli military's investigation, did Orme write a story that covered the possibility that Al-Dura had not been killed by the Israeli soldiers.[21] Orme provided only four full quotations. One is from a spokesman for Arafat, who condemned the Israeli army investigation as an attempt to distort the facts. Another quote is from an Israeli general who, in the days immediately after the incident, mistakenly said Israeli soldiers had been responsible for the death. The third quote came from the Palestinian cameraman, Abu-Rahman, who shot the footage of the day. And the last quote is from left-wing Israeli newspaper, *Haaretz*, which called the Israeli military's investigation (which turned out to be accurate) "stupid and bizarre."

Observant readers of the *New York Times* in 2000 and 2001 may have wondered how two different reporters, William Orme and Deborah Sontag, could consistently produce articles that were so consistent with one another. In the case of Hiroshima and Nagasaki, even William H. Lawrence ran a story that contradicted the other William, William L. Laurence, on the issue of death by radioactivity before Lawrence was reined in by the *Times*'s higher-ups. But Orme and Sontag seemed always to be in lockstep, with their stories complementing one another's. Orme's Al-Dura narrative buttressed Sontag's insistence that Sharon started the intifada, and Sontag's "blame Sharon" line provided a political stage-setting for Orme's stories about an innocent child murdered by the Israeli military. For the readers who might have wondered about these parallels, there is an important fact that was unknown to the vast majority of *Times* readers: Deborah

Sontag was not just William Orme's bureau chief, she was also his wife. The two made an effective reporting team in the early days of the Palestinian uprising, getting big stories and lots of attention.

Not long after the intifada, Sontag got a chance to write for the *New York Times Magazine*, where writers get more leeway to choose stories, an ability to write with more of an "edge," and considerably more space for each story. Sontag took the opportunity. Orme also left Israel for greener pastures. For him, it was a little heard-of but hugely important section of the United Nations called the United Nations Development Program (UNDP). The UNDP, which receives funding of billions of dollars, began to get involved in the Gaza Strip more heavily after Israel withdrew its army and citizens from the territory in 2005. During the pullout, the UNDP provided Palestinian groups with money to disseminate information to Palestinians about the withdrawal (sometimes called the disengagement). Not long after, Palestinian brochures and fliers appeared, which contained unadulterated propaganda. The main slogan on the printed pamphlets read, "Today Gaza, tomorrow the West Bank and Jerusalem." The Palestinians used the pamphlets to position Israel's withdrawal from Gaza as a military victory that would be reproduced and urged Palestinians to push on. And the United Nations funded it.

When the pamphlets were revealed to the outside world, the UNDP went into damage control mode. They knew that they had a scandal on their hands, as the press was lighting up and United States ambassador to the United Nations, John Bolton, condemned the funding of the propaganda in strong terms. The UNDP turned to a veteran reporter who had demonstrated ability working with the press on sensitive Palestinian issues: William Orme Jr. Orme, who had become a spokesman for UNDP, swooped in to deny that the agency was political in its operations or intentions. However, he refused to say whether or not the agency stood behind the slogans printed on pamphlets that it funded.[22] The former *Times* reporter took a position, in relation to Palestinian propaganda, with which he was well acquainted on account of his days at the *New York Times*. The refusal to apologize for shoddy reporting and the over-eagerness to apologize for Palestinian propaganda—or, more precisely, to not recognize it as propaganda—was all too evident. Five years earlier, Orme had not only refused to acknowledge a major piece of propaganda but had been one of the main avenues for its distribution. His failure to look into the Al-Dura killing or examine the Palestinian narrative of the event critically, was a serious dereliction of his journalistic responsibilities. In the midst of the twenty-first century, a century of information, digital recording, and codified journalistic standards, the New York Times, seemingly eager for the story, had bought a narrative that Jewish soldiers were out for the blood of Arab children—hook, line, and sinker.

Orme's immediate boss, Deborah Sontag, did no better. Being married to her reporter would admittedly make it difficult to gain objectivity about his work. However, as Sontag's staid insistence on the simplistic claim that Ariel Sharon started the intifada demonstrated, Sontag was not eager for objectivity. Her landmark July 26, 2001 article, with its "lazy reporting, errors of omission, questionable shading," showed a doggedness to stick to a particular line, even though one of its main premises, the "Sharon cause," had been flatly rejected by an international commission of statesmen and scholars just months beforehand.[23]

Nevertheless, the Al-Dura narrative persisted in the hearts and minds of millions. The story of the innocent Palestinian boy murdered in cold blood by Israeli soldiers was invoked, almost like a magic spell. It resulted in jihadis decapitating Wall Street Journal reporter Daniel Pearl.[24] It was used to justify the sickening lynching of two Israeli reserve soldiers and the desecration of their bodies. It has been used to motivate countless suicide bombings and attacks. And for years after, it served as the rallying cry, the chant of global jihad.

The truth is that we will likely never know precisely what happened at the Netzarim junction that day. It was, unquestionably, a tragedy—a terrible conflict consumed the life of a young boy. Nonetheless, the evidence is not nearly sufficient to condemn Israel as the Palestinians, France 2, and the New York Times quickly did. We have only a blurry video that does not prove Israeli responsibility, the testimony of two witnesses, one of them profoundly biased and the other an interested party, and a narrative formulated by a reporter who wasn't there. That narrative has been seriously questioned by many, including an independent expert. And even if it were true, it is not an excuse for the *Times*'s uncritical parroting of the Palestinian narrative, which helped to spark a jihadist frenzy around the world.

The narrative persisted, but the *New York Times* and its reporters moved on. For William Orme, it was a publicity job at the United Nations. Deborah Sontag, however, was rewarded for her neglectful and sometimes dishonest reporting with further work at the *Times*. Sontag, as we will soon see, remained in the business of creating myths, and unsurprisingly, the *New York Times* was still in the business of printing them.

8

The Plame Game:
"A Misbegotten War"

𝕴n the weeks after a news scandal that rocked the *New York Times* in 2003, Arthur Ochs Sulzberger Jr., the newspaper's publisher and chairman of The New York Times Company (and grandson of "Jew"-avoiding Arthur Hays Sulzberger), rented a theater in New York.[1] The idea was to bring together hundreds of members of the *Times*'s staff so he and the then executive editor Howell Raines could explain what was going on and answer the questions of worried employees.

The theater meeting was a good idea—air the dirty laundry, starting with the people who were manning the ship, before going to the public. That day, Arthur Sulzberger Jr. strode onto the theater stage holding a bag. No one knew what was inside the mysterious bag. Sulzberger, according to Seth Mnookin's *Hard News*,[2] stopped on stage and removed something from the bag. It was a toy stuffed moose, something a child keeps in a crib or on a bed. Sulzberger tossed the toy to Howell Raines, who caught it awkwardly, not knowing what was going on. Then Sulzberger explained.

Back in the old days, a group of *Times* executives and top editors were at a company retreat in the woods. They were sitting in a cabin when nearly all of the editors and executives in the room noticed a huge moose standing outside the window. But no one mentioned the moose.

"Today," Sulzberger explained with his court jester smile and Barney Fife earnestness, "we're talking about the moose." The staff were nonplussed. Here was the captain of the *New York Times* in the middle of one of the roughest storms that the paper had experienced in recent years, and he was going on about a stuffed moose. Although Sulzberger managed to mix an indefinite number of metaphors and clichés ("the cat's out of the bag," "the pink elephant in the room," "the moose at the cabin," etc.) to make a vague point, Sulzberger's metaphor turned out to be oddly appropriate.

As this book has shown, the *New York Times* has a disturbing history of keeping quiet about the major world-changing errors, lies, and fabrications that have been made on its pages. The proverbial moose has often—too often—gone unnoticed. But on occasion, the moose comes rampaging through the glass façade of the *Times* building on Eight Avenue, crashing through barriers of journalistic politesse.

This is exactly what happened in 2003 when a junior staff reporter named Jayson Blair resigned from the paper. By that point, Blair had lied, fabricated, plagiarized, and committed just about every other conceivable journalistic sin during his short career at the *New York Times*. And it was at that moment that a series of articles by a highly regarded veteran *Times* reporter named Judith Miller concerning the presence of weapons of mass destruction (WMDs) in Iraq started to unravel in a very serious way.

Jayson Blair rose to national prominence in the fall of 2002 when a sniper of unknown identity began murdering people in the Washington D.C. area. The story gripped the country as the sniper continued his rampage and the police seemed powerless to stop him. Blair's reporting on the D.C. Sniper—as the figure came to be called by the media (though, in reality, it was a team of two men)—kicked off his own editorial rampage against established journalistic norms. But it was Blair's later coverage of a topic of much greater import, the war in Iraq, that proved to be his downfall—as it did for the *Times*'s star foreign correspondent, Judith Miller, at almost exactly the same time.

◆ ◆ ◆

The story of Jayson Blair is by now well known. It has been the subject of books, a documentary, and endless analysis by journalism schools and segments of media that cover journalism. Like its diminutive, then cherub-faced main character, Blair's story has a tragic flare to it. Blair had been a rising star at the *Times*, which had recruited him out of journalism school at the University of Maryland. The *Times* had selected Blair for a prestigious internship, which led to a second internship and finally an offer to join the paper as a staff reporter. By all accounts, Blair was a devoted, charming and dogged figure. According to an exposé in the *Baltimore Sun*, Blair would put in extra hours at college, stuffing envelopes or doing photocopying work that, presumably, other students were less than enthusiastic about.[3] "Jayson was a guy who put his head into every door," one of Blair's former journalism professors told the *Baltimore Sun*.

As an editor and reporter of his college newspaper and a news service associated with the university, Blair started to attract the wrong kind of attention. Problems started to crop up in his reporting, according to the *Baltimore Sun*, including when Blair took an internship with the *Boston Globe*. Editors at the *Boston Globe* reported serious issues with Blair's spelling and accuracy. Blair, who was made editor-in-chief of his college paper, the *Diamondback*, began falling behind in school. Questions about sourcing cropped up. In one case, he carelessly attributed the death of a student on campus to a cocaine overdose, when there was no evidence to support the claim. Serious financial issues regarding the newspaper also began to emerge, with Blair paying editors significantly more than reporters, some of whom were earning a mere $13 per story.

It was against this background that the *Times* tapped Blair in 1998 for a prestigious fellowship for minority reporters. A year later, the offer for the second internship arrived, despite the issues that were still cropping up concerning Blair's reporting. By the end of 1999, Blair was made a reporter at the *New York Times* even though he was still a full year from completing his journalism degree.[4]

For the next two years, Blair would report on metro stories, like the development of a new electricity substation in New York, the death of a local African-American leader, a decision by a phone company to offer service in New Jersey, and dozens of other bread-and-butter stories of this kind. Blair occasionally reported on the TV and tech industries but, for the most part, New York and its environs were his domain.

That all changed on October 24, 2002 when Blair reported that a man and a seventeen-year-old boy were taken into police custody under suspicion they were involved in the killings taking place in the D.C. area.[5] After that initial article, Blair shifted into overdrive, writing almost twenty stories in as many days. This was a dizzying, almost superhuman level of journalistic output, with stories by Blair frequently appearing on consecutive days. Blair reconstructed the search for the sniper in a series, "The Hunt for a Sniper." He covered legal issues surrounding the case and reported on other crimes linked to the snipers. The feverish pace of Blair's reporting combined with the national profile of the case put Blair on the map of American journalism.

Blair continued to cover the sniper case through the beginning of 2003. But it was in March of that year—just two days after the United States invasion of Iraq—that Blair kicked off a series that would have implications not just for him and the *New York Times* but for the entire country. The series was called "A Nation at War" and its first installment was "Tough News: Bearing the Worst News, Then Helping the Healing."[6] The article focused on the grim moment when military officials show up in full dress uniform to inform next of kin about a soldier who has fallen in battle. The article reported on the officers of bases around Hampton Roads, Virginia who had the difficult duty of telling spouses and children about their loved ones who had perished in the fighting.

Three days after the initial "Bearing the Worst News" story, Blair did another war tragedy piece, this one under the headline, "Families; Watching and Praying as a Son's Fate Unfolds."[7] The article, reported from Hunt Valley, Maryland, told of a Martha Gardner whose son was a marine scout in Iraq. Blair wrote of Mrs. Gardner's almost paralyzing fear and her constant need to check the news in the hope that the war would be over. The story also told of Corporal Gardner's father, Michael Gardner, who commented to Blair about watching the news, "It shows you the animalistic nature of what we are dealing with," and even included an oblique reference to Vietnam, in the form of a quote by Mr. Gardner.

On April 1, the *Times* ran a piece by Blair about bringing soldiers' bodies back to the United States.[8] On April 7, the *Times* ran another war tragedy story about a pastor with a son who died in Iraq, struggling to come to grips with why his only child was killed in a foreign war.[9] In an April 15 piece, "The Spouses; A Couple Separated by War While United in Their Fears," Blair presented an increasingly familiar portrait of a military family lost in grief. The wife of a servicemen was quoted as saying, "I am not sure what's worse, the fear or the loneliness." The story made the front page of the *Times*.[10] Four days later, Blair furthered the *Times*'s war tragedy narrative in an April 19 article, "Veterans; In Military Wards, Questions and Fears from the Wounded."[11]

The April 19 article told the story of a marine lance corporal named James Klingel who had been wounded in an RPG attack in Iraq. The Blair article reported that the corporal was thankful to be walking again but that he would have to walk with a limp and use a cane for the rest of his life. In the sixth paragraph of the article, Blair summed up a viewpoint reflective of much of the *Times*'s position on the effects of the war on soldiers who fought in it:

> In news conferences and television appearances carefully orchestrated by military officials, many wounded service members here and at other hospitals displayed self-assurance and confidence in response to questions about their fears and futures. But in long conversations, many patients here tell of visits to chaplains and other counselors, as well as fright, remorse and other hard-to-explain feelings as some of the long-term physical and emotional effects of the war become evident.[12]

The idea behind the paragraph and train of reporting was clear: what you have seen on TV about soldiers being confident in their duty and their recovery is "carefully orchestrated by military officials" or, in other words, fake. The truth, excavated by Blair and the *New York Times* through "long conversations" involved "fright, remorse and other hard-to-explain feelings."

Blair wrote of another serviceman in the article, Marine Staff Sergeant Alva, who, Blair reported, was feeling "anger that he directed inward and toward the news media that he said were too hard on soldiers and a public that he said that did not really understand the costs of war." But, Blair reported, it was this Sergeant Alva who had recently appeared before the media promising that despite "losing his leg," he would one day run a marathon. The self-confidence to move forward, Blair claimed, "was revealed in private moments" to be a façade. In reality, according to the *Times* reporter, the soldier was gripped by a misdirected anger that Alva harbored against the public and the media.

For his part, Corporal Klingel, the wounded veteran covered by Blair's April 19 article, had been visited by President Bush and had reported to the media that he felt encouraged by the visit and the president's message that the wounded men were heroes. But, Blair noted when he interviewed the wounded solider, Klingel revealed he did not feel like a hero at all. He said that his sense of safety and security had been "taken away in an instant" and that he was suffering from disturbing dreams and mental images that, he feared, would be with him long after his physical wounds had healed. After telling the horror stories of a few other servicemen, Blair returned to Klingel to close the article. The marine was being flown to his parents' home by a navy charity and even though he was looking forward to being at his parents' home and standing on their porch, the article quoted him as saying, "I am still looking over my shoulder. I am sure I will be standing on the back porch and worry about who might come shooting at me out of the bush. It's changed me."

The series of articles on the devastating effects of the war unfolded with relentless consistency. Articles by Blair appeared on March 25, 27, and 31 followed by installments on April 3, 4, 5, 6, 7, 11, 13, 15, and 19. Incredibly, Blair continued to report stories on the D.C. sniper case, with five sniper-related stories running during the same period. In some cases, he published stories about the sniper case and the Iraq war on the same day.

The pace of this output is not simply exemplary but unprecedented and almost impossible to understand. Blair's articles from this period were reported from places as far away as Hunt Valley, Maryland; Palestine,

West Virginia; Dover Air Force Base, Delaware; Marmet, West Virginia (a two-hour drive from Palestine, West Virginia); Los Fresnos, Texas, and Bethesda, Maryland. The reporter would have been coordinating schedules, conducting interviews, traveling, writing his stories, and repeating the cycle with ferocious intensity for weeks on end in order to achieve this herculean output of journalism. Not even the most adept veteran reporters could manage a schedule like this, let alone a journalist who had been in the saddle for barely three years.

Oddly, management at the *Times* did not find this physics-defying pace unusual—or, if they did, no one did anything about it. On the contrary, Blair's stories got more and more play, with two of them making the front page of the *Times*. The reason for the intense focus on these articles was not only their relevance but the larger narrative they were sculpting. Again and again, Blair's reports told a story of loss, tragedy, fear, and shame resulting from the weeks-old war.

The problem was that virtually all of Blair's reporting from the period was fraudulent—either plagiarized, embellished, or completely fabricated. Importantly, it was not the *Times* that clocked on to the fact that Blair's reporting was massively problematic. Rather, it was a reporter from a different newspaper, Macarena Hernandez of the *San Antonio Express-News*, who realized Blair had plagiarized significant pieces of her story[13] for his April 26 article, "Aftereffects: The Missing; Family Waits, Now Alone, for a Missing Soldier."[14]

Blair's article had, again, made the front page of the *Times*, sprawling across three columns of "the most valuable real estate in journalism."[15] Ironically, Hernandez, the reporter Blair plagiarized, had been one of the other three minority reporters with whom Blair had completed his *New York Times* internship before being hired by the paper. According to Seth Mnookin's reporting for Vanity Fair, Hernandez alerted the *Times* recruiter who had hired her and Blair, who in turn alerted the newspaper's managing editor. That revelation set off a chain of events that would expose Blair as a journalistic fraudster.

Times editors began looking into the plagiarism more carefully and uncovered an almost endless series of breaches that the junior reporter had been perpetrating for years. The story of the Gardners had been mostly fabricated. While the Gardners were real people with a real son in the Marine Corps in Iraq, Blair had never gone to Hunt Valley to interview them. He had spoken to them on the phone, though no one knows for how long, but that was all. Similarly, Blair's initial "Bearing the Worst News" story was also made up. At the time that Blair had supposedly been in Virginia talking to somber military officers and even more somber military families, he had actually been in New York. Reporting on the family of Jessica Lynch, the young army soldier who had been captured in Iraq, had similarly been compromised. Blair, whose article was supposedly reported from the Lynches' home in Palestine, West Virginia, had actually never been to interview the Lynch family. In addition to plagiarizing an Associated Press report, Blair had taken the liberty of making up a story that Lynch's mother, Deadre, had a dream that Jessica left her unit to save an Iraqi child. Mrs. Lynch later told the *Times* she had never had any such dream.[16]

There was virtually no aspect of the sprawling front-page April 19 veterans' article that was untainted by fabrication, false shadings, and blatant lies. Blair, of course, had never been to the National Naval Medical Center in Bethesda, Maryland, where the "long, private conversations" supposedly had taken place. Sergeant Alva, who had confidently promised to one day run the Marine Corps marathon, had not lost his leg, as Blair had written—he had had his lower leg amputated below the knee. The main subject of the article, Corporal Klingel, denied ever having told Blair about nightmares. He never said, "I am still looking over my shoulder" or that he worried about people coming out of the "bush" to kill him. And, far from being disheartened because of a limp and lifelong use of a cane, Corporal Klingel was neither limping nor using a cane when *Times* reporters returned to him to learn the extent of Blair's lies.

All this happened right under the noses of *Times* editors who worked with the reporter on a daily basis and, at least in theory, read his stories. Worse, a number of editors had spotted Blair's fabrications and lies and reported them to newsroom managers.

One such person, metropolitan editor Jonathan Landman, wrote to *Times* managers in April 2002, a full year before Blair was actually caught.

"We have to stop Jayson from writing for the *Times*. Right now."[17] Even still, it took the *New York Times* months to catch on to Blair's lies and plagiarism. Yet there was an almost endless list of signs that should have tipped off someone (other than Jonathan Landman) that things were not right. There was the pattern of Blair's spelling and factual mistakes (which the paper caught) but, more incredibly, no one thought it strange that a reporter who supposedly crisscrossed the country for his job never filed expense reports.

However, if Blair's breaches were so egregious that they led Jonathan Landman to write to senior editors that Blair must be stopped, what possibly could have led the newspaper to continue printing the reporter's fraudulent stories—or at least prevented editors from looking more carefully into his writing? One critical clue lies in something that all other accounts of the Blair scandal omit: exactly what Blair had been writing about between April 2002, when Jonathan Landman issued his unequivocal warning, and May 2003, when Blair was finally forced to resign from the paper.

In the *New York Times*'s own in-depth report on the Blair scandal, *Times* reporters gave an honest and accurate account of the failures, conducting interviews with more than a hundred people and spending weeks getting the facts straight. The reporters, however, never mentioned the publisher of the paper in a substantive way until the end of the massive article. They quoted Arthur Sulzberger Jr., who remarked that "The person who did this is Jayson Blair. Let's not begin to demonize our executives—either the desk editors or the executive editor or, dare I say, the publisher."[18]

How Sulzberger felt that he, as the paper's publisher and the person who stood to gain and lose the most from the newspaper, was beyond blame is difficult to imagine. He displayed a certain amount of gall in explicitly exculpating himself in the article about one of the paper's greatest failure under his leadership. But, to be fair, he also noted that the desk editors and executive editors were not to be demonized either—emphasizing that what Blair had done was what *Blair* had done—and it was not something for which any of the other executives or editors (or he, himself) was responsible.

Yet, just one month after the Blair scandal broke, Sulzberger fired the very executives he'd insisted could not be blamed, including the *Times*'s top two editors, executive editor Howell Raines and managing editor Gerald Boyd. Sulzberger, in an almost admirable feat of media spin, played the firing of the two senior editors as a decision by the men to do the right thing. Sulzberger announced to *Times* staff that he wanted to "applaud Howell and Gerald for putting the interests of this newspaper, a newspaper we all love, above their own." He also remarked that he accepted their resignations "with sadness."[19]

It is not clear why Sulzberger felt that he had to make the firings into a public relations event, complete with slick corporate statements about "sadness" and fables about the people who got the ax putting company (or in this case newspaper) interests before their own. It is also not clear why Sulzberger thought that the firing of two men who had been with the newspaper for decades would stay swept beneath the rug of the "noble resignation" line. But the illusion was not to last. Little more than a year later, Raines wrote in the *Atlantic* about his being "dismissed as executive editor" and remarked in the first paragraph of that piece that he was a "casualty" of the Blair scandal.[20]

◆ ◆ ◆

When the *New York Times* published a photo in 2001 of an Israeli soldier screaming and holding a stick in the air as he approached a bloodied young man, the *Times* revealed its operating assumptions about the conflict. As we discussed earlier in this book, in the caption to the photo, the *Times* reported that an Israeli soldier was approaching a Palestinian man on the Temple Mount, ready to beat him. This incident provided a glimpse into how the *New York Times* saw the situation, since the paper's choice of caption, which was so far from the truth that it ignored the presence of a gas station in the photo's background, ruling out the possibility that the scene occurred on the Temple Mount, revealed its assumptions.

Jayson Blair did very much the same thing as that photo and its false caption. Sulzberger told *Times* reporters that Blair was the single culprit for the deception. But for a newspaper that is known as being the most hawkeyed when it comes to finding and correcting spelling mistakes, grammatical slips, and other "errata" each day, it is almost beyond belief that the *Times* missed the fact that Blair was misspelling the names of important roads and of the people whom he interviewed, while describing tobacco fields and cow pastures where there were none.

The paper had found a number of mistakes, and editors had identified Blair as a notorious offender of the *Times*'s standard for maintaining a low error rate. But Blair continued to report, and continued, even, to get praise from top editors. The question that many of the *Times* staff who gathered in the theater after the Blair scandal came to light is the question many media observers and *Times* readers were also asking: How could this have happened?

It requires no stretch of the imagination to think that American servicemen were coming home with difficult emotions caused by their war experience. But in the series of articles by Blair which frequently received coveted front-page placement in the paper, the *Times* was presenting an either/or situation: either soldiers who show "self-assurance" and confidence about their "fears and futures" are part of a military-orchestrated press extravaganza (they're putting on a show) or they're not feeling confident and self-assured and are actually afraid, remorseful, and confused.

The more likely case is that soldiers return home with a complex set of feelings that include pride and confidence as well as fear and frustration. But this was not what the *Times*'s articles were saying. In and of itself, there was no problem with the intentions behind the approach to covering the story of veterans coping with war. The *Times* felt that readers should get a look at how the war was affecting individuals involved in it. The problem, however, is that Blair wrote endlessly on this topic. More importantly, the *Times* published this flow of war tragedy stories, despite all the mistakes and despite the recommendations of editors like Jonathan Landman. It was as if the *New York Times* would pursue this narrative about the tragedies of the Iraq war no matter what the cost.

◆ ◆ ◆

Right at the time that the extensiveness of Blair's lies and deception was coming to light, another scandal was unfolding at the *Times*. For months, *Times* veteran reporter Judith Miller had been writing stories about Iraq's secret caches of WMDs. These stories were great scoops, and many of them, filled with details about secret nuclear, biological, and chemical weapons facilities, landed on page one with gripping headlines.

Getting big scoops, or exclusive reporting on important topics, is an important part of any newspaper's operations, especially for the *New York Times*. But it had become even more important when Howell Raines ascended to the editorial throne of the paper in the early fall of 2001. Raines had been competing for the position with a more richly experienced *Times* reporter named Bill Keller. Raines, a southerner who was not known for his finesse or people skills in the newsroom, made Arthur Sulzberger an excellent pitch for the job. He told the paper's publisher of great plans to go national and eventually global, to increase the paper's web presence, and most importantly, to raise what he called the paper's "competitive metabolism." This meant getting scoops.[21]

The *Times* won an astonishing four Pulitzer Prizes during Raines's first year as executive editor, all of them reporting on the aftermath of 9/11. Unsurprisingly, Judith Miller was a member of the group of *Times* reporters who had written the prize-winning stories. As part of this post-9/11 reporting, the *Times* published an October 27, 2001 story that reported a meeting between the 9/11 mastermind Muhammad Atta and an Iraqi agent in Prague.[22] The story became almost a linchpin for the case that Iraq was connected to Al-Qaeda. However, not long after the initial *Times* report on the Prague meeting, the story was debunked, most notably by James Risen in an October 21, 2002 *New York Times* article.[23] Risen's article was published on a Monday, which, according to a *New York Magazine* piece by Franklin Foer, meant that Raines did not have time to properly "vet" it. After it ran, Raines was unhappy. Foer reported that according to a *Times* editor, Raines "wanted to throw off his liberal credentials and demonstrate that he was fair-minded about the Bush administration. This meant that he bent over backwards to back them often." Worse, a former *Times* editor told Foer:

In the months before the war, Raines consistently objected to articles that questioned the administration's claims about Iraq's links to Al-Qaeda and September 11 while never raising a doubt about Miller's more dubiously sourced pieces about the presence of weapons of mass destruction.[24]

On May 4, 2003, nearly two months after the United States-led invasion of Iraq and subsequent hunt for Iraqi WMDs, the *New York Times* ran a spectacular headline. The page-one story, written by Judith Miller, blared, "U.S. Experts Find Radioactive Material in Iraq."[25] The headline, and its page one positioning, had all the trappings of a major scoop: the much sought-after evidence of Iraqi weapons of mass destruction had finally surfaced. More than that, it was *"radioactive"* evidence. For people on the street passing a news stand and glancing at a copy of the *Times*, for online news readers checking out the day's headlines, and for TV news viewers following the news "tickers" running at the bottom of the screen, this all must have seemed cut and dry: Iraq had indeed been developing WMD.

But the article *Times* editors gave the sensational headline and front-page positioning to told a very different and much less exciting story. Miller's article was about radiation in Iraq, but it had nothing to do with WMDs. In fact, the story was about the detection of some radiation at the nuclear facility where the Osirack reactor had sat before Israel had destroyed it in a bombing run. The radiation being emitted by the site was, the article reported, "consistent with industrial or research use" or, in other words, consistent with what Saddam Hussein's regime had claimed about its nuclear facilities before the war.

The May 4 article bore all of the features of failure that the greater debacle of the *Times*'s reporting on Iraqi WMDs showed. It was written long after the unsuccessful search for weapons began, but it did not really touch on the fact that pre-war evidence about WMDs had been bad. It was given front-page prominence and a bold, attention-getting headline. However, it had little to say in terms of facts.

Miller was no newbie when it came to reporting on WMDs. She'd begun her reporting on Iraqi WMDs as early as 1998, when she reported on the Iraqi nuclear scientist defector Khidir Hamza, who was willing to spill secrets about Iraq's quest for nuclear weapons. Four years later, in spring and summer of 2002, Miller had cultivated a group of sources, many of whom were Iraqi defectors, centered around the leader of the Iraqi National Congress, Ahmed Chalabi. But it was only on September 8, 2002, as the country was approaching its first 9/11 anniversary, that Miller, along with *Times* reporter Michael R. Gordon, hit a journalistic home run with the first story about concrete evidence regarding WMDs in Iraq. The story ran in the lead spot of the *Times*'s front page under the headline, "Threats and Responses: The Iraqis; U.S. Says Hussein Intensifies Quest for A-Bomb Parts."[26]

The story focused on the aluminum tubes that would become an infamous part of the media's misreporting on WMDs in Iraq. According to the *Times* article, these tubes were precisely the ones needed for uranium-enriching centrifuges. With this idea as a starting point, Miller and Gordon went on to offer ominous warnings, almost all issued by the Bush administration (though none were attributed to named sources). The article was peppered with claims that were quietly tucked into the narrative, which made them seem as if they should be taken for granted. For example, Miller and Gordon wrote about "renewed Iraqi interest in acquiring nuclear arms"; they mentioned, almost casually, that "acquiring nuclear arms is again a top Iraqi priority"; that "Mr. Hussein had also heightened his efforts to develop new types of chemical weapons"; that "the acquisition of nuclear arms might embolden Mr. Hussein and increase the chances that he might use chemical or biological weapons," and, finally—and most terrifyingly—"The first sign of a 'smoking gun,' they argue, may be a mushroom cloud."

Miller and Gordon covered their bases by qualifying their claims and noting some of the facts were in doubt. But even these qualifying statements of "however" sounded ominous. As an example, the sentence from the article, "While there is no indication that Iraq is on the verge of deploying a nuclear bomb..." implies that since Iraq is not on the *verge of deploying* a nuclear weapon, such a scenario must be in the realm of possibility. In other words, if the *New York Times* could assert that there was no indication Iraq might *use*, or "deploy," a bomb, there had to be reason the country had the ability and intention to acquire one.

The September 8 article served as a kind of template for much of Miller's later reporting on WMDs in Iraq. Front-page (or otherwise prominent) stories gave readers the definite sense that Iraq was in possession—to some extent—of WMD and was pursuing more weapons of that kind. But many of these reports had serious flaws. An April 21, 2003 article by Miller, which followed a string of stories reporting that no weapons and no "smoking gun" had been found in Iraq, suddenly took a different tack.[27] The report claimed that there indeed had been WMDs in Iraq and the weapons had been kept there (the headline stated) till the "eve of war." This was a big claim, since it meant that even though nothing was turning up a month into the search for WMDs, the Bush administration, and importantly, the *New York Times*, had been correct about their initial claims that Iraq had WMDs. But the report itself admitted to not having access to the main source for the claim that WMDs had been present in Iraq but were subsequently moved. In fact, Miller wrote in the April 21 article, "While this reporter could not interview the scientist, she was permitted to see him from a distance."

This statement bears some consideration. What Miller was referring to was a moment when, from hundreds of feet away, the reporter was able to look at a guy wearing a baseball hat who pointed at the ground where alleged WMDs were buried. That was the big scoop—and that was the source she relied on to salvage the claim that there were WMDs in Iraq. This level of sourcing would not pass muster at the average college newspaper, never mind at a national newspaper that prided itself on its standards of sourcing—and for good reason: any one of us can claim to have seen at a distance any number of people. But that is a far cry from interviewing them in a journalistic context. Furthermore, from that distance, Miller had no way of verifying the man's identity. He could have literally been anyone. Yet, the *Times* editors responsible for overseeing Miller's reporting ran the story anyway.

Miller followed up this doubtful article with another. According to her reporting, unidentified "military officials" had been told by unidentified

Iraqi scientists that Hussein regime officials had set fire to an unidentified biological weapons research and storage facility four days before the war. Miller believed this was a major scoop. Apparently, so did her bosses at the *Times*. Miller went on Jim Lehrer's PBS show, *NewsHour*, the next day claiming the April 21 article did not represent just a smoking gun but a "silver bullet."[28]

Miller might have been gulled into believing this claim for many reasons. It could have been on account of deception by her sources, overconfidence that resulted from her long reporting on Iraq's WMDs, her extensive knowledge of the early Hussein regime and its brutality, or a combination of all of the above. But agreeing to the journalistically untenable terms set by the United States military—for example, not to meet, interview, or even approach the source of the April 21 WMD article—was a failure no matter what the cause. Staking so much on such thin evidence and declining to follow up with more investigation before turning in her great "scoop" amplified this failure to an almost historic scope.

But the more astonishing fact is that the *Times* printed the story on page one. Somehow, editors at the *Times* thought that a man pointing at the ground constituted evidence for a front-page article about the most consequential story of the early twenty-first century. What is worse is that while the *Times* had been reporting in this way until that point, the newspaper continued to publish reports based on very little evidence well into the spring of 2003, when Miller was still writing articles about mobile bio-weapon trailer-facilities and following them up with "maybe not" stories weeks later.

By the time the *Times* ran a Miller story (reported with Douglas Jehl) in September 2003 that reported on a weapons inspector's investigation findings showing no signs of WMDs in Iraq in recent years, the damage had already been done.[29] The *Times* had published a long and influential series of reports on the presence of WMDs in Iraq. Once it became clear there were no such weapons, the newspaper—just as it had done in the wake of the Al-Dura affair—kept quiet.

The *New York Times,* under its new executive editor Howell Raines, had indeed "bent over backwards" to not appear to be going after the

Bush administration. Raines's hunt for Pulitzers and his drive to raise the paper's "competitive metabolism" put the paper into even weirder contortions than that. And even though Judith Miller's experience with Iraq and WMDs (and her recently won Pulitzer Prize) seemed to make her the perfect fit for reporting on a post-9/11, pre-Iraq war world, in truth she was the worst person to have done so specifically *because* of her history with the topic and her boundless ambition that earned her that history.

But despite all this, the *New York Times*, which is as proud of its liberal values as it is well known for them, still had to provide some counterweight in its wartime reporting. Balance had to be shown, especially since Judith Miller had been going after the Iraqi WMDs story for close to a year. So, after Miller had delved into her Iraqi WMDs scoops, and after critics had begun to allege that the *Times* had done too much to make the case for war, Jayson Blair stepped in with his string of stories about the suffering of soldiers who had returned from the very same war.

◆ ◆ ◆

The war tragedy narrative was a reasonable one to tell. More than this, covering the health and concerns of American soldiers returning home was not just an acceptable thing for a newspaper to do but an honorable one. The problem was that Jayson Blair showed that the *Times* intended to do more than just report on soldiers' homecoming. Blair's stories between April 2002, when Landman issued his stark warning about Blair, and May 2003, when Blair was caught and forced to resign, were not about the "after-effects" of the war on soldiers. Blair's articles told only one aspect about the war's effects: the war was crippling the bodies of American soldiers, ruining their minds, and sinking their families into a quagmire of fear and despair. Had Blair told the whole story, he would have included (even in his fabrications) stories about soldiers coming home proud, determined to overcome injury, and full of courage just as often as they were crestfallen, anxious, and frustrated.

More so, if the *New York Times* wanted to cover the story, to report on what was actually going on with a topic as complex as the emotional and physical state of large numbers of soldiers returning from war, they would not have assigned a relatively new reporter to cover the story, especially not a relatively new reporter who already had serious red flags to his name. Like with the WMDs in Iraq, the *Times* was striving to show something specific, even if it was not there. And even if the paper's management and senior editors did not know it at the time, Jayson Blair was the perfect person to take on a task like this one. The paper certainly did not assign Blair to this story because he was a fantasist and a fabricator, but it did assign him to the story (and kept him on the story) because, simply put, he delivered the goods.

But the *Times*'s take on the returning veterans, and, thus, on the war itself, invites the question of where these views came from. No matter how charming Blair might have been, no reporter—and certainly not one as junior as he was—would have been able to push through so strong a narrative if it conflicted with the principles and beliefs of the newspaper's owners and top executives. To understand this question, we have to return to the moose in the room.

The attitude that the newspaper's highest echelons of power took toward the war in Iraq is no secret. Arthur Sulzberger Jr., the *Times* publisher during the WMD debacle and the Blair scandal, fervently opposed the war in Iraq, just as he had fervently opposed the war in Vietnam. But when Sulzberger gave a commencement speech at SUNY New Paltz in 2006, he revealed the extent to which he did not just oppose the war, as many people did, but felt that it was something for which he had to *personally* apologize.

In what might be one of the most depressing graduation speeches in modern history, Sulzberger started with a few opening remarks that led up to a lone, stark, and troubling statement:

> I'll start with an apology. When I graduated from college in 1974, my fellow students and I had just ended the war in Vietnam and ousted President Nixon. Okay, that's not quite true. Yes, the war did end and yes, Nixon did resign in disgrace but maybe there were larger forces at play.[30]

According to the *Times* publisher, the world in the wake of Sulzberger and his fellow students' partial involvement in Nixon's being "ousted" was supposed to be a better and brighter place, one in which the children of Sulzberger's generation would never know the "futility of war" or the "stench of corruption." But, most poignantly, Sulzberger went on to tell the graduating students, "You weren't supposed to be graduating into an America fighting a misbegotten war in a foreign land." This was the big failure that demanded an apology from Sulzberger's generation to the next generation of college graduates.

What the publisher of the *New York Times* neglected to mention was that a good deal of public support for the "misbegotten war in a foreign land" had been won by his newspaper's false reporting on WMDs, which created the impression that the "foreign land" probably possessed the weaponry and the willpower to wipe out a good deal of the United States. But the *Times* publisher did not entirely forget to mention his newspaper.

> Yes, it's important that those of us at the New York Times have the courage of our own convictions and defend the rights of our journalists to protect their sources or, after much debate and discussion, publish the news that our government is bypassing its own legal systems to tap into phone calls made to and from the United States.

So, Sulzberger pointed out, the *New York Times* stood up to the government when it had to, particularly when it came to the "rights of our journalists to protect their sources."

Sulzberger's speech was not as glum as it first seemed. Rather, it was a call to action—or, more accurately, a show of action. What Sulzberger was referring to was two separate occasions when the *New York Times* had stood up to the government of the United States under his watch. One of those was specifically related to a journalist's right to protect their sources, a principle which lies at the very foundation of free speech. That, at least, was what the paper wanted to show when it stood up for the journalist to whom Sulzberger was referring, a year before the commencement speech. The journalist was none other than Judith Miller, one of a small handful of reporters who had learned from a source in the Bush administration the identity of an undercover CIA agent by the name of Valerie Plame.

◆ ◆ ◆

By the summer of 2005, the *New York Times* was in a bad state. The Jayson Blair scandal had given the paper a "black eye," as Sulzberger himself put it. In truth, with the Blair scandal coinciding (almost to the day) with the emergence of its failure in its reporting on Iraqi WMDs, resulting in the firing of the *Times*'s newly hired top editor, Howell Raines, and his managing editor, Gerald Boyd—the first African-American to serve in that role—the paper, more accurately, had been beaten to a pulp.

Just when it seemed that matters could not get any worse, another major journalistic issue cropped up at the *Times*. In October 2003, directly in the wake of the Miller failure, the Blair scandal, and the Raines-Boyd firings, the Ukrainian-American community, along with a group media watchdogs, started to make noise about what *Times* management had likely considered to be a long-forgotten dark chapter in the story of the *New York Times*: Walter Duranty.

Since the 1986 release of Robert Conquest's damning book on the Ukrainian famine, *Harvest of Sorrow*,[31] a steady stream of articles by dozens of high-profile media critics had appeared in the media. Pressure had been building, and, with it, the outrage of the Ukrainian-American community rose. By 2003, that pressure came to focus on Duranty's ill-gotten Pulitzer. To throw oil on the waters, the *Times* hired a consultant to review the history of Duranty's reporting and advise the paper on the appropriate steps the paper should take. The consultant, a highly regarded historian named Mark von Hagen, recommended that the *Times* should return the prize. "For the sake of the *New York Times*'s honor, they should take the prize away," Hagen told the Associated Press.[32]

But the *Times*, following the instructions of its publisher, Arthur Sulzberger, refused to do so. Sulzberger (as we saw in Chapter 2) wrote a long, strange cover letter for the consultant's report, providing three bizarre reasons why the newspaper should not give back the prize. At the time, it was difficult to understand why the newspaper had not done the right, straightforward and simple thing by returning the prize. Now, the reason for its refusal is crystal clear.

At any other moment in time, the newspaper probably would have made the ethically and optically sound choice to give up the prize in order to correct the record and rectify its failure of reporting on the Ukrainian famine. The move would have been applauded by the Ukrainian-American community and by most *Times* readers, and even some critics of the *Times* would have admitted it to be a difficult yet honorable decision. But in the wake of Jayson Blair's Duranty-esque escapades, Judith Miller's seeming collusion with the American government, and the dismissal of the paper's top two editors, giving up Duranty's Pulitzer was not an option. To give back the prize at that moment would have caused the *Times* to connect its problematic 2002–2003 reporting to the gross failure of its 1930s Russia reporting. This was not a hit the beleaguered newspaper could withstand. The *Times* knew that it had to dig itself out of a deep hole, and it needed to do so in a very public way. So when Judith Miller received a federal subpoena to reveal the name of a confidential source, the newspaper saw an opportunity for the equivalent of a public relations makeover.

On July 14, 2003, conservative columnist Robert Novak revealed that the wife of the former ambassador to Iraq, Joseph Wilson, was an undercover CIA operative named Valerie Plame.[33] The disclosure of Plame's true identity, Valerie Wilson, meant a federal law that prohibits exposing undercover agents had probably been violated. A grand jury investigation was launched to figure out where the leak had come from and who had committed the crime. Judith Miller was one of a small handful of journalists to be subpoenaed to testify in the leak case. A few days before Novak revealed Plame's identity, Miller had interviewed the source of the leak, Vice President Dick Cheney's chief of staff, Scooter Libby, for a story about the absence of WMDs in Iraq. It was during this sequence of interviews with Libby that, at least according to Miller's notebook (which misidentified Wilson's wife as "Valerie Flame") that Miller learned about the undercover operative.

Miller, however, never wrote the story. When she received her subpoena in August 2004, she refused to testify purely because she felt she could not betray a source who had provided her with information on a confidential basis. The *Times* was swift in coming to the side of its reporter. But its enthusiasm belied other motivations than the desire to defend its reporter. The newspaper hired one of the country's top First Amendment attorneys, Floyd Abrams, indicating it wanted to make the case a free speech issue at least as much as it wanted to defend Judith Miller.

As a free speech issue, the case was, at best, flawed. Miller was not protecting the identity of a federal whistleblower by refusing to testify. In fact, on the contrary, she was protecting the identity of someone who may have broken a federal law and, even more egregiously, someone who had done so while sitting in the executive branch of government. Worse still, Miller's confidential source, Libby, had provided her with a waiver that stated she was free to reveal his identity by testifying. Miller and the *Times* alleged the waiver had been granted by Libby under allegedly coercive circumstances. A July 19, 2005 *Times* editorial made this point harshly saying, "In fact, these documents were extracted by coercion, so they are meaningless."[34]

But the waiver was not coerced. In fact, the opposite was true. Libby wrote a second waiver that all but begged Miller to testify. Libby's second letter was genuine and heartfelt and told Miller her testimony would actually help his case. Libby wrote, "I would like to dispel any remaining concerns you may have that circumstances forced this waiver upon me...I waived the [confidentiality] privilege [in order] to cooperate with the Grand Jury, but also because the reporters' testimony served my best interests. I believed a year ago, as I believe now, that testimony by all will benefit all."[35]

Miller was held in contempt of court for refusing to testify and was thrown in jail on July 6, 2005, specifically because she felt that the first round of waivers, as the *Times* editorial wrote, were "meaningless." The reporter sat in jail for nearly ninety days until September 29, 2005. She was released that day because, after all the claims about coercive waivers and, more critically, the larger issue of the rights of reporters and the need to protect sources, she agreed to testify before the grand jury.

Sulzberger seized the opportunity. He spoke loudly about his determination to support Miller but, according to him, saw the issue as an issue of the freedom of speech. The previous fall, when the scandal was starting to erupt, Sulzberger co-authored an October 10, 2004 editorial in the *Times* titled, "The Promise of the First Amendment," in which he argued:

> The press simply cannot perform its intended role if its sources of infor-
> mation—particularly information about the government—are cut off.
> Yes, the press is far from perfect. We are human and make mistakes. But,
> the authors of our Constitution and its First Amendment understood all
> of that and for good reason prescribed that journalists should function
> as a "fourth estate."[36]

The problem with this was that Judith Miller was not protecting a source from government prosecution because that source had information about a crime. Miller was protecting a source who was in the government (at the top level, no less), and who was the person who had ostensibly *committed* the crime. But Sulzberger was energized. He wanted to have hundreds of buttons made bearing the rally cry, "Free Miller. Free Press." He was willing to foot Miller's estimated $1.5 million legal bill. And when he went on Charlie Rose's show to do an interview about the "Plamegate" affair, he painted a grim, brutal picture of the conditions in which Miller was imprisoned, making her out to be a dissident shut away in a Soviet gulag.[37]

During the hour-long interview with Charlie Rose, the question of Miller's motivations for going to jail came up, as they inevitably would. One of the *Times*'s own columnists, Maureen Dowd, wrote in a column, "Woman of Mass Destruction," asking whether some might wonder whether Miller's "stint in the Alexandria jail was in part a career reha-bilitation project."[38] In response to this claim, Sulzberger was passionate. He described the Alexandria Detention Center in extreme terms, saying, "I was not sitting there day after day in what is truly a despicable place, the Alexandria Detention Center. I mean if anyone in your audience has a sense that this is some kind of a country club, this is a grim place. And I've been at Riker's Island and I've been other places—as a reporter, not as an inmate—and this is as grim as any place I've been." Charlie Rose responded incredulously to the comparison to Riker's Island, one of the United States' most notoriously harsh prisons, saying, "As grim as Riker's Island?" And Sulzberger nodded back enthusiastically with, "Uh-huh!"

Strangely, Miller who (as Sulzberger duly noted) was actually the one sitting in the Alexandria Detention Center, did not find it to be the "grim" "despicable" place Sulzberger made it out to be. If anything, she described it in terms somewhat opposite to Sulzberger's. Speaking to Larry King in an interview—the same night Sulzberger went on Charlie Rose—Miller said:

> It was a very professional place. It was very well-run. The staff took enormous pride in their work. The inmates were for the most part a diverse and interesting group of women, some of whom had made bad mistakes, but they were—I never felt threatened. It was a fascinating experience for me, and especially some of the counselors who were there, working part-time. These were amazing men and women. They were—they gave me a lot of personal encouragement. They encouraged other women. And the place would have been a lot poorer and more depressing without them.[39]

Sulzberger's claim that Miller couldn't possibly have gone to jail for "career rehabilitation" reasons on account of the extremely "grim" "despicable" conditions at the detention center went out the window when Miller almost praised conditions at the prison. But the publisher's passion when speaking to Charlie Rose, his need to cast the incident in extreme colors of black (the government's prosecution of Miller and its draconian punishment) and white (the New York Times and its fight for freedom of speech) is even more glaring, especially when it becomes apparent that in cases such as the Alexandria Detention Center, Sulzberger was not entirely honest.

After all the hoopla, Miller got out of jail. She decided she wanted to spend some time at her home in Sag Harbor to rest and "put on some weight" before returning to reporting at the paper—or so she thought. Just three weeks after being released, Miller was testifying before the Senate Judiciary Committee about federal shield laws for journalists when the Times's executive editor, Bill Keller, sent the newspaper's staff a memo saying that part of the trouble with the Plamegate episode was that Miller had gotten into an "entanglement" with her source, Scooter Libby. The sexual innuendo in the memo, following Maureen Dowd's attack on Miller as an opportunist, pointed in a very definite direction where Miller's future at the *Times* was concerned. It was almost as if the paper's management were paving the way for a very different approach to Miller and the paper's fast fading free speech crusade on her behalf. And, indeed, just a few days after her Capitol Hill testimony, Miller was in negotiations with the *New York Times* regarding the terms of her departure from the newspaper.

For Arthur Sulzberger, Miller had to leave because, he told Charlie Rose, she had "become the story." Actually, when first addressing this issue, Sulzberger said, "The truth is this the right time. She's become too entangled with the story." Realizing he had just brought up Bill Keller's "entanglement" reference, he corrected himself quickly. What really happened with Miller, he said with a smile, was a case that exemplified a pattern: "When a *New York Times* reporter becomes the story, becomes entwined with the story, it's very hard to continue as an independent journalist and Judy is simply too much aligned now with the story."

If this book has demonstrated anything, it is exactly that when a *New York Times* reporter becomes a story, it is, in fact, "hard" if not impossible for that reporter to do their job correctly. But the episodes chronicled in this book have also shown that in practice, the *New York Times* has never found it problematic for a journalist to become part of the story. Time and again, the paper featured its own reporters as not just a part of the story but the story itself. From Walter Duranty, who was trumpeted on the pages of the *Times*, whose books and lectures were the topics of articles, whose travel plans were the subject of *New York Times* news articles; to Herbert Matthews, who wrote himself into the fable of Fidel Castro on the pages of the Gray Lady; to William Laurence, who, like Duranty, eventually became the subject of *Times* articles as much as he was the author of them, the *New York Times* has consistently displayed an unrelenting affinity for making its reporters into rock stars and then reporting on the arcs of these stars through the media universe.

Judith Miller followed the same pattern. Her books were reviewed in the *New York Times,* and her stories splashed on the front page over the period of decades. But more than anything, the *Times* deliberately made her the story when they chose to convert the Valerie Plame leak into a public relations Hail Mary. Almost in the same breath that he claimed Miller had to leave the paper because she was too much a part of the story, Sulzberger continued to stitch Judith Miller into that story with fabulous (and ridiculous) tales of her dark, "grim" imprisonment in a detention center that Miller, the one actually serving time, described as "professional" and "diverse."

Worse still, in the midst of all this, when the *Times* had the opportunity to correct the damage of a reporter who had been indisputably entangled with his story, they chose not to do so. The *New York Times* would fire Judith Miller but just two years earlier it adamantly refused to return a fraudulent Pulitzer Prize. In firing Judith Miller, the *Times* hoped the multiple scandals associated with her name would be forgotten; in refusing to return the Ukrainian famine Pulitzer Prize, they hoped Walter Duranty would remain largely unremembered.

Sulzberger revealed as much in his interview with Charlie Rose when he told Rose that in his opinion Judith Miller and WMDs was a "small-bore" issue that would be forgotten, but the *New York Times*'s fight for journalists' rights would be remembered. So far, that has not been the case. But even at the time of the interview, when Charlie Rose interjected that Miller's reporting on WMDs could not possibly be a "small-bore" issue for a newspaper, the statement had the desperate feel of wishful thinking.

◆ ◆ ◆

The *New York Times* is, in theory, too intelligent an institution and too rich in resources to allow a reporter to systematically rely on faulty sourcing. It is too seasoned in journalistic procedure to publish the brazenly fake articles of a junior reporter. It is too savvy a media player to fall into disarray and internal conflict over a single subpoena. Looking at each of these scandals as isolated events provides no real explanation for any of them. If any one of them had occurred without the other it could be explained as a technical glitch, or a cog momentarily slipping off the journalistic mechanisms of the paper. But looking at each one of them in their actual context—that they all took place within two years—demands a more realistic explanation.

These scandals, missteps, and errors of judgment were not technical glitches, as Sulzberger made them out to be, that could be solved by a careful examination and oiling of the machine. Rather, these episodes were organic—they were outgrowths or, in a more negative sense, symptoms of something deeper. They were the product of an organization brimming with talented reporters, experienced editors, and endless resources but one that has flaws in its roots.

The *New York Times* is a massive, complex organization that has an immeasurable impact on American life. But unlike other such organizations, it is led by one family, one group of people, who are not subject to the oversight of an independent boardroom or even the opinions of major shareholders. To the extent the media is considered the "fourth estate" of American government, and to the extent the *New York Times* has long been identified (even if in jest) as being the very incarnation of the fourth estate, the *Times* lacks one of the most critical underpinnings of American public life: checks and balances.

The irony of the owners of the *New York Times* deciding, against the advice of their own consultant, to refuse to return a Pulitzer Prize won for corrupt reporting just months after the *Times* was struck by another bout of tainted journalism is almost palpable. But looking carefully at what actually happened and at who was in control during these episodes makes it clear that the irony is only surface level and that, given what happened with Walter Duranty, the Jayson Blair scandal should almost have been expected.

Walter Duranty admitted to a United States embassy official that the *New York Times* itself had been in collusion with the Soviet government regarding its coverage of Russia. The jilted coverage of the Ukrainian famine was not the "slovenly" reporting (as Arthur Sulzberger Jr. called it) of a rogue journalist. Rather, it was the newspaper itself that was responsible for the disastrous reporting. The *Times* believed a certain narrative about socialist Russia, and that narrative is the one Walter Duranty reported. By his own account, Duranty knew the devastation of the Ukrainian famine. However, as he confessed to a State Department official, he had been directed by his newspaper to cover it up.

When it came to Jayson Blair's reporting between April 2002, when, per the almost frantic pleas of a senior editor, he should have been fired, and May 2003, when he was fired, the personal convictions of the *Times* leadership played a similar role to the role those convictions played during the Ukrainian famine. As he noted in his somber commencement speech at SUNY New Paltz, Sulzberger had protested strongly against the Vietnam War. The then-young son of the publisher of the *New York Times* went so far in his anti-war convictions that he had gotten himself arrested on multiple occasions for anti-war demonstrations in which he had partaken.

It was after one such incident when Sulzberger's father Arthur Ochs Sulzberger, known as "Punch," decided to sit down with his son, who after all, was heir to the throne of the *New York Times*, in order to find out what was going on. In this father-son conversation, Punch Sulzberger asked Arthur Jr. a crucially important question. The younger Sulzberger, however, later said it was "the dumbest question I've ever heard in my life." The question Punch asked was if, during the Vietnam War, a single American soldier were to encounter a single North Vietnamese soldier, who would he, Arthur Sulzberger Jr., prefer to be killed in the inevitable fight? Arthur responded without hesitation: "I would want to see the American get shot. It's the other guy's country."[40]

It seems that well into 2003, when Jayson Blair was writing stories about American soldiers wracked by mental and physical pain, he was well in keeping with a preference long held by the publisher of the *New York Times*. In the case of the Iraq War, it was, without question, "the other guy's country." Arthur Sulzberger Jr.'s stated preference would be for the American to get shot—for the American to lose the moral battle symbolized by his father's question. Jayson Blair presented just this view—that of the American getting shot, the American soldier bearing the moral consequences for the Iraq War.

Unfortunately, the end of the successive scandals of missing WMDs, Jayson Blair's fabrications, and Judith Miller's false reporting at the *New York Times* is not the end of this story. Jayson Blair and Judith Miller are gone, but Arthur Sulzberger Jr. remained for another fifteen years. With

him remained the *Times*'s dogged desire to show the apparent justness
of seeing the American soldier getting shot rather than "the other guy."

The subsequent scandal at the *Times* presents just this narrative. It picks
up where Jayson Blair left off and, shockingly, it displays many of Jayson
Blair's tendencies toward fiction, Judith Miller's willingness to transcribe
rather than investigate, and of course, the Ochs-Sulzberger family's belief
that history is a malleable thing that can be bent to their will.

◆ ◆ ◆

When, in a rented theater packed with *Times* employees, Arthur Sulzberger
took a moose out of a bag, the gesture referred to the major problem
everyone involved knew existed but no one was willing to address. For
Sulzberger, the moose was the paper's failure in stopping Jayson Blair before
too much damage could be done. The moose might have also referred to
Judith Miller's highly flawed reporting on WMD in Iraq, which the Bush
administration used to sell its "misbegotten war" (in Sulzberger's words)
to the American public.

What Sulzberger was not able to see was that the real moose in the
room was the dynasty he represented. It was a senior member of that
dynasty which forbade the word "Jew" from appearing in the pages of
their newspaper during the Holocaust. It was a member of that dynasty
who directed Walter Duranty to skew his coverage. And it was that
dynasty which was thanked "profusely" by Fidel Castro for helping to
bring about the Cuban Revolution.

The moose is still in the *Times* newsroom. It always has been, and
it likely always will be. Only now it is clear what that moose actually
represents and why of the hundreds of people sitting in a New York theater
when Sulzberger pulled out his moose, and the thousands who read about
it in the media, only Sulzberger himself was able to appreciate the real
meaning behind the gag.

9

Crazy Vets:
"Extensive, Unprovoked Killings"

"I don't remember all of it," a twenty-seven-year-old former navy constructionman named Amorita Randall explained to a *New York Times Magazine* reporter about an IED attack in which she was injured. "I don't know if I passed out or what, but it was pretty gruesome."

Randall, the *Times Magazine* story recounted, had been traveling in a Humvee in Iraq when a roadside bomb exploded, killing the driver of the vehicle and injuring Randall. But the IED attack was not the only reason that the magazine reporter, Sara Corbett, had included Randall in the sprawling 12,000-word story: Randall claimed she had been raped in the military—not once, but twice—before being shipped off to Iraq.

The problem is that Amorita Randall was never in an IED attack. How can we be certain? For one, she was never in Iraq. The *Times* distributed the magazine with the story, "The Women's War," on Sunday, March 18, 2007.[1] One week later, on March 25, an "editor's note" was printed in the newspaper, which said that Randall had not been in Iraq.[2] Strangely, however, editors at the *Times* knew about the mistake before the Sunday magazine hit the stands. Three days before the magazine went to press, on March 9, a *Times* fact-checker had some "back and forth" with a navy spokesperson who informed the fact-checker there was no record of Randall receiving danger pay (which military personnel receive when serving in war zones) and that Randall's commander had confirmed that their unit had never been in combat. The navy spokesperson also noted that there was no record of Randall ever having filed a rape report.

These seriously alarming discrepancies were written into the story, but only as irrelevant tidbits. Corbett noted the navy's claim that Randall had never been in an attack but still wrote, "and yet, while we were discussing the supposed IED attack, Randall appeared to recall it in exacting detail—the smells, the sounds, the impact of the explosion."

This was a strange thing for Corbett to write since most of the journalist's description of Amorita Randall involved the woman's faulty memory. At one point in speaking about her memory, Randall went so far as to tell Corbett, "Nothing is ever clear." But for Corbett, what *actually* happened to Randall was somewhat irrelevant. The *Times* reporter wrote that Randall might have been in combat, or she might have just been "reacting to some more generalized recollection of powerlessness. Either way, the effects seemed to be crippling."

The *Times* learned definitively that Randall had not been telling the truth three days after the magazine went to print. This meant that between the time that editors learned of the error, on March 12, and the distribution date of the magazine on March 18, there was enough time to send a corrected version of the story to the printers. Whether it was a consideration of cost or just the conclusion that such a move was unnecessary, it did not happen.

The "Women's War" story in itself is an important one to tell. Women are serving in America's armed forces in greater numbers than ever before, and many of these women are being placed in or around active combat zones, even if it is in a combat support role. But in an age when a clear front line has disappeared, the risk of being exposed to combat or combat-like situations while serving in a support role has drastically increased. This exposure to the risk of trauma coupled with the atrocious trends of rape or sexual harassment in the military make the story more than worthy of the 12,000 words the *Times* devoted to it. Without question, the story is one that needs to be told.

But the problem is that the *New York Times* ran with a story that had a serious flaw in it. Amorita Randall might have been too traumatized to remember what actually happened (or did not happen) to her, or she might have concocted a story maliciously, or she might have claimed to have been in Iraq for a thousand other reasons. The fact remains: Randall's admittedly sketchy memory and the tendency of her "speech to slow down and sometimes stop altogether," as Corbett wrote, when speaking about a difficult subject should have raised enough questions to at least cut down her significant contribution to the story.

The *Times*'s fact-checker's March 6 "back and forth" with the navy spokesperson should have resulted in Randall's story being struck from the piece altogether. And the *Times*'s later confirmation that Randall's account was indeed false should have resulted in the paper at very least running a correction to the story the next day—not a full week later. More than all this, it was the still-fresh scandals of recent years—especially since they directly involved the Iraq War—that should have given pause to somebody at the *New York Times* to reflect that, given what had happened at the paper just a few years ago, maybe it would be better to err on the side of caution. But that is not what happened.

It's in a quote from a professor of sociology that the reader feels the pointy end of the "Women's War" story. In an attempt to explain an extremely confusing, complex, and serious pattern of sexual harassment and rape in the military, the sociologist Corbett chose to quote boiled things down to a simplistic formula:

> You have a male population that fits a perpetrator profile. They are mostly under twenty-five, often developmentally adolescent, and you put them together. What do you think will happen? The men do the damage, and the women get damaged.[3]

The import of the quote cited by the *Times* reporter is that not only do American male soldiers fit a "perpetrator profile," but they are also "often developmentally adolescent." It is an out-and-out dishonest formulation of the problem, since the expert seems to imply that a perpetrator profile means being a male who is under twenty-five, in which case half of all

American college students fit a "perpetrator profile." In claiming that soldiers are "developmentally adolescent," the quoted expert not only fails to cite a statistic that speaks to what percentage of soldiers fit this description—and so implies that all male American soldiers are "developmentally adolescent"—but neglects to discuss what being developmentally adolescent actually means and why soldiers might be considered as such.

Either way, there is no hidden innuendo, no insinuation to tug out of a metaphor, no scientific or sociological nuance to understand. The expert made her case in blunt words: "The men do the damage, and the women get damaged." American male soldiers, that is, are aggressors and victimizers of other Americans—in this case, American women on the battlefront.

It is a broad, bold, and charged claim to make, especially when many of those soldiers are risking their lives in a war. But it is a claim the *Times* was willing to make, even if it meant printing a faulty story to make it. More so, it is a claim the *Times* was determined to prove, no matter what the cost to truth, no matter how many facts are twisted around, turned inside out, or simply thrown by the wayside: American soldiers were warped beyond repair by the Iraq War. The war, the *New York Times* seemed to say, turned our servicemen into crazy vets.

Less than a year after "The Women's War," the *New York Times* kicked off a series called "War Torn" about American combat soldiers coming home from the war in Iraq and Afghanistan. The *Times*'s own description of the series made no bones about what it was to be about: "A series of articles and multimedia about veterans of the wars in Iraq and Afghanistan who have committed killings, or been charged with them, after coming home."

The first installment in the series, "Across America, Deadly Echoes of Foreign Battles," was published on the *Times*'s front page on January 13, 2008.[4] The article immediately jumped into the action, telling the story of a former "battle-weary grenadier" named Matthew Sepi who went out in Las Vegas one night and shot two people, killing one of them. The article's authors wrote that Sepi spoke in military terminology, later asking police who he had "taken fire from" and explaining that after the shooting he "broke contact with the enemy."

The article went on to explain that Sepi's case was not unique—it was part of a "patchwork picture of a quiet phenomenon, tracing a cross-country trail of death and heartbreak." The "trail of death," the reporters wrote, was marked by 121 cases that the *New York Times* found "in which veterans of Iraq and Afghanistan committed a killing in this country, or were charged with one, after their return from war." The article provided some horrifying statistics about the nature of the killings: more than fifty percent of the killings "involved guns," while the others were "stabbings, beatings, strangulations, and bathtub drownings." The number of the victims was even more chilling, as the reporters told readers that a third of the victims of these killings were the spouses, girlfriends, children, or relatives of the murderous veterans.

Furthermore, the article said, the reporters' own research found that since the beginning of the wars in Iraq and Afghanistan, there had been an eighty-nine percent increase in cases of murder committed by active-duty members of the American armed forces. The *Times* noted, however, that because the Pentagon does not compile these numbers (most of the cases are prosecuted in civilian [not military] courts), the newspaper arrived at its own numbers after it "conducted a search of local news reports, examined police, court, and military records and interviewed the defendants."

To do their due diligence, the reporters also asked the Pentagon to comment on the staggering eighty-nine percent increase in the number of murders committed by active-duty soldiers. The Pentagon refused to comment, but it did provide a reason for its refusal, saying that comparing killings on the basis of news reports does not factor into account the fact that during a war there is more news coverage of the actions of military personnel, meaning more murders would be reported now than before the war even if the actual murder rate was unchanged. The Pentagon's spokesperson "also questioned the value of 'lumping together different crimes such as involuntary manslaughter with first-degree homicide.'"

Nevertheless, the *New York Times's* "War Torn" series reporters were not deterred. They explained that certain unnamed veterans' groups "deplored" the way that stories about vets in trouble—such as those psychologically damaged enough to commit murder—get covered in the media, as if these veterans organizations were trying to silence the coverage of an important trend. According to the reporters, one of those organizations, the American Legion, had gone so far as to advise journalists "to subordinate whatever slight news value there may be in playing up the ex-service member angle in stories of crime or offense against the peace."[5] This was pretty damning: a government-chartered organization was telling journalists how to cover veterans returning from war who had been involved in crimes. But there was one important detail regarding the statement by the American Legion that might have been overlooked by *Times* readers: it was made just after the end of the First World War, a *hundred years* before the "War Torn" series saw print. Still, the reporters felt it was representative of contemporary cultural norms surrounding veterans returning from war.

Taken as the *Times* article presented it, the "War Torn" series presented a gripping and terrifying narrative. Well-trained and often well-armed veterans were supposedly killing civilians almost *twice* as frequently as they had before the wars in Iraq and Afghanistan. What is worse is that these killer vets were killing their wives, children, and girlfriends by shooting them, drowning them in bathtubs, and stabbing them to death. And, it seems, the Pentagon was not even looking into the matter, maybe because veterans groups like the American Legion were trying to quash such talk since it could hinder veterans in their search for jobs or hurt morale in the armed services. It was a powerful story indeed.

But looking back at the coverage, a simple question strikes even the most casual reader. The *Times*'s description of the "War Torn" series billed itself as, "A series of articles and multimedia about veterans of the wars in Iraq and Afghanistan who have committed killings, or been charged with them, after coming home." Veterans who have committed killings "*or been charged with them*"? Surely there is a difference between someone who has been convicted of murder and someone who has been accused of it. No homicide statistic in America includes people who were just accused of the crime.

But from there things got worse very fast. A closer look at the statistics, prompted by the disturbing phrase "or been charged with them," shows that for all the numbers tossed around on the first page of the January 13 article (which, bear in mind, was on the front page of the newspaper)— including numbers like the fifty percent of vets who killed with a gun and the thirty percent of victims who were spouses, children, relatives, or acquaintances of the killer vets—the authors of the article never spoke about what their statistic of 121 American soldiers who committed a killing, or were accused of it, meant in context of the non-military population. Were these numbers higher or lower than those related to crimes committed by civilians? That, it seems, would be the critical question. But it was one the *Times* reporters did not address.

This glaring omission did not go unnoticed by other news agencies. The *New York Post* was one of the first to comment on the strange, even whimsical use of homicide statistics by the *Times*. In one article, "Smearing Our Troops," *Post* reporter Ralph Peters pointed out the lack of any context for the 121 figure and wrote about how he ran the numbers himself. He found that a conservative estimate of the number of United States troops in Iraq and Afghanistan between 2003 and 2007 was 350,000 (without double counting those who served multiple tours). On the other hand, on the basis of the Justice Department's statistics of the number of homicides committed in the United States each year, active-duty American soldiers would had to have committed 150 murders a year, Peters said, just to *match* the rate of civilian homicide in the United States for the age group relevant to soldiers. Between 2003 and 2007, that is, returning soldiers would had to have killed between 700 and 750 people at home to equal the average United States homicide rate.[6]

What does this mean? It means that on the basis of the *New York Times* article's number of 121 murders committed by active-duty soldiers, military men returning home are *far less likely* to kill than men their age in the general population. In the article's defense, the reporters noted that 121 is the minimum number of murders that were committed (or possibly committed) by active-duty servicemen who had returned home from the wars. But still, as a *Weekly Standard* article noted, the magic 121 number cited by the *Times* translated to a homicide rate that was significantly below that of the general civilian population.[7]

Despite this glaring omission in the basic journalistic duty of providing relevant context, things still deteriorated. Taking a look at a list of some of the veterans included in the *Times*'s 121, we see that many of these men did not commit violent crimes at all, and that the violent crimes of the others had very little (if anything) to do with their having been in a war. For example, one former soldier on the list, Brian Epting, was convicted of vehicular homicide. His crime? He lost control of his car while drag racing and ended up hitting a man who was killed by the impact. This can hardly be considered a violent crime connected to an experience of war trauma. Two others on the list had histories of schizophrenia. One had a history of abuse—*before* he went to war. And one other, Larry Jaimall, was a known member of the violent street gang, the Crips.

The last case brings us back to Matthew Sepi, the main character in the anecdote the *Times* reporters began their "War Torn" piece with. The night that Sepi went out and shot two people in Las Vegas, it is not certain that he really lost control in a war-induced post-traumatic stress disorder (PTSD) panic. In fact, the evidence suggests the opposite. The article itself noted that the two people Sepi shot were gang members. Both were "large," both were armed, and both approached Sepi as he tried to get to a 7-Eleven store to buy beer (or have beer bought for him, since he was underage). In a situation in which two armed gang members approach a third armed non-gang member, it is far from obvious that the subsequent shootout has anything to do with the third person's experience in a war, at least not more than it has to do with the other two people's active involvement in a street gang.

The rest of the article goes on to discuss the impact of PTSD and chronicles the stories of other former servicemen who were involved in a civilian death back home. There is the story of a man who got drunk at a party and thrust his gun into a fellow party-goer's car. During the ensuing scuffle, the gun went off, and a young man was left dead. Another story is about a former marine who inhaled ether and drove down the freeway until he collided with another car, killing one person.

The stories are dramatic and tragic. They make a big impact. But the series of which the article was a part was not about dramatic and tragic stories of the post-war lives of servicemen. It is about trends and patterns of returning veterans. If it had not been, the authors of the first article in the series would not have bothered to provide any statistics at all, let alone the specious 121 number, which purported to show that killings by veterans who returned from the Iraq or Afghanistan war were on a rampant increase.

Without the implication of a worrying trend, the story would only have been a chronicle of the lives of a few men and the crimes they committed. It would have been a good topic for a film, a novel, or a magazine article, but certainly not news, which is exactly why the article's reporters strained so hard to make something out of the 121 alleged murders.

But like the "The Women's War" article by Sara Corbett, the faulty reporting cast a shadow over the entire article. After seeing that such a solid number had no basis—and, when properly construed, proves exactly the opposite of what the *Times* reporters were trying to show—what could a reader think about the rest of the article, or the rest of the series? Similarly, after learning that the *Times Magazine* reporter had been so easily taken in by Amorita Randall's tales of Iraq despite having plenty of evidence that cast doubt on the woman's stories, how could a reader be expected to believe that the allegations of sexual harassment, military rape, and combat-related PTSD reported in the article were any more free of journalistic problems than Randall's story was?

The context of the reporting reveals further cracks in the foundation. As the previous chapter showed, Jayson Blair had reported along the same costs-of-war narrative of which the "Women's War" article and the "War Torn" series were a part. Unsurprisingly, similar errors can be found in all three instances. Of course, Jayson Blair was the case of extreme dysfunction since he lied systematically, and knew it, and, for this reason, the reporters of the "Women's War" and "War Torn" articles should not be compared to Blair. But, unfortunately, the stories that they reported reveal parallels to Blair's reporting that simply cannot be ignored.

◆ ◆ ◆

The "War Torn" series continued despite the problems found in the first installment. The public editor of the New York Times, Clark Hoyt, wrote an editorial about the first story in which he argued that even though the first article did use "squishy numbers" and "colorfully inflated language" (e.g. "trail of death"), the article's stories are "powerful and important," and, he wrote, he hoped they would "goad the military to figure out what went wrong."[8] Once again, the New York Times was making an effort to quarantine the problem, limiting its extent to a few minor flaws.

Some Times readers might have been reminded by this incident of the problems in Jayson Blair's articles. Many undoubtedly would have thought about Judith Miller's flawed reporting. And some may have even remembered Sara Corbett's article from 2005, in which Amorita Randall's version of events was transcribed rather than investigated. But very few people (if any) paid attention to the authors of the story. One of them we already know: Deborah Sontag. Sontag was the Times's Jerusalem bureau chief who spent a good deal of her time reporting that the Israeli military had killed a Palestinian boy named Muhammad Al-Dura. It was the creation of this narrative of the Palestinian boy murdered by Israeli soldiers that has since justified countless suicide bombings, jihadist operations, and was even invoked in the beheading of Wall Street Journal reporter Daniel Pearl. But when an independent French ballistics expert found that there was no way that Israeli gunfire could have killed the boy that day—and that there was cause to think the entire episode had been a hoax—Deborah Sontag and the New York Times stayed silent.

Sontag had also written endlessly (and incorrectly, according to both the Mitchell Committee and the Palestinian leadership itself) that the then-Minister of Transportation, Ariel Sharon, had set off the years of violence between Israel and the Palestinians by visiting the Temple Mount. In story after story, Sontag and her bureau's reporter William Orme Jr., her husband, inserted the truism that Sharon, the military man, had started the intifada that led to the death of the Palestinian boy.

The overarching themes in Sontag's "War Torn" reporting were not all that different from her reporting on Israel. The first "War Torn" article advanced the notion that on the basis of the New York Times's research,

American soldiers were committing more murders of Americans once they returned home from war. In her faulty reporting on the Israeli soldiers who killed a Palestinian boy, the same general notion was called into play: soldiers do not just kill on the battlefield, where killing is a terrible but sometimes necessary part of their job—they kill their "spouses, children, [and] girlfriends" at home, and they kill Palestinian children at protests.

But the facts do not support this thesis, and never did—at least not concerning the death of the Palestinian child or the trend of American servicemen committing murder Stateside. Given that the *Times* never ran a story to report that contrary to Sontag and Orme's reporting—i.e. that the Israeli military had not killed the boy (in fact, the paper never ran a story that even mentioned that as a possibility, once the French ballistics expert's testimony was published and the court's verdict returned)—it is unlikely the *Times* had actually paid attention to the fact that it had gotten one of the most important Middle East stories of the last ten years completely wrong. And if editors and executives at the newspaper were aware of this, it can only be concluded that either they did not want to admit the error, or that the error was not worth being corrected on their pages. It was not, as the *Times* front page famously asserts, "All the news that's fit to print."

The second installment of the "War Torn" series, written solely by Sontag, did away with any attempt to show through the use of evidence or statistics that there was a trend or pattern of Iraq or Afghanistan war veterans committing violent crimes at home. Instead, the whole article, more than 6,000 words of it, focused entirely on one former soldier who had murdered his girlfriend.[9] Again, the story is as dramatic as it is tragic. But drama and tragedy are not the stuff of newspapers, at least not traditionally. People form their opinions on the basis of what they read in reputable newspapers. When they read dramatic tales taken out of context, they form opinions that are equally out of context. Maybe there actually is a disturbing trend of combat soldiers increasingly committing acts of violence after they have endured trauma or have been damaged by the experiences of America's wars. If there is, it is a story that the American public must hear. But it is not the story the *New York Times* told in the articles of the "War Torn" series.

Rather, these stories are anecdotal: They might provide an example of a larger pattern, or they might not. The people at the center of the stories are not subjects as much as they are archetypes—in this case, soldiers who have been so damaged by the wars abroad that they come home broken and even homicidal. When Sara Corbett reported her article, "The Women's War," she included a woman named Abbie Pickett, a former soldier in the Army National Guard, as one of the examples of female soldiers who suffered trauma in Iraq, in addition to being sexually assaulted by a fellow soldier. Like the stories of the men in the "War Torn" series, Pickett's story is difficult to read, sometimes even difficult to believe, not because Pickett seems to be lying but because the story is so tragic and so extreme that someone who has not experienced it can barely imagine it.

Pickett related to Corbett her experience of being raped while serving in Nicaragua on a humanitarian mission. She described the humiliation of being the constant butt of sexist jokes and the difficulty of being constantly confronted by pornography, especially in the latrines. At one point, Pickett describes the level of desperation she reached during her service. There was a mortar attack on her unit's base one night, during which she, as a medic, had to care for a number of bleeding soldiers in the dark. Looking back on that harrowing night, Pickett told Corbett, "For a long time, I wished I had died that night." It is a powerful thing to say and a difficult thing to hear from a young woman who enlisted in the army because she had a genuine desire to serve her country.

For the *New York Times*, it seemed too powerful to resist. In a November 26, 2005 article, "The Struggle to Gauge a War's Psychological Cost," the reporter, Benedict Carey, wrote about the young men and women fighting in the Middle East who were experiencing various kinds of psychological damage.[10] About a quarter of the way into the article, Carey puts the reader straight into the boots of a soldier, writing that on an October 2003 night, mortars started to fall on a base in Iraq. The report detailed that a young medic named Abbie Pickett who rushed to help bleeding soldiers, "plugging and chugging," to try save the lives of the wounded men.

Pickett was quoted by Carey in the article saying, "I would say that on a weekly basis I wish I would have died during that attack." Almost two years later, in her 2007 article Sara Corbett wrote that Pickett told her, "For a long time, I wished I had died that night." In two different articles separated by more than a year and a half, the *Times* not only used the same soldier to prove a point (actually, two different points) or trend, but the paper published basically the same quote in support of claims about the level of damage done to young soldiers fighting, in this case, in Iraq.

Technically speaking, using the same quote twice is not problematic. What likely happened is that the two different reporters interviewed the same source who gave a similar account of a very important, relevant and memorable event in her life. However, the paper's use of the same source, the same incident, and nearly the same quote twice shows just how much its costs of war narrative relies on anecdotal evidence in place of hard facts. Pickett's story is a particularly dramatic one—so dramatic that it projected her all over the media and even temporarily earned her an official role as an adviser on military issues for MTV's "Rock the Vote" campaign. But the *Times* articles on the effects of the war—the human costs of the war—were supposed to be about real trends that were occurring and provable by data. If reporters wanted to color or illustrate the data for readers by providing stories of individual people as examples, that would have been fine. But in fact, they did the opposite, using individual stories, and only the most dramatic ones, to attempt to prove the existence of a trend.

In the sense that professional psychologists and cognitive science professors refer to the common-sense approach to explaining psychological phenomena as folk psychology, it would be appropriate to call the *Times*'s reporting on the effects of the war—as found in the "War Torn" series and the "Women's War" article—as "folk journalism." Like folk psychology, folk journalism does not rely on data or reliable investigation to arrive at a conclusion or to make a connection between two things. Rather, it draws conclusions out of personal intuition and preconceived belief and then fits real life examples into the mold it has already sculpted.

The difference, of course, is that people who do folk psychology are not psychologists. But the *New York Times*, which has practiced folk journalism on the crucially important topic of war veterans, is not just another newspaper—it is supposed to be the pinnacle of the journalistic field, the best, most experienced, and most professional journalistic organization in the country. Often, the paper lives up to its reputation. The *Times* deploys a staggering amount of resource to help a pool of talented reporters do an excellent job at reporting the news and the facts from all over the world. But things go wrong when the beliefs and convictions of the *Times*'s monolithic ownership get in the way of accurate reporting.

We have seen that time and time again, from Soviet Russia to Castro's Cuba to the Holocaust to the atomic bombs in Japan, that when the top power structure at the *New York Times* got involved in a story, the story got blown in the worst possible way. In the case of America's wars, especially the war in Iraq, the then-publisher of the paper and chairman of The New York Times Company made no attempt to hide or dilute his opinion about America's wars. So strongly did Arthur Sulzberger Jr. feel about the situation that he was compelled to personally apologize for America's involvement in the "misbegotten war in a foreign land" to a group of college graduates of 2006. And he also once expressed his more youthful, more passionate view that when it comes to an American soldier fighting in a foreign country, he would prefer the American to be shot, explaining, "it's the other guy's country."

Much the same happened with the *Times*'s still ongoing "War Torn" storyline. The third installment in the "War Torn" series is a good example of the rest of the series. The January 27, 2008 article, "In More Cases, Combat Trauma Takes the Witness Stand,"[11] is about yet another alleged trend involving war veterans.[12] This time, the so-called trend relates to veterans who commit a violent crime and then take the stand, armed with a PTSD and combat-trauma defense.

Sontag was once again on the byline of the article, as was the co-author of the first article, Lizette Alvarez. The article jumps straight into the trial of a former National Guardsman who, after returning from Iraq, had gotten into a fight that ended up with him shooting a man to death. The reporters made the point of the article very clear. They wrote,

> When combat veterans like Mr. Gregg stand accused of killings and other offenses on their return from Iraq and Afghanistan, prosecutors, judges and juries are increasingly prodded to assess the role of combat trauma in their crimes and whether they deserve special treatment because of it.

But other than the word "increasingly" in the phrase "prosecutors, judges, and juries are increasingly prodded to assess the role of combat trauma," there was no indication in the entire article as to what extent this trend occurred—or if it existed at all. In fact, in the nearly 3,000 words devoted to the article about the "Combat Trauma Defense," Sontag and Alvarez did not cite even one statistic, one figure, or one bit of formal data from the military, the Justice Department, or any other agency, organization, or study group. There was just the story of one National Guardsman whose sentence was affected by a consideration of combat trauma. Other than that, readers were left to themselves to ponder the meaning of the word "increasingly."

By the fourth article of the series, "When Strains on Military Families Turn Deadly," which ran on February 15, 2008, Sontag and Alvarez had managed to make their approach to the "War Torn" articles into a formula. Once again, the article opened with a shocking, even gruesome account of a veteran committing a violent crime. This time, it was domestic violence.

"He struck her, choked her, dragged her over a fence and slammed her into the sidewalk," the article recounted. And when the battered woman finally moved away from home, made all the right moves, and took all the correct legal action, the army veteran, who had served in Iraq, found his wife in a small Texas town and shot her in the head, just before shooting himself.

The article focused on violent crime committed by male veterans of the wars in Iraq and Afghanistan against their spouses, girlfriends, and even children. Once again, the stories were chilling, horrific and tragic. But, once again, the article, in refusing to cite reliable statistics in order to show a pattern or trend, left the stories lingering in a gray area between storytelling and news reporting. About a quarter of the way into the more than 4,000-word article, the reporters wrote that the *Times* had done its own "examination" of the data and found "more than 150 cases of fatal domestic violence or child abuse in the United States involving service members and new veterans during the wartime period that began in October 2001 with the invasion of Afghanistan." But this time, the reporters were quick to note that only one-third, or fifty, of those cases *definitively* involved servicemen who had been deployed in Iraq or Afghanistan. The other two-thirds either had not been in combat in Iraq or Afghanistan or their involvement in the wars could not be verified.

Further, the reporters seemed to put a disclaimer on the only shred of data that they offered in the entire piece, saying, "It is difficult to know how complete the *Times*'s findings are." (Given the reporters' track record in the previous three installments of the "War Torn" series, that last statement might have been the most reliable one in their many thousand words of reporting.)

The fifth and last article in the series, "After the Battle, Fighting the Bottle at Home," turned to a fairly old hat when it comes to military stories as it tackled alcohol abuse among soldiers.[13] The story, written and reported by Lizette Alvarez, took a more conservative approach than the four other articles in the "War Torn" series. However, as with the other four articles, Alvarez jumped into the story with a tantalizing hook—a former marine who was so traumatized by his experience in Iraq that he suffered flashbacks, frayed nerves, and explosions of aggression. But it was the former marine's trouble sleeping that caused him to start drinking.

The story went on to claim that the marine's case was "part of a growing body of evidence that alcohol abuse is rising among veterans of combat in Afghanistan and Iraq, many of them trying to deaden the repercussions of war and disorientation of home." Clearly, Alvarez was making two separate but interconnected claims in the article: that alcohol abuse was increasing and that the causes for the increase were war trauma and the "disorientation" of returning home.

Unlike the other four articles, Alvarez referred to reliable sources to make claims based on the findings of expert researchers. She included both military representatives and health professionals to speak about the increase of alcohol abuse in the military since the beginning of the Afghanistan and Iraq wars. She also cited Pentagon studies and conversations with people who have knowledge of a large group of relevant subjects (such as base commanders), and she used individual cases as illustrations of the trend rather than as substitutes for evidence.

But Alvarez occasionally slipped into the bad habits of her earlier reporting—specifically by *referring* to her earlier reporting. At one point in the final "War Torn" article, Alvarez tried to make that final critical leap that would connect the increase in alcohol and drug abuse caused by war stress to an increase in violent crimes committed by veterans. "Sometimes, though, substance abuse becomes a factor in major crimes," she wrote. "This year, a *New York Times* examination of killings in this country by veterans of Iraq and Afghanistan found that drinking or drug use was frequently involved in the crimes."

Her first statement, that substance abuse "becomes a factor in major crimes" says nothing beyond what is already known by the vast majority of readers—alcohol and drugs correlate with crime. The second statement about the *Times*'s examination is supposed to provide the evidence and support for this bigger claim that veterans are drinking more because of their war trauma and that the substance abuse leads to more civilian deaths. However, as we saw, the *Times*'s first "examination of killings" was dubious at best. Moreover, Sontag and Alvarez provided no clear numbers in their original article on how many of those killings involved substance abuse, and Alvarez, in this final article, made no effort to fill in the blanks. Rather, she reverted to the chosen tactic of the two reporters in their earlier articles of the series—filling the gaps with anecdotes, which is exactly what she did in the next paragraph. After making her reference to the first, flawed "War Torn" article, Alvarez immediately told the reader about a soldier from Fort Bliss, near El Paso, who was accused of killing a woman in a drunk-driving incident.

Once again, however, Alvarez was relying on allegations and accusations. She wrote, "a soldier at Fort Bliss, outside El Paso, was charged with killing a woman in a drunken-driving accident." But the claim would prove more than merely problematic. The soldier she wrote about, Deron Kemp Rodriguez, was initially charged with intoxicated manslaughter after he hit four women crossing the street on which he was driving in Central El Paso. But the charges of intoxicated manslaughter and intoxicated assault were dropped three days after Alvarez's story was published. The reason was that the blood sample taken from Rodriguez just after the accident showed that he, in fact, had not been driving drunk: He was below the legal limit of .08% blood alcohol.[14]

But Alvarez was so convinced of her conclusions that that was not the only significant error she made in the piece. Alvarez reported that the main subject of the article, a former marine corporal named Anthony Klecker (the soldier who had been drinking himself to sleep), had been thrown out of a substance abuse program for pulling a knife on other patients. That's an extreme allegation, one which would amount to very serious criminal charges. More importantly, it offered an anecdotal illustration of the claims Alvarez was pushing about veterans, which she had been unable to make with hard evidence. The problem is it wasn't true. A correction to the article made by the *Times* noted that, according to prosecutors, though Klecker did indeed possess a knife, he never threatened anyone in the program with it.

Similarly, Deron Rodriguez might have committed some kind of crime, but it was not the crime Alvarez implied he had committed. Even though the reporter wrote that the soldier had only been "charged" with killing the woman, by including Rodriguez's story just after her statement about the *Times*'s "examination of killings," which showed that alcohol was sometimes involved in violent crime, readers were led to believe that Rodriguez had actually committed the crime. And by citing the alleged crime, Alvarez also used the incident to provide an example of the trend she was citing. The result is what philosophers call circular logic—two unsupported claims are craftily positioned to support each other. But with the slightest critical breeze, both claims fall.

The very next statement in the report takes the case even further as Alvarez wrote that not only were these alcohol-abusing, post-combat soldiers a danger to others, but they were also a danger to themselves.

She wrote, "Substance abuse frequently figures in suicides, which reached a high in the Army last year; alcohol or drugs were cited in 30 percent of those 115 cases, the Pentagon reported."

However, a more careful look at the Pentagon's reporting on suicide once again reveals the opposite of what the *Times* reporter was trying to show. The Army Suicide Event Report (ASER) of 2007 provides a detailed look at suicide trends among soldiers in the army, the branch of the United States armed forces that Alvarez cited as suffering an all-time record for annual suicides. The report looked at multiple factors such as where suicide victims lived, their marital status, their substance abuse histories, and their combat experience.

While Alvarez's article is about the rise in alcohol abuse as a consequence of the stresses of serving in war, which she connected to the increased suicide rate, the facts tell quite a different story. According to the 2007 ASER, only twenty-four percent of army soldiers who had committed suicide experienced direct combat. Thirty-seven percent of the suicide victims did not see combat, while thirty-nine percent of the victims' combat experience was undetermined.

A much better suicide predictor than combat experience in the army is marital status. The ASER showed a very strong correlation between failed relationships with a spouse and suicide, as a full fifty percent of the study's sample who had committed suicide had experienced failed relationships with their spouses. In fact, the correlation between suicide and failed relationships with a spouse vastly outstrips the correlation with any other factor, including sexual abuse (2% positive correlation), physical abuse (7% correlation), sexual harassment (0%), excessive debt (9%), and a family history of mental illness or suicide (10%).

With all this in mind, a reader of this last piece in the *Times*'s "War Torn" series is left wondering: Why focus on the connection between combat and suicide, as Alvarez did, when the connection between suicide and failed marriage is so much stronger? In fact, given the very strong correlation between failed marriage and suicide versus the relatively much lower correlation between suicide and alcohol (thirty percent), there is the question of why Alvarez did not write a story about the stresses and mental health effects of being married while in the military.

◆ ◆ ◆

By the time she reported the "War Torn" series, Lizette Alvarez had worn a number of hats at the *New York Times*, including her position as a reporter for the metro desk and for the national desk. She came to the *Times* in 1995 after a stint at the *Miami Herald,* which culminated in her winning Harvard University's Goldsmith Prize for a story she co-reported about America's immigration policy.

Months after Alvarez's arrival at the *Times*, she was reporting on a subject whose trail had already been blazed by the *Times*'s staff and publishers. In October 1995, Fidel Castro made his first visit to the United States since 1979. The occasion was the fifty-year anniversary of the United Nations, and leaders from all over the world poured into the city for the diplomatic celebration. Alvarez covered Castro's visit to New York for the *Times*. She wrote "Visiting Castro to Meet Both Cold Shoulder and 'Fidelmania'" on October 20,[15] and her October 23 story was entitled "Castro Back in Fatigues in Harlem."[16] The first story was a fairly straightforward account of how Castro might be received, stating there were people who supported him and people who did not.

But the story "Castro Back in Fatigues in Harlem" took a more romantic look at the Cuban dictator. Alvarez opened the piece with an account of Castro at the Abyssinian Baptist Church in Harlem, where an "adulatory" crowd of "1,300 admirers" applauded and cheered the Cuban leader. The *Times* reporter devoted a full paragraph to quoting Castro, who lamented that after all the time that had passed, he was still being "expelled"—meaning he had not been greeted by President Clinton nor had he been invited to any official state or city events. Alvarez also provided an excerpt from Castro's United Nations speech, in which he said:

> We lay claim to a world without ruthless blockades that cause the death of men, women and children, youths and elders, like noiseless atom

bombs. We lay claim to a world of peace, justice and dignity where everyone, without exception, has the right to well-being and life.

Despite Alvarez's inclusion of Castro's bombastic claims about the "right to well-being and life," the reporter saw fit to include only one critical view of Castro and did so in a mere two sentences, when quoting the statements of the head of the San Carlos Institute. The rest of the quotes in the piece were of Castro or his supporters, such as a man who told the *Times* reporter that Castro was "a principled man and he doesn't bow down. He did a whole lot for Africans."

"We have shed our blood to fights [sic] against colonialism," Alvarez quoted Castro as saying and finished off the piece with Castro's claim that the people, even in New York, support him and his revolution. "And he pointed to the crowd in Harlem," she wrote, "who obtained tickets through churches, black groups and social advocacy groups, as proof that the real people are on his side, even if the politicians remain hostile. 'Others might change because they are not in the right,' he said. 'We won't because we are right. The best evidence is your presence here.'"

For all of Alvarez's talk about Castro's style of dress, reporting as if he were a celebutante in that he first wore a black suit then changed back into his fatigues, and for all of Castro's self-adulatory quotes that Alvarez included in the piece, she neglected to speak about one important aspect of Cuban life under Castro: human rights. In fact, none of the pieces by Alvarez or other *Times* reporters who covered the visit touched directly on Cuba's horrendous human rights record. A fairly puffy Week in Review piece, "A Little Hope Pumps up an Attitude," on the situation in Castro's Cuba at the time of his 1995 visit, quotes a Human Rights Watch report as saying, "the Cuban Government is trying to improve its human rights image," even if "positive developments might be fleeting."[17] But the *Times* story left out the meat of the Human Rights Watch report on Cuba, which included dismal evaluations of Cuba's policies on the right to free speech; the right to work and freely associate, and most sharply, the status of political prisoners. While Alvarez reported on and quoted from Castro's lofty, self-righteous speech made inside of an American church, she, just like she did in her "War Torn" stories, neglected to provide the key piece in the puzzle: context. She did not speak about the thousands of political prisoners held by Castro in Cuba's prisons. The article made no mention of prisoners like Reidel de la Torre Calero, a Cuban political prisoner who told the Inter-American Commission on Human Rights that he suffered "the cruel, inhuman and degrading conditions" of his prison's "punishment cells."[18] It made no mention of Omar del Pozo Marrero and Joel Alfonso Matos—both of whom, like Torre Calero, were put in prison without trial for disagreeing with government policy, or other prisoners who were beaten, degraded, and sometimes tortured.[19]

Alvarez, however, did include an account of one of the more eyebrow-raising parts of Castro's visit: just as he had done decades before, the Cuban dictator made his now traditional visit to the *New York Times* building to meet with the paper's publisher. According to Alvarez's article, "Giuliani? He Wouldn't Get Castro's Vote," Castro sat with the *New York Times*'s publisher along with "several editors."[20] This time, the man at the helm of the newspaper was Arthur Ochs Sulzberger Jr., who strolled down the halls of the newspaper with Castro—just as his grandfather, Arthur Hays Sulzberger, had done forty years before. According to Anthony DePalma, Castro jokingly asked Arthur Sulzberger Jr., "Where is Matthews?" referring to Herbert Matthews, the *New York Times* reporter who had launched Castro onto the world stage with the famous front-page article in 1957. Castro even repeated the story of how he paraded his troops around in circles to give Matthews the impression that there were dozens, or even hundreds of them, instead of the eighteen or so that Castro claimed there actually were.[21]

Given that the *Times* had been so badly burned by Fidel Castro, and given that Herbert Matthews had tarnished the paper's reputation so irrevocably, it's strange to think that the dictator would be welcomed in the *New York Times* building yet again. But only five years after the 1995 visit, in September of 2000, Castro, in New York for the Millenium Summit, was again given the VIP treatment by the *New York Times*. Once again, he strolled the hallways of the *Times* buildings repeating ad nauseam his socialist theory of revolution and his adventuristic take on history. And, once again, the *Times*'s publisher was there, listening to the Cuban dictator's tales.[22]

(In a flourish of irony only the *Times* could achieve, the newspaper ran an article impugning the ethics of another newspaper, the *New York Daily News*, which had run a composite photo of Castro about to shake hands with President Clinton.[23] The handshake did take place, but there was no photograph of it. The *Times* report stated, without citing any sources, that the photo had "some in journalism questioning the newspaper's ethics." The author of the article? None other than Jayson Blair, one of the most notorious violators of journalistic ethics in recent memory.)

The same day of Alvarez's "Giuliani" story, October 26, the *Times* ran an editorial about Cuba, speaking about Castro who "dropped by" the newspaper, bearing his "disarming sense of humor and an unbending allegiance to Cuban Socialism."[24] The main thrust of the editorial was very clear: end the embargo against Cuba. The editorial's authors referred to the embargo as an "archaic" and "tired policy" and claimed that it "has clearly served Mr. Castro's political interests, providing him with an excuse for economic privation." Though, as Chapter Four of this book showed, the "economic privation" that existed in Cuba under Castro prevailed long before the United States stamped an embargo on the Caribbean island. And with a revolutionary-communist economic policy that was closely modeled on the kind of policies that Stalin employed in the early days of the USSR (the ones that led directly to the Ukrainian famine), it would be difficult to see how Cuba could have wound up prosperous and free—even if the United States had not enacted an embargo.

Either way, a *Times* editorial that advanced the same policy approach that Castro was advancing, printed a day after the paper's publisher strolled through the *Times* building with the Cuban dictator, raises serious questions, especially given the *Times*'s sordid history with Cuba and Fidel Castro. But, as with so many other journalistic failings at the *Times*, these questions were not addressed, let alone answered. And the "War Torn" series, and others like it—so intent on casting America's wars and the soldiers returning from them under a shadow of psychological damage, rape and murder that the articles not only failed to live up to the *Times*'s own journalistic standards but flouted them at almost every turn—became a critical support in the media's emerging narrative about those "misbegotten wars in foreign lands."

Woke History:
"Our Founding Ideals Were False"

On August 14, 2019, the *New York Times* launched one of the most ambitious and far-reaching initiatives in the history of the paper. Called "The 1619 Project," the endeavor would encompass the entire hundred pages of the *Times*'s *Sunday Magazine*, spanning tens of thousands of words and dozens of photos devoted to a single topic. The issue, conceived and overseen by *Times* reporter Nikole Hannah-Jones, included essays, poems, and rare archival photography, all of which reached deep into history to bring the past roaring into the present.

There is no denying the scale, complexity, and sophistication of The 1619 Project. Despite this—or maybe because of it—the project's authors at the *Times* made understanding the aim of the project exceedingly simple. On the first non-advertising page of the issue, the *Times*'s *Sunday Magazine* editor, Jake Silverstein, spelled out why the newspaper had invested what amounts to millions of dollars in print and digital real estate into a single topic. In the third paragraph of his Editor's Note, Silverstein wrote:

> The goal of the 1619 Project is to…reframe American history by considering what it would mean to regard 1619 as our nation's birth year. Doing so requires us to place the consequences of slavery and the contributions of black Americans at the very center of the story we tell ourselves about who we are as a country.[1]

The online version of The 1619 Project carried the same preamble to the piece, though with a subtle distinction. It stated the aim of The 1619 Project was "to *reframe* the country's history[2] by placing the consequences of slavery and the contributions of black Americans at the very center of our national narrative" (author's emphasis). The name of The 1619 Project is a direct expression of this aim. Rather than locating the founding of America in the nation's Declaration of Independence, which was adopted by the Second Continental Congress on July 4, 1776, the Project sought to replace the traditional history of the founding of America with the date the first slave ship arrived to the colonies around August 1619. This is a momentous shift, as it was intended to be. Rooting the founding of America in slavery, not liberty, would invert the entire project of America and the national story we tell about the country. It would make the world's oldest democracy into its most durable slavocracy. With this stroke of the *Times*'s historical pen, July 4, 1776 became not a day to mark the triumph of liberty but the scourge of human bondage.

This fully explains the seemingly cryptic opening statement of Nikole Hannah-Jones's main essay in the magazine: "Our founding ideals of liberty and equality were false when they were written." And it's precisely this subversion of history that the *Times* had in mind when it declared its intent to reframe the history of the United States in terms of the historical realities and—much more importantly—the *consequences* of slavery. What we see is that far from an *exploration* of this kind of theoretical framework, with The 1619 Project the *Times* set out to change history as we know it.

For any institution, organization or even government, changing accepted history is quite an aim. It took the Maoists of China and communists of Russia generations, and countless lives, to pull off. To think the *Times* could reframe the country's history with a single magazine issue, no matter how long or in depth, seems a little hubristic. An undertaking of this scope would require a massive ideological effort, the likes of which the world has only seen in major national or cultural revolutions.

But the scale of this "reframing" is only one of the critical elements of The 1619 Project. The other is its content. The *Times*'s opening salvo, which came in the form of Silverstein's note, made clear in no uncertain terms that the aim of the project is to reframe American history such that slavery would become the taproot of American history. Silverstein's statement, elegantly simple as it is, holds back an ideological torrent. Accepting its premise means changing our understanding of and approach to every element of American life, economy, culture, society, and of course, history. Slavery becomes everything, and everything becomes slavery.

And that is precisely the challenge that The 1619 Project rose to meet. It was and still remains the guiding intention behind the Project itself. The landmark issue of the *Times Magazine* ranges across all of the above topics, speaking of how slavery not only affected but determined the course of American economics, politics, culture, entertainment, music, healthcare, and dozens of other spheres of life. But the *Times*, cognizant of the breadth of its mission, would not stop at a single magazine issue. Far from it. The issue was intended to be merely the *launch* of the wider project, which would include slavery-based school curricula, educational programs, and even entertainment projects. It would be an all-encompassing approach to an all-encompassing mission.

Looking back at the history of slavery in America, including by reading the 1619 issue itself, it is not difficult to understand why someone would make a claim of this sort. Slavery was (and still is) a grossly immoral, malicious, and malign institution. It rests on breathtaking hypocrisy and boundless cruelty. The extent, both in terms of the use of slaves in America and the length of time the institution was perpetuated, not to mention the crimes perpetrated against freed slaves and later ordinary black citizens by American institutions after slavery's abolition, make it seem inevitable that its impact would be a long-lasting (if not permanent) feature of American life. The essays in the *Times* reflect the gravity and urgency of addressing a topic of this importance. By reconnecting present-day political and cultural experiences with a part of American history that would be easy to ignore or wish away, the authors of the Project were bringing to the surface a horrific and shameful past that, if left to linger, will only rot. And this connecting of past to present was exactly what the essays attempted to do. For example, one essay by sociologist Matthew Desmond asserts that

American capitalism was formed by slavery and remains a contemporary manifestation of that system.[3] Another essay traced the failings of America's present-day healthcare system, including a lack of universal healthcare,[4] back to post-Civil War policies. A third essay connected today's traffic jams to slavery in the South.[5] Another tied America's sugar-laden junk food to (by now you will have guessed) slavery.

But it was the lead essay of the magazine issue that set the stage for all the other essays. The nearly 8,000-word essay was written by the creator of The 1619 Project, Nikole Hannah-Jones, and made the most sweeping, sometimes shockingly radical claims about American history, including that Abraham Lincoln was an unrepentant racist who blamed black people for the Civil War; that the war was fought not to end slavery but solely to keep the Union together; that American democracy and the liberty on which the system is based was birthed by black Americans alone; and, in Hannah-Jones's own words, that, "Anti-black racism runs in the very DNA of this country."[6]

While the claims were so far from the mainstream dialog on American history so as to be nearly unimaginable to most *Times* readers, the ideas were presented not as theory or hypothesis but hard fact. One reason the *Times* was able to present radical ideas as historical gospel has to do with the way they were presented. True to *Times* form, The 1619 Project special issue was executed with a level of sophistication and style that is virtually impossible to find in any other American media outlet—and certainly not in another newspaper. From the photos to the contributor's stylized headshots to the quality of the writing and the eminence of the contributors, the issue was almost flawless. Almost.

◆ ◆ ◆

As virtually any media consumer or news industry observer could have predicted, The 1619 Project ignited a firestorm. After all, if this book has shown anything it's that the *Times* is no stranger to controversy. But this time something was different. While *Times* coverage often elicits strong responses from the right and the left, very rarely does it provoke outrage from both sides at the same time. Yet, that is exactly what happened with The 1619 Project as outlets as diverse as the conservative *National Review* to the arch-leftist World Socialist Web Site (WSWS) came out swinging. For all the conservative criticism of the project, it was the latter source—published by the self-described "leadership of the world socialist movement"—that put its finger on the most sensitive of The 1619 Project's many editorial pressure points.

The WSWS, which opposes what it calls a "racialist" reading of history, began interviewing preeminent American historians whose specialties include slavery, the American South, the Civil War and other topics relevant to the Project. This group of historians included Gordon Wood, a Pulitzer Prize-winning professor of American history who has taught as Harvard, Brown, and Cambridge; Victoria Bynum, Distinguished Professor Emeritus of History at Texas State University, who specializes in race relations in slavery-era South; James McPherson, another Pulitzer Prize-winner who was Jefferson Lecturer in the humanities at the National Endowment for the Humanities, and James Oakes, the Lincoln Prize-winning Distinguished Professor of History and Graduate School Humanities Professor at the Graduate Center of the City University of New York.

Each historian took issue with a major aspect of the claims and arguments made by The 1619 Project, each according to his or her own area of expertise. James Oakes objected strongly to the idea put forward in the issue by Matthew Desmond that slavery formed the basis of American wealth and therefore became the foundation of the United States economy. "Slavery made the slaveholders rich. But it made the South poor," Oakes told WSWS. "And it didn't make the North rich. The wealth of the North was based on the emerging, capitalist internal market that allowed the North to win the Civil War."[7] Victoria Bynum took issue with the Project's broad-stroke approach to the issue of slavery and race, arguing that the complexities of race relations concerning slavery in the South cannot be reduced to simple dichotomies, like the *Times*'s frequent claim that slavery was upheld by all whites and all whites benefited from it.[8] Gordon Wood, in his interview, countered that far from being motivated by slavery, the American Revolution had likely limited slavery to the South and possibly even served the trigger of forces that would eventually end slavery: "To somehow turn this around and make the Revolution a means of preserving slavery is strange and contrary to the evidence."[9] Finally, James McPherson, who characterized the Project as "a very unbalanced, one-sided account, which lacked context and perspective on the complexity of slavery," questioned (as did many of the other historians) the Project's oft-repeated claim that racism is somehow connected to America's "DNA."[10] He also took issue with specific claims, including the one made in the preamble to Hannah-Jones's lead essay, which asserts that regarding the "false" founding ideals of liberty and equality, "Black Americans fought to make [these ideals] true. Without this struggle, America would have no democracy at all."

Another preeminent American, Princeton professor of history Sean Wilentz, found problems with the Project's core claims, as well as many of its details. Wilentz, Bynum, Oakes, McPherson, and Wood co-authored and signed a letter to express their misgivings of the historical inaccuracies, mischaracterizations, and lack of proper context to many of the claims of the piece. The letter was sent to A.G. Sulzberger, the then-recently appointed publisher of the *Times* (and son of Arthur Ochs Sulzberger Jr.), and three top *Times* editors.[11] The authors of the letters wrote:

> We write as historians to express our strong reservations about important aspects of The 1619 Project...[We] applaud all efforts to address the enduring centrality of slavery and racism to our history...some of us have devoted our entire professional lives to those efforts, and all of us have worked hard to advance them...Nevertheless, we are dismayed at some of the factual errors in the project and the closed process behind it.

Both the tone and content of the historians' letter reveal their exasperation at the audacity of some of the claims made by The 1619 Project. The letter cited two specific instances of major claims they found not just unsupportable but possibly made in bad faith. The first is the Project's claim that the American Revolution was motivated by a desire to protect slavery, which the authors rejected out of hand as simply "not true." They note that "every statement offered by the project to validate [this claim] is false." They also noted that the Project's claim that Abraham Lincoln was essentially a racist in abolitionist clothes, made by Hannah-Jones in her essay, was "misleading" and ignored "his conviction that the Declaration of Independence proclaimed universal equality, for blacks as well as whites, a view he upheld repeatedly against powerful white supremacists who opposed him."

The letter's authors addressed a further claim that had emerged amid the controversy set off by The 1619 Project: that the Project presents nothing more than the views and opinions of the essayists who contributed to the issue. In reality, the historians wrote, the Project:

> ...is offered as an authoritative account that bears the imprimatur and credibility of the *New York Times*. Those connected with the project have assured the public that its materials were shaped by a panel of historians and have been scrupulously fact-checked. Yet the process remains opaque. The names of only some of the historians involved have been released, and the extent of their involvement as "consultants" and fact checkers remains vague. The selective transparency deepens our concern.

The historians signed off by asking that the *Times*, "according to its own high standards of accuracy and truth, issue prominent corrections of all the errors and distortions presented in The 1619 Project."

The historians' letter represents a devastating critique. When we consider that it comes from leading scholars of American history, all of whom expressed clear and enthusiastic support for the Project's intention of addressing head-on the consequences of slavery and ongoing racism in America, the letter takes on even greater significance. That significance—and the fact that the letter was written by eminent historians and published not in a conservative but a hard-left outlet—was not lost on the *Times*, which waited nearly three weeks to publish the damaging letter.

Given this, and knowing what we know about the *Times*'s own high standards (which the historians refer to in their letter), we have to ask how could a project so ambitious, so bold, and so fraught with editorial, not to mention political, implications risk getting it so wrong? Surely there would have been fact-checkers to ensure the kinds of fundamental historical errors the Project had been accused of making?

Surely the *Times* would have reached out to a broad swath of experts for comment, nearly all of whom would be willing to lend their expertise to the Gray Lady on an endeavor of this importance? With all this, we're left asking: what went wrong?

◆ ◆ ◆

In the three weeks between the historians' submission of their letter and its publication by the *Times*, the *Times Magazine*'s Editor-in-Chief Jake Silverstein penned a lengthy, 2,000-word response that, in the online edition of the newspaper, appeared directly below the original letter.[12] In his response, Silverstein pushed back against the historians, denying their request for a correction and after acknowledging that neither he nor other *Times* staffers are historians, went on to rebut some of the historians' arguments. Silverstein's response presented a mini-history lesson that spanned a few paragraphs to argue the claim, which Gordon Wood in his letter had called "astounding," that slavery was the motivating cause of the American Revolution. Silverstein also acknowledged that Hannah-Jones had not presented the full context about Lincoln's view of African-Americans on account of space limitations in the piece.

But it was earlier on in Silverstein's response that the editor touched on the essence of the Project. Silverstein wrote:

> The project was intended to address the marginalization of African-American history in the telling of our national story and examine the legacy of slavery in contemporary American life…In the case of the persistent racism and inequality that plague this country, the answer to that question led us inexorably into the past.

Side by side, these two sentences present a strange formulation of the Project's mission. The first sentence claims the Project intended to address the disproportionate role black Americans play in America's "national story." In other words, the *Times* wanted to look *back* in order to right historical wrongs. But the second sentence seems to contradict this. In that sentence, Silverstein wrote that it was the *Times*'s observation of persistent racism and inequality *of the present* which led them to examine the past.

Again, the *Times* took an approach to the Project that provoked more questions than it answered, namely, how could readers reconcile these two seemingly contradictory motivations behind the Project and why would an editor as sharp as Silverstein specify conflicting motivations in the first place?

A little less than twelve weeks after the historians' letter was published in the *Times*, on March 6, 2020, news site Politico ran an opinion piece related to the Project.[13] Unlike most of the other opinion pieces published in the media, which argued for one view or another, this one did not seek to convince readers of a certain ideological standpoint. Rather, it offered critical background information regarding the Project and the editorial processes that produced it. The Politico piece opened with a shocking admission by its author:

> On August 19 of last year I listened in stunned silence as Nikole Hannah-Jones, a reporter for the *New York Times*, repeated an idea that I had vigorously argued against with her fact-checker: that the patriots fought the American Revolution in large part to preserve slavery in North America.

In the following paragraphs, the author of the piece, Leslie M. Harris, identified herself as one of the expert historians the *Times* had consulted as part of their research for The 1619 Project. Harris, a Stanford-trained professor of American history and slavery-era South at Northwestern University, revealed that a *Times* research editor had sent her a number of statements from the Project to evaluate for historical accuracy. But the one statement that stood out made a staggering assertion that cut to the core of not just The 1619 Project, but virtually all of American history. The claim was:

> [A] critical reason that the colonists declared their independence from Britain was because they wanted to protect the institution of slavery in the colonies, which had produced tremendous wealth. At the time there were growing calls to abolish slavery throughout the British Empire, which would have badly damaged the economies of colonies in both North and South.

Harris "disputed the claim vigorously" and objected to the *Times*'s overall characterization of revolutionary-era slavery, which she asserted was more typical of the later antebellum era.

It is important to note that Harris takes serious issue with some of the five historians who wrote and signed the letter discussed above, in particular Wilentz and Wood, whose histories, she argued, "underrepresent the centrality of slavery and African Americans to America's history." Despite her scholarly and ideological differences with Wilentz, Wood, and the other historians who authored the letter to the *Times*, Harris similarly had voiced similarly "anxious" concerns about the radical and unsupported claim made by The 1619 Project. The *Times*, Harris wrote in Politico, published the claims about the American Revolution "anyway."

It could be argued that though these six historians—Wood, Oakes, Wilentz, Bynum, McPherson, and Harris—are distinguished, even field-defining experts, they are, after all, only six people. But it did not take long for that number to burgeon. On January 26, 2020, another letter was published objecting to the core claims of The 1619 Project, the *Times*'s "reframing" of American history in terms of slavery, and the major errors and mischaracterizations found throughout the Project.[14] This letter, published in George Washington University's History News Network, was signed by a dozen historians from institutions as regionally and intellectually diverse as Princeton, Yale, University of Notre Dame, Loyola University, University of Illinois, Springfield, Michigan State University, Western Kentucky, University of Delaware, Washington & Lee University, University of Alabama, Villanova University, and the Rochester Institute of Technology.

Noting that "It is not our purpose to question the significance of slavery in the American past," or to doubt the "scarred legacy of slavery," the authors and signatories of the second historians' letter went on to express their serious concerns about the Project's historical claims. The letter notes that the Project claims "every aspect of American life has only one lens for viewing, that of slavery." It reduced "history to metaphor," with essays like the one explaining traffic jams in America by tracing their supposed causes back to slavery. And it left the professional historians "dismayed" at the way "major issues and personalities of the Founding and Civil War eras" were presented. After noting the seriousness of these issues, including the *Times*'s evident failure to consult with—and accept the expert guidance of—a wide group of academic historians, the authors of the second historians' letter made a particularly dramatic demand: that the *Times* stop publishing and distributing materials from the Project until all the major issues connected with it had been addressed.

This request by academic historians from the country's leading universities and history departments is significant, if not completely unprecedented. Only under the most serious of circumstances would academics in a free and open society request the country's top newspaper stop distributing material related to an important topic. Furthermore, as we have seen throughout this book, the *Times* is no ordinary newspaper. Its reach, in terms of its influence and power, is unmatched. In publishing their letter and making this solemn request, the historians were going far out on a limb at the risk of their own reputations and academic security. The *Times* (to no one's surprise) did not cease to produce or distribute the Project. But more to the point, it also refused to publish the second historians' letter, which had been crafted and addressed to the newspaper as a Letter to the Editor.

According to academic experts on both sides of an ideological divide in the study of history, the *Times* had gotten both the details and the general thrust of their account completely wrong. One of its own consultants who had been called on to fact check for the Project objected "vigorously" to major claims made in some of the Project's key essays—and was ignored. Historians from universities around the country voiced not just concern but "dismay" at the extent to which the Project distorted and warped American history. Their letter went unpublished by the *Times*.

What we can glean from this is a willfulness on the part of the *Times* to make these claims and assertions *at all costs*. For the paper, historical truth—the accuracy of facts, events, cause-and-effect extrapolation, raw data, and, most importantly, context—was not at stake. This is what explains Silverstein's strangely paradoxical comment in his response to the original historians' letter that on the one hand, the Project "was intended to address the marginalization of African-American history" and on the other hand, its aim was to answer the question of "persistent racism and inequality" in present-day America by tracing it to the past. The deeper intention of the *Times* in pursuing The 1619 Project was not to find the truth *but to create it*. It was to prove the present-day thesis that racism is systemic and that it touches on every element and aspect of American life by attempting to prove that America's very history is one of thoroughgoing racism. This is what explains the Project's continued reliance on the concept of a national and historical "DNA." Over and over, the Project stated that America's DNA is racist. "Anti-black racism runs in the very DNA of this country," Hannah-Jones wrote in her essay. Matthew Desmond offered a quote from historians Sven Beckert and Seth Rockman, who wrote, "American slavery is necessarily imprinted on the DNA of American capitalism." Contributor Khalil Gibran Muhammad quotes a black farmer who says, "To this day we are harassed, retaliated against and denied the true DNA of our past."[15] The notion that history or a country has DNA is one that many of the letter-writing historians found puzzling—even concerning. As a metaphor, it might make sense, indicating that a quality or trait is part and parcel of something else. But in an account of a national history, the idea that an institution as complex, varied, and changing as slavery can, with genetic efficiency, be a determining factor in the entire unfolding of a country is bizarre. On closer inspection, the claim is virtually incomprehensible—until we do what the authors and creators of The 1619 Project were widely accused of failing to do and consider the broader context.

◆ ◆ ◆

On July 14, 2020, the *New York Times* ran an article reporting one of its own editors had resigned.[16] This was an extremely unusual occurrence, as rarely does the *Times* report on staffing changes within its own ranks, news it instead releases in corporate statements or announcements. But this was different. The editor, Bari Weiss, had become a *bête noire* in America's rising hard-left social justice movement by thrusting her editorial hand onto a number of political and cultural third rails. She broke taboos about feminism, gender, the Israel-Palestine conflict, and "cancel culture," and each time she did it, animus against her from the far left intensified.

In truth, the vast majority of the opinion pieces Weiss penned were innocuous, if interesting, intelligent, and relevant. They included politically down-the-middle pieces, like one criticizing Donald Trump's use of the world "disloyal" to describe certain Jewish Americans;[17] alarming trends related to the rise of global anti-Semitism;[18] an exploration of how coronavirus affected American cultural debates;[19] an enthusiastic look at former Democratic presidential contender Andrew Yang,[20] and similar articles. While Weiss had been "hired as part of the paper's effort to broaden the ideological range of its opinion staff after President Trump's inauguration," according to the *Times* article on her resignation,[21] she was hardly a flag-waving, MAGA hat-wearing right-wing firebrand. Far from it.

When Weiss resigned from the *Times*, it was not, by her own account, because she had better opportunities to pursue or wanted to explore new career options. Rather, in a 1,500-word resignation letter, Weiss described an "illiberal work environment" where terms like "unlawful discrimination, hostile work environment, and constructive discharge" could apply. Weiss detailed various forms of abuse she suffered as a *Times* staffer, including derogatory comments about the subjects of her writing (that she was "writing about the Jews again"), being "openly demeaned" on internal communications channels like Slack, and being called a "liar and a bigot" by other *Times* employees on public forums, like Twitter. "I do not understand how you have allowed this kind of behavior to go on inside your company in full view of the paper's entire staff and the public," Weiss wrote, addressing A.G. Sulzberger, the paper's publisher. Weiss went on to say that she wished her case was unique, "But the truth is that intellectual curiosity—let alone risk-taking—is now a liability at the *Times*."

Exactly one week prior to news breaking about Weiss's departure, the *Times* announced another high-profile resignation. On July 7, 2020, the *Times* ran a news article reporting that James Bennet, then editor of the paper's Editorial Page, had resigned.[22] In this case, however, the resignation seems to have been more of a corporate euphemism for a firing. The article, written by media reporter Marc Tracy, quoted A.G. Sulzberger, who explained the reason for the resignation by noting, "Last week, we saw a significant breakdown in our editing processes, not the first we've experienced in recent years." The breakdown Sulzberger was referring to was the publication of a June 3 op-ed by United States Senator Tom Cotton, in which Cotton argued that the government should send the military to disperse protests that had erupted around the country in the wake of the killing of a black man named George Floyd.[23] The op-ed ignited an intense controversy, not only—or even principally—concerning Cotton's argument but more related to the *Times*'s decision to publish it. Responding to growing criticism, Bennet responded the next day on Twitter with an explanation regarding his decision to publish the op-ed.

> I want to explain why we published the piece today by Senator Tom Cotton…*Times* Opinion owes it to our readers to show them counter-arguments, particularly those made by people in a position to set policy… We understand that many readers find Senator Cotton's argument painful, even dangerous. We believe that is one reason it requires public scrutiny and debate *(@JBennet, June 4, 2020).*

This seems like a sound argument, especially coming from the opinion editor of a newspaper. A serious issue rising to the forefront of national politics should be discussed, especially when one of the sources of the idea is a powerful United States senator. But this was not the approach the debate surrounding Cotton's *Times* op-ed would take.

While there was public controversy surrounding the op-ed, the real pushback came from within the *Times*, where 800 staffers signed a letter of protest addressed to the paper's management. Three hundred non-editorial staffers staged a "virtual walkout" by not showing up to work as a form of boycott. A *Times* staffer told *Vanity Fair*, "I've not experienced a backlash like this before, internally or externally."[24]

The paroxysm of rage and fear prompted by the op-ed led the *Times*'s top editors to convene an all-hands town hall meeting, where publisher Sulzberger walked back his previous defense of the piece, saying, "It should not have been published."[25] The piece was pulled from running in the *Times*'s print edition, and a lengthy editor's note was added to the digital version explaining the piece "fell short of our standards."

One of the main places this backlash unfolded was on Twitter, where dozens of *Times* staffers tweeted an identical statement: "Running this puts Black @NYTimes staff in danger." *Times* reporters, editors and other staffers tweeted the phrase over and over.[26] But pausing to consider the language of the tweet reveals it to be a strange formulation. While the case could be argued that Cotton's call to send military forces to break up the protests would put black lives *in general* in danger, it is hard to understand why running the op-ed specifically put black *New York Times* staffers in danger. Were black *Times* staffers attending protests at a disproportionate rate to black people who did not work at the *Times*? Did staffers fear that, as the result of a single op-ed, military riot police would line up at the banks of elevators at the *Times*'s skyscraper on Eighth Avenue and, going floor by floor, search for the paper's black staff members and act violently with them? Obviously, they did not.

The answer to this linguistic conundrum rests on the specialized jargon of the social justice movement, including two of its key definitions, those of the word "danger" and "safety." For years, the United States and the Western world has heard the term "safe space" being widely used, particularly in academic and campus settings. Safe spaces have become battlegrounds where ideological skirmishes are fought over who is permitted to enter the safe space, who is not, and why. A good example of this is the 2019 controversy that erupted over the presence of a statue of a Confederate soldier, "Silent Sam," on the campus of the University of North Carolina at Chapel Hill. When the then-chancellor of the university decided to have the statue removed, she explained it by saying that "The presence of the remaining parts of the monument on campus poses a continuing threat both to the personal safety and well-being of our community and to our ability to provide a stable, productive educational environment...No one learns at their best when they feel unsafe."[27] No one, not even the wary chancellor, feared that a statue would somehow spring to life and cause physical harm to the students. That is clear. But it was not the students' *physical* safety that was at stake.

The concept of non-physical safety and danger emerged out of an academic movement called critical theory. The roots of critical theory lie in an approach developed by a group of Marxist social theorists in 1930s known as the Frankfurt School, who held that a "'critical theory' may be distinguished from a 'traditional' theory according to a specific practical purpose: a theory is critical to the extent that it seeks human 'emancipation from slavery,' acts as a 'liberating...influence,' and works 'to create a world which satisfies the needs and powers' of human beings."[28]

The job of critical theory was to look at the power structures that lie beneath *any* theory and how those theories work to oppress others. A critical theory thus became one that did not aim first and foremost at finding "truth"—something critical theory holds is *produced* according to the needs of a power structure—but, instead, at effecting social change. "Because such theories aim to explain and transform *all* the circumstances that enslave human beings," this applies equally to any theory, whether it pertains to gravity, mathematics, biology, literature, culture, chemistry, physics, art, psychology, or any other field of study. It is not the subject matter that is important. What is important is a theory's ability to "explain what is wrong with current social reality, identify the actors to change it, and provide both clear norms for criticism and achievable practical goals for *social transformation*" (author's emphasis).

Academics and activists took up the mantle of critical theory by applying it to specialized areas of study, including the LGBTQ and women's rights movements, for whom it became a core ideological framework. Out of this shift rose the notion of a safe space. Moira Kenney explains in her book, *Mapping Gay L.A.*, that the term "safe space" was born in reference to gay bars in the 1960s, when being openly gay, especially in public places, was not an option. Gay bars became a place where gay people could feel safe.[29]

What is crucial to note is that the bars did not provide physical or legal safety. Quite the opposite was true, since these bars were frequently raided by police, who often did not hesitate to use violence as they sought to enforce anti-sodomy laws. In that sense, staying home would have been the safe option. What bars and other safe spaces could provide was *ideological* safety. "As developed in the context of the women's movement, the notion of safe space implies a certain license to speak and act freely, form collective strength, and generate strategies for resistance," Kenney wrote.

The idea here is that safety, in the context of critical theory and the social justice movement that sprang from it, is a matter of being free from ideological constraint, conflict, or challenge so the group in question can plan, strategize, and take action to fight oppression. Key to this is the idea that those sheltering in safe spaces constitute a group of ideological fellow travelers. While they may harbor internal debates or dissent about finer aspects of their theory, on the whole, they are in agreement about the major points of the theory and what it means for the world around them. And they are safe because the ideas they hold sacrosanct cannot be challenged in that space.

This is what the *Times* staffers meant when they claimed, in unison, that the *Times*'s decision to run the Cotton op-ed posed a danger to black *Times* staffers. The piece threatened not the *Times* staffers' physical well-being but their ability to be in a workplace where their most fundamental ideological assumptions were not up for debate. And this was precisely the charge Bari Weiss leveled when she resigned from the *Times,* where, she claimed, "If a person's ideology is in keeping with the new orthodoxy, they and their work remain unscrutinized. Everyone else lives in fear of the digital thunderdome."

But the Cotton op-ed did more than just challenge ideological assumptions at the *Times*. Plenty of op-eds do that, often with the *Times*'s own emphasis on how important it is to present readers with ideas that differ drastically from their own. When Bennet decided, some five months before, to publish an op-ed by a representative of one of the world's most gruesome and deadly Islamist terror groups, the Taliban, there was no such backlash. The *Times*'s own publisher made this very point in initially defending the decision to run the Cotton op-ed, writing in an email to staff, "I believe in the principle of openness to a range of opinions, even those we may disagree with, and this piece was published in that spirit." But outrage on an unprecedented level had to be about more than a disagreement of ideas and opinions. And it *was* about more than that—much more. What crossed the red line was a southern senator whose surname is the very product that sits at the center of one of the central arguments of The 1619 Project—that America was built on a cotton economy fueled by slave labor—demanding what critical theorists would call the instruments of state power (the military and police) break up black protests. The metaphor could only be too clear, and too striking: a white enslaver was readying a posse to lynch enslaved black people for daring to protest their enslavement, and the *Times* had willfully served as the scaffold.

Not by coincidence, Nikole Hannah-Jones was among the first to register her outrage, tweeting on June 4, "as a black woman, as a journalist, as an American," she was "deeply ashamed" the *Times* ran the piece. That Senator Cotton is a distinguished graduate of Harvard and Harvard Law School (hardly bastions of racist ideology) who clerked for a federal court judge before serving in Iraq and Afghanistan (which, according to the *Times*'s post-war reporting, would make him more likely to be homicidal or otherwise "predatory") was immaterial. It was the metaphor that mattered most.

◆ ◆ ◆

In religious practice and worship, there is a concept that is directly equivalent to the social justice movement's idea of a safe space, and that is "the sacred." In a sacred space, rules are emplaced to prevent outsiders from profaning the space with foreign practices or alien ideas. As guardians of the sacred, true believers will go to any lengths to protect the sacredness of that space, since open violation of that space amounts to the religion's fundamental tenets being not just questioned but contradicted.

In the case of the *New York Times*, it was not merely the publication of a countervailing view that sent the *Times* staff into open revolt. It was that a safe space had been violated, and (for them) in the most egregious way. And this points to the deeper ideological foundations from which an endeavor like The 1619 Project could spring. In religious terms, a sacred ideal seemed to have not just emerged at but taken hold of the *Times*. And, indeed, leading commentators have begun to identify that one common thread among the different approaches to critical theory is their strongly religious aspect. Columbia University professor John McWhorter pointed out this trend in the area of what is now known as anti-racism. "Anti-racism as currently configured has gone a long way from what used to be considered intelligent and sincere civil rights activism. Today, it's a religion. And I don't mean that as a rhetorical feint, I mean that it actually is what any naive anthropologist would recognize as a faith."[30]

McWhorter details that the social justice movement's now popular idea that "responsible" white people must acknowledge their racism is equivalent to biblical notions of original sin. Similarly, the idea that America will one day "come to terms" with its racist history "corresponds to Judgment Day." When we use the word "problematic"—a key term in critical theory that identifies wrong thinking—it is actually the word "blasphemous" that's being hurled. McWhorter also notes that, like in religious belief, in the realm of critical theory, "there's an extent to which logic is no longer to apply." In this, McWhorter puts his finger on the heart of the matter. As we have seen, for adherents to critical theory, truth is not the aim. In fact, for these believers, there is no such thing as truth as it has been understood by Western culture for thousands of years. The "traditional" theories against which critical theory defines itself all have one thing in common: they exist in order to best approximate (or come closest to) objective truth. They may have recognized that pure, perfect truth is a human impossibility, but these theories are based in the idea that real, objective, knowable reality is the ultimate aim.

In science and public life (including politics and governance), this approach was developed over the course of the Enlightenment. Emerging from a long era where truth was defined by religious dogma, Enlightenment thinkers turned to reason as the compass that would guide them along a clear path of truth through the desert of falsehood. Critical theory rejects this objective conception of truth out of hand. As McWhorter points out, critical theory considers logic, reason's most fundamental tool, to be a social construct that serves power.

According to this line of thinking, the system of logic that deduces seemingly self-evident concepts like 2 + 2 = 4 is only true because power structures have enforced its truth. The *real* reality, critical theorists claim, is that 2 + 2 = 4 is not necessarily any more true than the statement 2 + 2 = 5. While this might seem like an exaggeration, this kind of thinking is very much central to critical theory, which holds that all our assumptions must not only be questioned, but deconstructed. The claim that 2 + 2 = 4 is just as suspect to critical theorists as the claim that the American Revolution was rooted in a pursuit of liberty. The disturbing part of this trend is that it is no longer confined to the halls of academic institutions, where esoteric theories play out every day, often with the assumptions that they are simply being proposed and tested.

In reality, critical theory has become so widespread in areas of American culture that the truth of the mathematical statement, 2 + 2 = 4, erupted into a social media controversy, with dozens of people using the hashtag #takebackmath to challenge the validity of basic mathematical propositions as "Western" and attempting to prove (though not by mathematical means) the opposite, that 2 + 2 = 5.

Mathematician James Lindsay, who has written extensively on critical theory, poked fun at this idea with an ironic Twitter meme, which was part of his humorous series, "Woke Minis," a tongue-in-cheek guide to woke culture for kids. In one of his Woke Minis cards, Lindsay wrote: "2 + 2 = 4: A perspective in white, Western mathematics that marginalizes other possible values." (@ConceptualJames, June 11, 2020).

While Lindsay's Woke Minis were designed to show the absurdity of claims like the ones above, proponents of the critical theory Lindsay was critiquing responded in force. True to John McWhorter's description of critical theory adherents as members of a religious sect, they were outraged that Lindsay would ridicule the idea of questioning arithmetical statements like 2 + 2 = 4, which (as we all know) is commonly used as shorthand to exemplify basic, unquestionable truth.

Most prominent among the people pushing back against Lindsay's meme was none other than Nikole Hannah-Jones, who tweeted, "Using Arabic numerals to try make a point about white, Western superiority is just so damn classic." (@nhannahjones, July 5, 2020). Hannah-Jones's tweet (which was later deleted) packaged into its assumption the idea that "white, Western superiority" is not only real but everywhere, including in math and, just as much, in tweets about math. But Hannah-Jones's almost reflexive decision to jump into the debate speaks to an idea that is essential to The 1619 Project itself. For Hannah-Jones and others crusading against 2 + 2 = 4, the objective accuracy of the mathematical statements was far less relevant than uncovering the cultural values used to assert it. What matters is questioning and dislodging the entrenched cultural and social values that govern existing theories, in this case, values of "white, Western superiority."

These were the intellectual foundations on which The 1619 Project was built. The historical accuracy of the Project's major claims were not nearly as important as the political goal the Project's creators were attempting to achieve. The Project was not about discovering truth or objective fact but *creating* a new narrative, a new truth, which, by challenging the power structures that govern American life, would be more valid than the ones that came before it. This is something Hannah-Jones, as the Project's creator, never tried to obscure. On the contrary, she touted it at every possible turn. In a Twitter thread with journalist Wesley Yang and political historian Phillip Magness in which the three were arguing over some of the historical issues concerning the Project (including some of James McPherson's criticisms, which we've seen above), Hannah-Jones offered a telling response (also subsequently deleted): "My point...is that there is no such thing as objective history so complaints that the 1619 is an illegitimate reframing of history deny that all history is framed." (@nhannahjones, November 21, 2019).

The idea that there is no objective truth to history, only competing interests vying for power, was a point Hannah-Jones would elaborate upon numerous times, and in many ways. On July 27, 2020, Hannah-Jones tweeted (and, again, deleted):

> The fight here is about who gets to control the national narrative, and therefore, the nation's shared memory of itself. One group has monop-olized this for too long in order to create this myth of exceptionalism. If

their version is true, what do they have to fear of 1619? *(@nhannahjones, July 27, 2020).*

The point Hannah-Jones was making is clear: the Project was not about historical truth—it could not be, since, in her view, there is no such thing—but about asserting political and social power by determining the "narrative" of America's history. It is this approach to history as a tool for political gain that explains not only the serious historical gaps and missteps of The 1619 Project and the *Times*'s unwillingness (or inability) to correct them but the entirety of the Project itself. It was not a search for truth but a subtle, self-aware, and very effective form of ideological activism. This answers one of the major unasked questions about the Project: Why was a newspaper producing history at all? The reason is that the Project was never about history. History was only a means to a broader end. As Hannah-Jones clarified in yet another tweet:

> I've always said that the 1619 Project is not a history. It is a work of journalism that explicitly seeks to challenge the national narrative and, therefore, the national memory. The project has always been as much about the present as it is the past. *(@nhannahjones, July 27, 2020).*

This also explains why the *Times* would extend past the boundaries of its own pages (print and otherwise) to develop educational materials, curricula, and other activities meant not to inform but influence. The point of the Project was not to produce a work that could illuminate dark areas of the past since its goal was expressly to change the course of the present, and thereby, the coming future.

The trouble with this approach to history is that it's not journalism either—it's activism. Although Hannah-Jones ran for cover by claiming transparency (by saying the Project's aims were all out in the open) when she came under intense intellectual fire from all sides, in reality The 1619 Project's magazine issue never offered an editorial disclaimer explaining that the ideas it passionately presented with unwavering conviction merely constitute one narrative among many. The issue offered no primer on critical theory, explaining it as one approach among many and advising the reader to be aware of this. Instead, those ideas were presented as absolute, concrete truth. The very cover of The 1619 Project's launch magazine proclaimed: "It's time to tell our story *truthfully*" (author's emphasis). But when we pause to consider it, this makes perfect sense. For the Project to succeed on its own terms—replacing the traditional understanding of American history with a new history—its main claims would have to be presented as historical fact, not an option, an opinion, or mere speculation.

But too often, that is exactly what those ideas were. While Hannah-Jones and other members of the *Times* staff, including Silverstein, readily admitted they were journalists and not historians, what they attempted to produce is, without doubt, a history. But unlike scholars of history who fight to prove the merit of their ideas in an academic arena where established principles and standards guide the development of historical ideas, the *Times* bypassed that critical step that helps filter errors, fill gaps, and engage in debate. Instead, America's most powerful news outlet leaned on its heft and reach to bring this new, unvetted and admittedly flawed history directly into an environment where its impact will be most felt: America's schools.

There is no doubt that the *Times* is well within its rights in doing so. It is a private company, not an official institution, and it can make whatever decisions serve its audience, who are its customers. The problem is that this approach to history leads us down a dangerous path, one from which it can be difficult, sometimes impossible, to return.

◆ ◆ ◆

As the nation's most prestigious and beloved news outlet, a "great, great American jewel" as even a detractor like Donald Trump put it,[31] the *Times* plays an outsized role in the ideas that govern the nation. In the 1930s, critical theory discovered a novel intellectual tool—questioning the power structures they claim gird all our assumptions and understandings of the world around us. From how a plant sprouts and seeds to the way a planet orbits a sun to the psychological structures that make up the human mind, and—of course—the flow of history in time, critical theory could call everything into doubt. But unlike the Enlightenment skepticism that fueled the creation of new frontiers of scientific inquiry, always asking why, how, and what, critical theory supplies its own answer: it is this way because people are being oppressed, and the current theory serves the oppressors.

The 1619 Project slots neatly into this framework. Few people in America, and even fewer around the world, have the privilege of an academic education rooted in a critical theory framework. For them, the highly tinted lens through which critical theory sees the world looks transparent, or as if it is not there at all. And this was, indeed, the goal. But—and this "but" is where the danger lurks—the swirling cultural energies of a given time and place, its zeitgeist, absorb ideas as potent as this one. No matter who we are, we see this new tool which is able to hammer out new "narratives" and novel "truths" based on personal preference and group interest, and we too want to pick it up and wield it to our benefit. After all, why should the other side get all the power?

This is where this approach becomes toxic. Only an information outlet with the experience and savvy of a century, like the *Times* (and, maybe, only the *Times* itself), could produce an initiative at the level of The 1619 Project. But all that means is that other self-serving, truth-questioning endeavors will meet a lower standard of production. The trend will be— and already is—a downward spiral as the moral and intellectual ease of declaring "This is *my* truth and these facts are *my* facts" becomes amplified. From a claim about "alternative facts" regarding crowd attendance at President Trump's inauguration to celebrities tweeting anti-Semitic messages based on "my truth," the ideology that holds truth is a substance to be molded to purpose is becoming dominant with frightening speed.

Conclusion

The *New York Times* was built with a very different standard in mind than the one embraced by the creators of The 1619 Project, who look at truth as a malleable substance, a "construct," in the terminology of critical theory. Adolph Ochs, founder of the *Times* dynasty that has owned and operated the paper for more than a century, boldly stated that the *Times*'s mission is "to give the news impartially, without fear or favor, regardless of party, sect or interests involved."[1] We've seen in this book that the *Times* failed in this regard—drastically and often tragically. Again and again, "party, sect or interests" were put above impartiality. These interests had direct influence over the *Times*'s most crucial reporting, whether it was a Nazi collaborator serving as the paper's Berlin bureau chief at the most sensitive moment in modern history, a communist propagandist helping to midwife American recognition of the Soviet Union, the creation of a jihadist boy-martyr almost out of thin air, the cover-up of radiation sickness resulting from the use of nuclear weapons, the overthrow of the war-time government in Vietnam, or, most disturbingly, the decision by the owners of the *Times* to wipe the Jews off the pages of their newspaper at the same time as the Nazis were attempting to wipe them off the face of the earth.

When it comes to criticism regarding the *New York Times*, we are often told that every news outlet makes these kinds of missteps and mistakes. Only (this argument goes) in the *Times*'s case, the spotlight is more intense so the shadows cast by these errors are longer. But as we've seen from reporting at the same times and places as the *Times*'s most egregious cases of misreporting, fabrication and distortion, this is not true. While Guido Enderis and Otto Tolischus were reporting favorably on Germany on the eve of the Second World War, almost trumpeting events that constituted great Nazi accomplishments, William Shirer was decrying those same events. While Walter Duranty was carrying water for the Soviet regime and bowing for the standing ovation he received for his efforts, Gareth Jones was doggedly reporting the truth—and was later murdered, likely by the Soviet secret police, on account of it. William Laurence worked hand in hand with the War Department to spin a tale about the benign effects of the Atomic bomb on the human body while reporters George Weller and Wilfred Burchett, reporting from Japan in the aftermath of the bomb, described an "atomic plague." Otto Tolischus, Walter Duranty, and William Laurence received Pulitzers for their reporting; the other report-ers—those who reported with accuracy, honesty and courage—did not.

The unavoidable reality is that *Times* was, and still is, different. It is considered a cut above, the pinnacle of journalism not just in the US but around the world. This is what makes it great. But great institutions, like great individuals, are prone to great failings. Maybe we can chalk up these major failings, which had an indelible impact on history's unfolding, to the phenomenon that being great means being alone, which leads us to error since there is no one there to check our mistakes or balance our thinking. And that may be the case. But if there is one overriding aim of this book it is not just to call attention to errors like the ones mentioned above but also, and more importantly, to show that our most seemingly infallible institutions are often prone to error. It is to imprint on our consciousness that we have to question not just our sources (since it is difficult to find a more sterling source than the *New York Times*), but also the content of their reporting. As critical theory would hold, it is incumbent on us to understand how interest and power affect the flow of information. But, very much *un*like critical theory, we have to search for a more objectively true account. We cannot assert in place of a flawed history an ever more flawed one that happens to advance our interests. Our history is shared and our humanity is shared with it. To believe that the truth is "mine" is to believe it does not exist. But it does. And this is where each of us bears a responsibility that grows more important every day. Just as we have a responsibility to safeguard our environment, our neighborhoods, and our communities, we have a responsibility to safeguard truth and history so they will be shared resources for generations to come, and not the purview of a small subset of special interests looking to make far too much of the present.

Notes

Introduction

1   "The Momentous Day," *New York Times*, November 8, 1864, 4, https://www.nytimes.com/1864/11/08/archives/the-momentous-day.html.

2   "The Momentous Day," 4.

3   William Shirer, *The Rise and Fall of the Third Reich* (New York: Simon and Schuster, 1990), 595.

4   Otto D. Tolischus, "Hitler Gives Word," *New York Times*, September 1, 1939, 1, https://www.nytimes.com/1939/09/01/archives/hitler-gives-word-in-a-proclamation-he-accuses-warsaw-of-appeal-to.html.

5   Abraham Lincoln, *Second Inaugural Address of the Late President Lincoln* (New York: James Miller, 1865), https://www.loc.gov/item/scsm000283/.

6   David W. Dunlap, "1896: 'Without Fear or Favor'," *New York Times*, August 14, 2015, https://www.nytimes.com/2015/09/12/insider/1896-without-fear-or-favor.html.

Chapter 1

1   "Hitler Tamed by Prison," *New York Times*, December 21, 1924.

2   Cyril Brown, "New Popular Idol Rises in Bavaria," *New York Times*, November 20, 1922.

3   Tolischus, "Hitler Gives Word."

4   "Otto D. Tolischus of the New York Times," The Pulitzer Prizes, accessed February 17, 2021, https://www.pulitzer.org/winners/otto-d-tolischus.

5   Elizabeth Glaser-Schmidt, "Between Hope and Skepticism," in *Transatlantic Images and Perceptions: Germany and America since 1776,* ed. David Barclay (Cambridge: Cambridge University Press, 1997), 211.

6   Glaser-Schmidt, "Between Hope and Skepticism," 211.

7   Christopher Ailsby, *The Third Reich Day by Day* (St Paul, MN: MBI Publishing, 2005), 112.

8   Charles Higham, *Trading with the Enemy: An Exposé of The Nazi–American Money Plot 1933-1949* (London: Hale, 1983).

9   William Shirer, *Berlin Diary* (Baltimore: Johns Hopkins Press, 2001).

10   William Stephenson, *A Man Called Intrepid* (New York: Ballantine Books, 1978).

11   "Woes of Austria Laid to Anschluss," *New York Times,* July 26, 1934, 5, https://www.nytimes.com/1934/07/26/archives/woes-of-austria-laid-to-anschluss-third-reichs-desire-for-unity-led.html.

12   David Clay Large, "The Nazi Olympics: Berlin 1936," in *The Palgrave Handbook of Olympic Studies,* eds. Helen Jefferson Lenskyj and Stephen Wagg (London: Palgrave Macmillan, 2012), 60-71. https://doi.org/10.1057/9780230367463_5.

13   "The Man behind Hitler: The 1936 Olympics," American Experience, accessed December 20, 2020, https://www.pbs.org/wgbh/americanexperience/features/goebbels-olympics.

14   "The Movement to Boycott the Berlin Olympics of 1936," United States Holocaust Museum, accessed December 20, 2020, https://encyclopedia.ushmm.org/content/en/article/the-movement-to-boycott-the-berlin-olympics-of-1936.

15   John Rodden and John P. Rossi, "Berlin Stories: Misreading the 1936 Olympics," *Commonweal,* August 3, 2016, https://www.commonwealmagazine.org/berlin-stories.

16   "Anti-Jewish Incitement and Riots in the Summer of 1935," Shoah Resource Center, Yad Vashem, accessed December 20, 2020, http://www1.yadvashem.org/odot_pdf/Microsoft%20Word%20-%203826.pdf.

17   Frederick T. Birchall, "Berlin Riots Mar Olympic Planning," *New York Times,* July 26, 1935, 1, https://www.nytimes.com/1935/07/26/archives/berlin-riots-mar-olympic-planning-assaults-on-jews-in-midst-of.html.

18   "Nazi Olympics, Berlin 1936: Exclusion of Jews," *United States Holocaust Museum,* accessed December 20, 2020, https://www.ushmm.org/exhibition/olympics/?content=exclusion_jews.

19   Arthur J. Daley, "Summer Olympics, Greatest Athletic Show in History," *New York Times,* December 27, 1936, 3, https://www.nytimes.com/1936/12/27/archives/summer-olympics-greatest-athletic-show-in-history-witnessed-by.html.

20   Clarence Lusane, *Hitler's Black Victims* (New York: Routledge, 2002), 225.

21 Haley Bracken. "Was Jesse Owens Snubbed by Adolf Hitler at the Berlin Olympics?" In *Encyclopaedia Britannica,* accessed December 20, 2020, https://www.britannica.com/story/was-jesse-owens-snubbed-by-adolf-hitler-at-the-berlin-olympics.

22 "The Nazi Olympics," Jewish Virtual Library, accessed December 20, 2020, http://www.jewishvirtuallibrary.org/jsource/Holocaust/olympics.html.

23 Terence Henry, "Olympic Highs and Lows," *Washington Post,* August 8, 2008, https://www.washingtonpost.com/wp-dyn/content/article/2008/08/07/AR2008080702180_pf.html.

24 Guido Enderis, "Berlin Is Relieved," *New York Times,* September 29, 1938, 1, https://www.nytimes.com/1938/09/29/archives/berlin-is-relieved-hopes-talks-on-czechs-may-lead-to-wider-european.html.

25 Shirer, William, *"This Is Berlin": Radio Broadcasts From Nazi Germany* (New York: Rosetta Books, 2014)

26 "Was Neville Chamberlain Really a Weak and Terrible Leader?" BBC News, accessed February 17, 2021, https://www.bbc.com/news/magazine-24300094.

27 "Nazi Demands Met," *New York Times,* September 30, 1938, 1, https://www.nytimes.com/1938/09/30/archives/nazi-demands-met-hitler-gets-almost-all-he-asked-as-munich.html.

28 Laurel Leff, *Buried by The Times: The Holocaust and America's Most Important Newspaper* (Cambridge: Cambridge University Press, 2005). doi:10.1017/CBO9781107050914.

29 Leff, *Buried by The Times,* 66.

30 Leff, *Buried by The Times,* 67.

31 Guido Enderis, "Group Formed by Papen," *New York Times,* January 31, 1933, 1, https://www.nytimes.com/1933/01/31/archives/group-formed-by-papen-nationalists-to-dominate-in-government-led-by.html.

32 Lynn Grove, "The American Internee Experience in Nazi Germany," Traces, accessed December 20, 2020, https://usgerrelations.traces.org/americaninternees.html

33 Grove, "American Internee Experience."

34 "Nazis Give Chateau to U.S. Prisoners," *New York Times,* December 15, 1941, 6, https://www.nytimes.com/1941/12/15/archives/nazis-give-chateau-to-us-prisoners-exchange-of-journalists-and.html.

35 Shirer, *The Rise and Fall of the Third Reich,* 897.

Chapter 2

1   Walter Duranty, "Russians Hungry, But Not Starving," *New York Times*, March 31, 1933, 13, https://www.nytimes.com/1933/03/31/archives/russians-hungry-but-not-starving-deaths-from-diseases-due-to.html.

2   *Oleh Wolowyna*, "Understanding Holodomor Loss Numbers," HREC Education, accessed December 20, 2020, https://education.holodomor.ca/understanding-holodomor-loss-numbers.

3   Georg Von Rauch, *A History of Soviet Russia* (New York: Frederick Praeger, 1957), 182.

4   Von Rauch, *History of Soviet Russia*, 182.

5   Von Rauch, *History of Soviet Russia*, 182.

6   Duranty, "Russians Hungry, But Not Starving."

7   Gareth Jones, "Famine Grips Russia Millions Dying, Idle on Rise, Says Briton," *Evening Post*, March 29, 1933, https://www.garethjones.org/soviet_articles/millions_dying.htm.

8   Duranty, "Russians Hungry, But Not Starving."

9   Roy A. Medvedev, *Let History Judge* (New York: Alfred A. Knopf, 1971), 95.

10   Medvedev, *Let History Judge*, 95.

11   "Duranty Predicts a Major War Soon," *New York Times*, June 7, 1934, 7, https://www.nytimes.com/1934/06/07/archives/duranty-predicts-a-major-war-soon-four-or-five-powder-magazines-in.html.

12   Jacques Steinberg, "Times Should Lose Pulitzer from 30's, Consultant Says," *New York Times*, October 23, 2003, 29, https://www.nytimes.com/2003/10/23/us/times-should-lose-pulitzer-from-30-s-consultant-says.html.

13   Barbara A. Anderson and Brian D. Silver, "Growth and Diversity of the Population of the Soviet Union," *Annals of the American Academy of Political and Social Sciences* 510 (1990): 155-177.

14   Walter Duranty, "New Zeppelin Raid on Paris Fails; 24 Dead, 30 Injured in Saturday's Raid; Majority are Women and Children," *New York Times*, January 31, 1916.

15   "Musical Play Gets the Pulitzer Award; Mrs. Buck, Pershing, Duranty Honored," *New York Times*, May 3, 1932, 1, https://www.nytimes.com/1932/05/03/archives/musical-play-gets-the-pulitzer-award-mrs-buck-pershing-duranty.html.

16   "Duranty Talks of Job," *New York Times*, April 17, 1936, 13, https://www.nytimes.com/1936/04/17/archives/duranty-talks-of-job-tells-foreign-correspondents-here-how-they.html.

17   "Walter Duranty Here," *New York Times*, May 9, 1934, 17, https://www.nytimes.com/1934/05/09/archives/walter-duranty-here-correspondent-reports-improved-conditions-in.html.

18 Medvedev, *Let History Judge,* 95.

19 Steinberg, "Times Should Lose Pulitzer from 30's."

20 Steinberg, "Times Should Lose Pulitzer from 30's."

21 Steinberg, "Times Should Lose Pulitzer from 30's."

22 Mikhail Heller and Aleksandr Nekrich, *Utopia in Power* (London: Hutchinson, 1986), 256.

23 Heller and Nekrich, *Utopia in Power,* 257.

24 "Shaw Praises Russia in Lecture in London," *New York Times,* November 27, 1931, 27, https://www.nytimes.com/1931/11/27/archives/shaw-praises-russia-in-lecture-in-london-soviet-communism-he.html.

25 Heller and Nekrich, *Utopia in Power,* 257.

26 Helmut Gruber, "Willi Münzenberg's German Communist Propaganda Empire 1921-1933," *The Journal of Modern History* 38, no. 3 (1966): 278.

27 Stephen Koch, "Lying for the Truth: Münzenberg and the Comintern," *The New Criterion* 12 (1993).

28 Ella Winter, "Soviet 'Shock Troops' Speed Up Industry," *New York Times,* August 2, 1931, 3, https://www.nytimes.com/1931/08/02/archives/soviet-shock-troops-speed-up-industry-a-soviet-shock-brigade-called.html.

29 Phillip Knightley, *The First Casualty* (London: Quarter, 1975), 195.

30 Knightley, *The First Casualty,* 196.

31 Joan Cook, "Ella Winter Stewart Journalist and Widow of Donald O. Stewart," *New York Times,* August 5, 1980, M10, https://www.nytimes.com/1980/08/05/archives/ella-winter-stewart-journalist-and-widow-of-donald-o-stewart-was.html.

32 Robert Conquest, "How Liberals Funked It," *Hoover Digest* 3 (1999), https://www.hoover.org/research/how-liberals-funked-it.

33 "Address by Litvinoff at Farewell Dinner Here," *New York Times,* November 25, 1933, 3, https://www.nytimes.com/1933/11/25/archives/address-by-litvinoff-at-farewell-dinner-here.html.

34 "The Editorial Notebook; Trenchcoats, Then and Now," *New York Times,* June 24, 1990, Section 4, 20, https://www.nytimes.com/1990/06/24/opinion/the-editorial-notebook-trenchcoats-then-and-now.html.

35 James Mace, "A Tale of Two Journalists: Walter Duranty, Gareth Jones, and the Pulitzer Prize," *Ukrainian Weekly,* November 16, 2003, http://www.ukrweekly.com/old/archive/2003/460315.shtml

36 Mace, "Tale of Two Journalists."

37 Marco Carynnyk, "The New York Times and the Great Famine," *Ukrainian Weekly* 37, no. LI, September 25, 1983, http://www.ukrweekly.com/uwwp/the-new-york-times-and-the-great-famine/.

Chapter 3

1   Herbert Matthews, *Castro* (Harmondsworth: Penguin, 1970), 105.

2   Herbert Matthews, "Cuban Rebel Is Visited in Hideout," *New York Times*, February 24, 1957, 1.

3   Herbert L. Matthews, "Rebel Strength Gaining in Cuba, But Batista Has the Upper Hand," *New York Times*, Feb. 25, 1957, 1, https://www.nytimes.com/1957/02/25/archives/rebel-strength-gaining-in-cuba-but-batista-has-the-upper-hand-rebel.html.

4   Peter Wyden, *Bay of Pigs* (New York: Simon and Schuster, 1979), 28.

5   Matthews, *Castro,* 155.

6   Anthony DePalma, *The Man Who Invented Fidel: Castro, Cuba, and Herbert L. Matthews of the New York Times* (New York: Public Affairs, 2007).

7   Theodor Draper, *Castro's Revolution: Myths and Realities* (London: Thames & Hudson, 1962), 21–22.

8   Wyden, *Bay of Pigs.*

9   Wyden, *Bay of Pigs.*

10   Wyden, *Bay of Pigs,* 26.

11   "Fidel Castro Visits Washington," *The Guardian*, April 17, 1959. Accessed via: https://www.theguardian.com/world/2015/apr/17/fidel-castro-visit-washington-cuba-1959.

12   DePalma, *The Man Who Invented Fidel.*

13   DePalma, *The Man Who Invented Fidel,* 162.

14   Alberto Sbacchi, "Poison Gas and Atrocities in the Italo-Ethiopian War (1935–1936)," in Italian Colonialism. Italian and Italian American Studies, eds. R. Ben-Ghiat and M. Fuller (New York: Palgrave Macmillan, 2005), 47-56. https://doi.org/10.1007/978-1-4039-8158-5_5

15   Knightley, *The First Casualty,* 184.

16   Herbert Matthews, *The Education of a Correspondent* (New York: Harcourt, Brace & Co: 1946)

17   Matthews, *Education of a Correspondent.*

18   Knightley, *The First Casualty,* 192.

19   Knightley, *The First Casualty,* 193.

20   Knightley, *The First Casualty,* 195.

21   Herbert Matthews, "Cuba: First Step to a New Era," *New York Times,* January 4, 1959, E6, https://www.nytimes.com/1959/01/04/archives/cuba-first-step-to-a-new-era-defeat-of-batista-only-the-start.html.

22   Herbert Matthews, "Now Castro Faces the Harder Fight," *New York Times Magazine*, March 8, 1959, SM22, https://www.nytimes.com/1959/03/08/archives/now-castro-faces-the-harder-fight-his-revolution-against-batista.html.

23   Theodore Draper, *Castro's Revolution, Myths and Realities* (New York: Praeger: 1962).

24   Draper, *Castro's Revolution*, 28.

25   Herbert L. Matthews, "Castro Has a One-Man Rule and It Is Called Non-Red," *New York Times*, July 16, 1959, 1, https://www.nytimes.com/1959/07/16/archives/cuba-has-a-oneman-rule-and-it-is-called-nonred-youthful-castro.html.

26   Draper, *Castro's Revolution*, 30.

27   Tad Szulc, "A Year of Castro Rule in Cuba: Leftists Speeding Vast Reforms," *New York Times*, December 17, 1959, 1, https://www.nytimes.com/1959/12/17/archives/a-year-of-castro-rule-in-cuba-leftists-speeding-vast-reforms-year.html.

28   Tad Szulc, "Cuba: Profile of a Revolution," *New York Times*, April 24, 1960, M117, https://www.nytimes.com/1960/04/24/archives/cuba-profile-of-a-revolution.html.

29   "Early Backers of Cuba Scored," *New York Times*, September 11, 1960, 1, https://www.nytimes.com/1960/09/11/archives/early-backers-of-castro-scored-herter-decries-senators-charge-early.html.

30   Wyden, *Bay of Pigs*, 153.

31   Wyden, *Bay of Pigs*, 154.

32   Wyden, *Bay of Pigs*, 155.

33   Phillip Benjamin, "Leader Tells of Hopes for Better Cuba," *New York Times*, April 22, 1959, 1, https://www.nytimes.com/1959/04/22/archives/leader-tells-of-hopes-for-better-cuba-city-gives-castro-a-noisy.html.

34   Benjamin, "Leader Tells."

35   Anthony DePalma. "Myths of the Enemy: Castro, Cuba, and Herbert L. Matthews of the New York Times" (working paper #313, Kellogg Institute Paper #313, July 2004).

36   DePalma, *The Man Who Invented Fidel*, 158.

Chapter 4

1   Neil Sheehan, "The Combatant," *The New York Times*, December 30, 2007, https://www.nytimes.com/2007/12/30/magazine/30lives-t.html.

2   Jack Shafer, "Portrait of the Pulitzer Prize-Winning Reporter as an Engorged Ego," *Slate*, April 24, 2007, https://slate.com/news-and-politics/2007/04/david-halberstam-1934-2007.html.

3   Richard Holbrooke, "A Loss for All of Us," *Washington Post*, May 2, 2007, https://www.washingtonpost.com/wp-dyn/content/article/2007/05/01/AR2007050101418.html.

4   Holbrooke, "A Loss for All of Us."

5   Holbrooke, "A Loss for All of Us."

6   "The Fog of War: Eleven Lessons from the Life of Robert S. McNamara,"
      directed by Errol Morris (2004; Sony Pictures Classics, USA).

7   "The Fog of War."

8   "The Fog of War."

9   Holbrooke, "A Loss for All of Us."

10   David Halberstam, "Diem Regime Under Fire," *New York Times*,
      July 7, 1963, E5, https://www.nytimes.com/1963/07/07/archives/diem-
      regime-under-fire-us-disaffection-with-the-government-mounts.html.

11   David Halberstam, "Police in Saigon Jostle Newsmen," *New York
      Times*, July 8, 1963, 3, https://www.nytimes.com/1963/07/08/archives/
      police-in-saigon-jostle-newsmen-us-reporter-is-felled-at-buddhist.html.

12   David Halberstam, "Another Buddhist Immolates Himself," *New York
      Times*, August 14, 1963, 1, https://www.nytimes.com/1963/08/14/
      archives/another-buddhist-immolates-himself-third-buddhist-ends-life-
      by-fire.html.

13   David Halberstam, "Repressions Are Seen Creating Sharp Divisions in
      Vietnam," *New York Times*, August 25, 1963, 3, https://www.nytimes.
      com/1963/08/25/archives/repressions-are-seen-creating-sharp-divisions-
      in-vietnam-increasing.html.

14   David Halberstam, "Anti-US Feeling Rises in Vietnam as Unrest
      Grows," *New York Times*, August 24, 1963, 1, https://www.nytimes.
      com/1963/08/24/archives/antius-feeling-rises-in-vietnam-as-unrest-
      grows-nhus-power-in.html.

15   Mark Moyar, *Triumph Forsaken: The Vietnam War, 1954-1965* (New
      York: Cambridge University Press, 2006), 234.

16   David Halberstam, "Plan Said to Be Nhu's," *New York Times,* August
      23, 1963, 1, https://www.nytimes.com/1963/08/23/archives/plan-said-
      to-be-nhus-lodge-arrives-in-saigon-some-in-saigon-believe.html.

17   Neil Sheehan, *A Bright Shining Lie: John Paul Vann and America in
      Vietnam* (New York: Vintage, 1988), 359.

18   Sheehan, *A Bright Shining Lie,* 359.

19   Ed Lasky, "Military-Haters in the Press," *American Thinker*, May
      20, 2005, https://www.americanthinker.com/articles/2005/05/
      militaryhaters_in_the_press.html.

20   David Rosenbaum, "Hunt Says He Fabricated Cables on Diem to Link
      Kennedy to Killing of Catholic," *New York Times*, September 25,
      1973, 28, https://www.nytimes.com/1973/09/25/archives/hunt-says-he-
      fabricated-cables-on-diem-to-link-kennedy-to-killing.html.

Chapter 5

1   Laurel Leff,, *Buried by The Times: The Holocaust and America's Most
      Important Newspaper* (New York: Cambridge University Press, 2005), 10.

2   "More Executed in Yugoslavia, Czechoslovakia & Poland—Jews' Toll 700,000," *New York Times,* June 27, 1942, 5, https://www.nytimes.com/1942/06/27/archives/big-rewards-paid-in-heydrich-case-two-czechs-get-5000000-crowns.html.

3   "Jews in Nazi-Occupied Countries: BBC: 700,000 Jews Killed in Poland," Jewish Virtual Library, accessed December 20, 2020, https://www.jewishvirtuallibrary.org/bbc-700-000-jews-killed-in-poland.

4   "Goebbels Spurs Abuse for Jews," *New York Times,* November 14, 1941, 11, https://www.nytimes.com/1941/11/14/archives/goebbels-spurs-abuse-for-jews-says-they-more-than-earned-hard-lot.html.

5   "Terror of Nazism in Balkans Told," *New York Times*, March 14, 1942, 7, https://www.nytimes.com/1942/03/14/archives/terror-of-nazism-in-balkans-told-relief-units-spokesman-here-says.html.

6   David Wyman, *The Abandonment of the Jews: America and The Holocaust, 1941-1945* (New York: Pantheon, 1984), 24.

7   "Nazi Punishment Seen by Roosevelt," *New York Times*, July 22, 1924, 1, https://www.nytimes.com/1942/07/22/archives/nazi-punishment-seen-by-roosevelt-says-hitler-will-be-held-to.html.

8   "Sees Freedom Even with War Censorship," *New York Times*, May 23, 1941, 10, https://www.nytimes.com/1941/05/23/archives/sees-freedom-even-with-war-censorship-arthur-h-sulzberger-replies.html.

9   "Miss Sulzberger Becomes a Bride," *New York Times*, July 9, 1941, 18, https://www.nytimes.com/1941/07/09/archives/miss-sulzberger-becomes-a-bride-married-on-lawn-of-parents-home-in.html.

10   "Ponary – The Vilna Killing Site," Holocaust Education and Archive Research Team, accessed Jaunary 7, 2020, http://www.holocaustresearchproject.org/einsatz/ponary.html

11   Wyman, *Abandonment of the Jews,* 11.

12   Wyman, *The Abandonment of the Jews*, 11

13   Wyman, *The Abandonment of the Jews,* 9.

14   Wyman, *Abandonment of the Jews,* 10.

15   "The Brandeis Nomination," *New York Times*, May 25, 1916, 12, https://www.nytimes.com/1916/05/25/archives/the-brandeis-nomination.html.

16   Amos Elon, *The Pity of it All: A Portrait of Jews in Germany 1743-1933* (London: Penguin, 2004).

17   Laurel Leff, "A Tragic 'Fight in the Family': *The New York Times*, Reform Judaism and the Holocaust," *American Jewish History* 88, no. 1 (March 2000): 3–51.

18   Leff, "Tragic 'Fight in the Family.'"

19   Ron Chernow, "Who's in Charge Here?" review of *The Trust: The Private and Powerful Family Behind the New York Times,* by Susan E. Tifft and Alex S. Jones, *New York Times*, September 26, 1999.

20   Gay Talese, *The Kingdom and the Power: Behind the Scenes at the New York Times: The Institution That Influences the World* (New York: Random House Trade Paperbacks, 2007).

21   Leff, *Buried by The Times*, 188.

22   Wyman, *Abandonment of the Jews*, 73.

23   Wyman, *Abandonment of the Jews*, 6.

24   "U.S. Refuses French Plea to Take Refugees," *New York Times*, January 9, 1941, 1, https://www.nytimes.com/1941/01/09/archives/us-refuses-french-plea-to-take-refugees-reich-curb-called-bar-to.html.

25   "The Refugee Problem," *New York Times*, January 12, 1941, E8, https://www.nytimes.com/1941/01/12/archives/the-refugee-problem.html.

26   "Refugees and Immigrants," *New York Times*, January 27, 1945, 10, https://www.nytimes.com/1945/01/27/archives/refugees-and-immigrants.html.

27   "Refugees and Immigrants."

28   "Oswiecim Killings Placed At 4,000,000; Soviet Commission Reports Death Camp in Poland Was Founded by Himmler," *New York Times*, May 8, 1945, 12, https://www.nytimes.com/1945/05/08/archives/oswiecim-killings-placed-at-4000000-soviet-commission-reports-death.html.

Chapter 6

1   Dan Kurzman, *Day of the Bomb: Countdown to Hiroshima* (New York: McGraw-Hill, 1986).

2   "B-29'S Hit Yawata; They Dropped First Atomic Bomb On Japan B-29'S Hit Yawata in 1,500-Ton Blow. Toyokawa Results "Excellent" Navy Privateers Rip Shipping Kenney's Planes over South Kyushu," *New York Times*, August 8, 1945, 1, https://www.nytimes.com/1945/08/08/archives/b29s-hit-yawata-they-dropped-first-atomic-bomb-on-japan-b29s-hit.html.

3   "William Laurence of The Times Dies," *New York Times*, March 19, 1977, 1, https://www.nytimes.com/1977/03/19/archives/william-laurence-of-the-times-dies-william-l-laurence-of-the-times.html.

4   William L. Laurence, "The Quest of Science for an Atomic Energy," *New York Times*, June 29, 1929, Section Radio, Automobiles, 122, https://www.nytimes.com/1930/06/29/archives/the-quest-of-science-for-an-atomic-energy-eddington-invites-new.html.

5   Kurzman, *Day of the Bomb*, 16.

6   Kurzman, *Day of the Bomb*, 20.

7   William L. Laurence, "Scientists to Build Atomic Siege Guns," *New York Times*, June 21, 1934, 20, https://www.nytimes.com/1934/06/21/archives/scientists-to-build-atomic-siege-guns-0ne-of-20000000-another-of.html.

8   William L. Laurence, "Artificial Radium Produced Cheaply," *New York Times*, April 25, 1935, 16, https://www.nytimes.com/1935/04/25/archives/artificial-radium-produced-cheaply-found-as-a-byproduct-of.html.

9   William L. Laurence, "Energy Multiplied 200,000,000 Times," *New York Times*, April 27, 1935, Section Religious News, 9, https://www.nytimes.com/1935/04/27/archives/energy-multiplied-200000000-times-yield-from-atom-increased-by.html.

10   William L. Laurence, "Force 40 Times That of Electricity Is Discovered in Hearts of Atoms," *New York Times*, May 2, 1936, 1, https://www.nytimes.com/1936/05/02/archives/force-40-times-that-of-electricity-is-discovered-in-hearts-of-atoms.html.

11   William L. Laurence, "Reports Particle of Trillion Volts," *New York Times*, April 23, 1939, 5, https://www.nytimes.com/1939/04/23/archives/reports-particle-of-trillion-volts-dr-arthur-h-compton-says-energy.html.

12   William L. Laurence, "Vast Power Source in Atomic Energy Opened by Science," *New York Times*, May 5, 1940, 1, https://www.nytimes.com/1940/05/05/archives/vast-power-source-in-atomic-energy-opened-by-science-report-on-new.html.

13   "Watched for Bomb Spies," *New York Times*, September 5, 1945, 4, https://www.nytimes.com/1945/09/05/archives/watched-for-bomb-spies-army-checked-circulation-of-article-by-wl.html.

14   Sidney Shalett, "New Age Ushered," *New York Times*, August 7, 1945, 1, https://www.nytimes.com/1945/08/07/archives/new-age-ushered-day-of-atomic-energy-hailed-by-president-revealing.html.

15   "Science and the Bomb," *New York Times*, August 7, 1945, 22, https://www.nytimes.com/1945/08/07/archives/science-and-the-bomb.html.

16   Sidney Shalett, "More Atom Plants Rise at Oak Ridge," *New York Times*, August 8, 1945, 6, https://www.nytimes.com/1945/08/08/archives/more-atom-plants-rise-at-oak-ridge-army-boss-reveals-expansion.html.

17   "War Department Called Times Reporter to Explain Intricacies to Public," *New York Times*, August 7, 1945, 5, https://www.nytimes.com/1945/08/07/archives/war-department-called-times-reporter-to-explain-bombs-intricacies.html.

18   William L. Laurence, "Atomic Bombing of Nagasaki Told by Flight Member," *New York Times*, September 9, 1945, 1, https://www.nytimes.com/1945/09/09/archives/atomic-bombing-of-nagasaki-told-by-flight-member-aftermath-of.html.

19   Y. Nishiwaki, "Fifty Years after Hiroshima and Nagasaki," *International Nuclear Information System*, 37, no. 2 (1996), 17-26.

20   Mark Selden, "Nagasaki 1945: While Independents Were Scorned, Embed Won Pulitzer," *Yale Global Online,* July 7, 2005, https://yaleglobal.yale.edu/content/nagasaki-1945-while-independents-were-scorned-embed-won-pulitzer.

21   Selden, "Nagasaki 1945."

22   William L. Laurence, "U.S. Bomb Site Belies Tokyo Tales," *New York Times,* September 12, 1945, 1, https://www.nytimes.com/1945/09/12/archives/us-atom-bomb-site-belies-tokyo-tales-tests-on-new-mexico-range.html.

23   "Topics of the Times," *New York Times*, September 12, 1945, 24, https://www.nytimes.com/1945/09/12/archives/topics-of-the-times-names-in-the-news.html.

24   William L. Laurence, "Drama of the Atomic Bomb Found Climax in July 16 Test," *New York Times*, September 26, 1945, 1, https://www.nytimes.com/1945/09/26/archives/drama-of-the-atomic-bomb-found-climax-in-july-16-test-drama-of-the.html.

25   "Story of Atom Bomb Told," *New York Times*, October 5, 1945, 4, https://www.nytimes.com/1945/10/05/archives/story-of-atom-bomb-told-wl-laurence-who-saw-it-tested-is-heard-at.html.

26   "William Laurence of The Times Dies."

27   Amy Goodman and David Goodman, *The Exception to the Rulers: Exposing Oily Politicians, War Profiteers, and the Media That Love Them* (New York: Hyperion, 2006).

28   Amy Goodman and David Goodman, "Hiroshima Cover-up: Stripping the War Department Timesman of His Pulitzer," *Democracy Now!* August 5, 2005, https://www.democracynow.org/2005/8/5/hiroshima_cover_up_stripping_the_war.

29   William H. Lawrence, "Honshu Badly Hit, Air Tour Reveals," *New York Times,* September 3, 1945, 1, https://www.nytimes.com/1945/09/03/archives/honshu-badly-hit-air-tour-reveals-25-to-68-per-cent-of-6-major.html.

30   William H. Lawrence, "Visit to Hiroshima Proves It World's Most Damaged City," *New York Times*, September 5, 1945, 1, https://www.nytimes.com/1945/09/05/archives/visit-to-hiroshima-proves-it-worlds-mostdamaged-city-tokyo-the.html.

31   William H. Lawrence, "No Radioactivity in Hiroshima Ruin," *New York Times,* September 13, 1945, 4, https://www.nytimes.com/1945/09/13/archives/no-radioactivity-in-hiroshima-ruin-what-our-superfortresses-did-to.html.

32   "After-Effects of the Bomb," *New York Times,* September 13, 1945, 19, https://www.nytimes.com/1945/09/13/archives/aftereffects-of-the-bomb.html.

33   "After-Effects of The Bomb."

34 Robert Jacobs, "The Bravo Test and the Death and Life of the Global Ecosystem in the Early Anthropocene," *The Asia Pacific Journal: Japan Focus* 13, no. 29 (2015).

35 Beverley Deepe Keever, "Suffering, Secrecy, Exile: Bravo 50 Years Later," *Honolulu Weekly*, February 25, 2004.

36 "The Bravo Test," AtomicArchive.com, accessed January 7, 2021, https://www.atomicarchive.com/history/cold-war/page-6.html.

Chapter 7

1 James Fallows, "Who Shot Muhammad Al-Dura?" *Atlantic*, June 2003, https://www.theatlantic.com/magazine/archive/2003/06/who-shot-mohammed-al-dura/302735/.

2 John Rosenthal, "France: The Al-Dura Defamation Case and the End of Free Speech," *World Politics Review*, November 3, 2006, https://www.worldpoliticsreview.com/articles/312/france-the-al-dura-defamation-case-and-the-end-of-free-speech.

3 William A. Orme, Jr., "Mideast Violence Continues to Rage; Death Toll Rises," *New York Times*, October 1, 2000, 1, https://www.nytimes.com/2000/10/01/world/mideast-violence-continues-to-rage-death-toll-rises.html.

4 William A. Orme, Jr., "A Young Symbol of Mideast Violence," *New York Times*, October 2, 2000, A12, https://www.nytimes.com/2000/10/02/world/a-young-symbol-of-mideast-violence.html.

5 Deborah Sontag, "Battle at Jerusalem Holy Site Leaves 4 Dead and 200 Hurt," *New York Times*, September 30, 2000, A1, https://www.nytimes.com/2000/09/30/world/battle-at-jerusalem-holy-site-leaves-4-dead-and-200-hurt.html.

6 "The Photo That Started It All," Honest Reporting, last modified February 2012, https://honestreporting.com/the-photo-that-started-it-all/.

7 "Corrections," *New York Times*, October 4, 2000, A2, https://www.nytimes.com/2000/10/04/nyregion/c-corrections-480142.html.

8 "Corrections," *New York Times*, October 7, 2000, A2, https://www.nytimes.com/2000/10/07/nyregion/c-corrections-542970.html.

9 William A. Orme, Jr., "As Arabs and Israelis Fight on, Albright Seeks Talks," *New York Times*, October 3, 2000, A1, https://www.nytimes.com/2000/10/03/world/whose-holy-land-the-overview-as-arabs-and-israelis-fight-on-albright-seeks-talks.html.

10 Judith Miller, "Neighbors Fear Turmoil Could Threaten Them," *New York Times*, October 13, 2000, A10, https://www.nytimes.com/2000/10/13/world/whose-holy-land-the-arabs-neighbors-fear-turmoil-could-threaten-them.html.

11 "Marwan Barghouti, Fatah-Tanzim, and the Escalation of the Intifada," Jerusalem Center for Public Affairs: *Jerusalem Issue Brief* 1, no. 16 (January 24, 2002).

12 Suleyman Demirel et al., "The Mitchell Report – Sharm el-Sheikh Fact-Finding Committee," *Middle East Policy* 8, no.3 (2001).

13 Deborah Sontag, "Quest for Mideast Peace: How and Why It Failed," *New York Times,* July 26, 2001, A1, https://www.nytimes.com/2001/07/26/world/and-yet-so-far-a-special-report-quest-for-mideast-peace-how-and-why-it-failed.html.

14 Robert Satloff, "Times Bomb," *New Republic*, August 13, 2001, https://www.washingtoninstitute.org/policy-analysis/times-bomb#main-content.

15 Satloff, "Times Bomb."

16 William A. Orme, Jr., "A Parallel Mideast Battle: Is It News or Incitement?" *New York Times,* October 24, 2000, A18, https://www.nytimes.com/2000/10/24/world/a-parallel-mideast-battle-is-it-news-or-incitement.html.

17 "Palestinian Anti-Semitism: Palestinian TV Calls for Killing Jews and Americans," Jewish Virtual Library, accessed January 7, 2021, https://www.jewishvirtuallibrary.org/palestinian-tv-broadcast-calls-for-killing-jews-and-americans-october-2000.

18 Deborah Sontag, "Israel in Shock as It Buries Mob's Victim," *New York Times*, October 14, 2000, A1, https://www.nytimes.com/2000/10/14/world/whose-holy-land-the-victims-israel-in-shock-as-it-buries-mob-s-victim.html.

19 Fallows, "Who Shot Muhammad Al-Dura?"

20 Adi Schwartz, "Ballistics Expert Supports Verdict in Al-Dura Libel Case: Gaza Child Wasn't Killed by Israeli Gunfire," *Haaretz*, last modified January 12, 2018, https://www.haaretz.com/1.4997964.

21 William A. Orme, Jr., "Israeli Army Says Palestinians May Have Shot Gaza Boy," *New York Times*, Nov. 28, 2000, A8, https://www.nytimes.com/2000/11/28/world/israeli-army-says-palestinians-may-have-shot-gaza-boy.html.

22 Jacob Gershman "United Nations Bankrolled Latest Anti-Israel Propaganda," *New York Sun*, August 17, 2005.

23 Sontag, "Quest for Mideast Peace."

24 Judea Pearl, "The Daniel Pearl Standard," *Wall Street Journal Europe*, January 31, 2008, https://www.wsj.com/articles/SB120165176905126961.

Chapter 8

1   Ken Auletta, "The Inheritance," *New Yorker*, December 12, 2015, https://www.newyorker.com/magazine/2005/12/19/the-inheritance.

2   Seth Mnookin, *Hard News: The Scandals at The New York Times and Their Meaning for American Media* (New York: Random House, 2004).

3   David Folkenflik, "The Making of Jayson Blair," *Baltimore Sun,* February 29, 2004, https://www.baltimoresun.com/bal-as.blair23-story. html.

4   Dan Barry et al., "Times Reporter Who Resigned Leaves Long Trail of Deception," *New York Times,* May 11, 2003, https://www.nytimes. com/2003/05/11/us/correcting-the-record-times-reporter-who-resigned-leaves-long-trail-of-deception.html.

5   Jayson Blair, "Police Questioning Man and Boy at an Undisclosed Location," *New York Times,* October 24, 2002, https://www.nytimes. com/2002/10/24/national/police-questioning-man-and-boy-at-an-undisclosed-location.html.

6   Jayson Blair, "Tough News: Bearing the Worst News, Then Helping the Healing," *New York Times,* March 22, 2003, B7, https://www.nytimes. com/2003/03/22/us/a-nation-at-war-a-tough-duty-bearing-the-worst-news-then-helping-the-healing.html.

7   Jayson Blair, "Families; Watching and Praying as a Son's Fate Unfolds," *New York Times,* March 25, 2003, B1, https://www.nytimes. com/2003/03/25/us/a-nation-at-war-families-watching-and-praying-as-a-son-s-fate-unfolds.html.

8   Jayson Blair, "The Mortuary; The Last Stop on the Journey Home," *New York Times,* April 1, 2003, B12, https://www.nytimes. com/2003/04/01/us/a-nation-at-war-the-mortuary-the-last-stop-on-the-journey-home.html.

9   Jayson Blair, "The Families; For One Pastor, the War Hits Home," *New York Times,* April 7, 2003, B1, https://www.nytimes.com/2003/04/07/ us/a-nation-at-war-the-families-for-one-pastor-the-war-hits-home.html.

10   Jayson Blair, "The Spouses; A Couple Separated by War While United in Their Fears," *New York Times,* April 15, 2003, A1, https://www. nytimes.com/2003/04/15/us/nation-war-spouses-couple-separated-war-while-united-their-fears.html.

11   Jayson Blair, "Veterans; In Military Wards, Questions and Fears from the Wounded," *New York Times,* April 19, 2003, A1, https://www. nytimes.com/2003/04/19/us/a-nation-at-war-veterans-in-military-wards-questions-and-fears-from-the-wounded.html.

12   Blair, "Veterans; In Military Wards."

13   Seth Mnookin, "Scandal of Record," *Vanity Fair,* April 29, 2008, https://www.vanityfair.com/style/2004/12/nytimes200412

14   Jayson Blair, "Aftereffects: The Missing; Family Waits, Now Alone, for a Missing Soldier," *New York Times,* April 26, 2003, A1, https://www. nytimes.com/2003/04/26/us/aftereffects-the-missing-family-waits-now-alone-for-a-missing-soldier.html.

15 Mnookin, Seth. *Hard News: The Scandals at The New York Times and Their Meaning for American Media* (New York: Random House, 2004).

16 Douglas Jehl and Jayson Blair, "Rescue in Iraq and a Big Stir in West Virginia," *New York Times,* April 3, 2003, A1, https://www.nytimes.com/2003/04/03/us/a-nation-at-war-the-hometown-rescue-in-iraq-and-a-big-stir-in-west-virginia.html.

17 Carl Swanson, "The Battle for the Newsroom," *New York Magazine,* May 16, 2003, https://nymag.com/nymetro/news/media/features/n_8722/.

18 Barry et al., "Times Reporter Who Resigned."

19 Jacques Steinberg, "Times' Two Top Editors Resign after Furor on Writer's Fraud," *New York Times,* June 6, 2003, https://www.nytimes.com/2003/06/06/nyregion/changes-times-overview-times-s-2-top-editors-resign-after-furor-writer-s-fraud.html.

20 Howell Raines, "My Times," *Atlantic,* May 2004, https://www.theatlantic.com/past/docs/issues/2004/05/raines.htm.

21 Raines, "My Times."

22 Patrick E. Tyler and John Tagliabue, "A Nation Challenged: The Investigation; Czechs Confirm Iraqi Agent Met With Terror Ringleader," *New York Times,* October 27, 2001, A1, https://www.nytimes.com/2001/10/27/world/nation-challenged-investigation-czechs-confirm-iraqi-agent-met-with-terror.html.

23 James Risen, "Threats and Responses: The View from Prague; Prague Discounts an Iraqi Meeting," *New York Times,* October 21, 2002, A1, https://www.nytimes.com/2002/10/21/world/threats-and-responses-the-view-from-prague-prague-discounts-an-iraqi-meeting.html.

24 Franklin Foer, "The Source of the Trouble," *New York Magazine,* May 28, 2004, https://nymag.com/nymetro/news/media/features/9226/.

25 Judith Miller, "U.S. Experts Find Radioactive Material in Iraq," *New York Times,* May 4, 2004, I24, https://www.nytimes.com/2003/05/04/world/aftereffects-search-for-weapons-us-experts-find-radioactive-material-in-iraq.html.

26 Michael R. Gordon and Judith Miller, "Threats and Responses: The Iraqis; U.S. Says Hussein Intensifies Quest for A-Bomb Parts," *New York Times,* September 8, 2002, 1, https://www.nytimes.com/2002/09/08/world/threats-responses-iraqis-us-says-hussein-intensifies-quest-for-bomb-parts.html.

27 Judith Miller, "Illicit Arms Kept Till Eve of War, an Iraqi Scientist Is Said to Assert," *New York Times,* April 21, 2003, A1, https://www.nytimes.com/2003/04/21/world/aftereffects-prohibited-weapons-illicit-arms-kept-till-eve-war-iraqi-scientist.html.

28 "Search for Evidence: Judith Miller Reports," archived July 23, 2017, Wayback Machine, transcript by PBS, April 22, 2003, https://www.pbs.org/newshour/show/search-for-evidence-judith-miller-reports.

29 Judith Miller and Douglas Jehl, "The Struggle for Iraq: The Weapons; Draft Report Said to Cite No Success in Iraq Arms Hunt," *New York Times*, September 25, 2003, A1, https://www.nytimes.com/2003/09/25/world/struggle-for-iraq-weapons-draft-report-said-cite-no-success-iraq-arms-hunt.html.

30 Arthur Sulzberger Jr., SUNY at New Paltz Commencement Address, video, May 21, 2006, https://www.c-span.org/video/?192696-1/suny-paltz-commencement-address.

31 Robert Conquest, *Harvest of Sorrow* (Hutchinson: London, 1986).

32 "N.Y. Times Urged to Rescind 1932 Pulitzer," *Associated Press*, October 22, 2003.

33 Robert D. Novak, "Mission To Niger," *Washington Post, July 14, 2003*.

34 "A Jar of Red Herrings," *New York Times,* July 19, 2005, A20, https://www.nytimes.com/2005/07/19/opinion/a-jar-of-red-herrings.html.

35 John Hinderaker, "Behind the Headlines," Powerline, October 1, 2005, accessed on December 21, 2020, http://www.powerlineblog.com/archives/2005/10/011671.php.

36 Arthur Ochs Sulzberger Jr. and Russell T. Lewis, "The Promise of the First Amendment," *New York Times,* October 10, 2004, https://www.nytimes.com/2004/10/10/opinion/the-promise-of-the-first-amendment.html.

37 "Arthur O. Sulzberger Jr.," Charlie Rose, October 11, 2005, charlierose.com/videos/18283.

38 Maureen Dowd, "Woman of Mass Destruction," *New York Times*, October 22, 2005, A17, https://www.nytimes.com/2005/10/22/opinion/woman-of-mass-destruction.html.

39 "Interview with Judith Miller," CNN *Larry King Live*, November 10, 2005. Transcript: http://transcripts.cnn.com/TRANSCRIPTS/0511/10/lkl.01.html.

40 Stanley Kurtz, "All The News That's Fit To Print," *National Review Online*, May 20, 2003, https://www.nationalreview.com/2003/05/all-news-thats-fit-print-stanley-kurtz/.

Chapter 9

1 Sara Corbett, "The Women's War," *New York Times Magazine,* March 18, 2007, https://www.nytimes.com/2007/03/18/magazine/18cover.html.

2 "Editors' Note," *New York Times Magazine,* March 25, 2007, A2, https://www.nytimes.com/2007/03/25/magazine/25ednote.html.

3 Corbett, "The Women's War."

4   Deborah Sontag and Lizette Alvarez, "Across America, Deadly Echoes of Foreign Battles," *New York Times Magazine,* January 13, 2008, 11, https://www.nytimes.com/2008/01/13/us/13vets.html.

5   Sontag and Alvarez, "Across America."

6   Ralph Peters, "Smearing Soldiers," *New York Post*, January 15, 2008. https://nypost.com/2008/01/15/smearing-soldiers/.

7   John DiLulio, Jr., "The Wacko-Vet Myth," *The Weekly Standard*, January 14, 2008, https://www.washingtonexaminer.com/weekly-standard/the-wacko-vet-myth-15688.

8   Clark Hoyt, "Stories That Speak for Themselves," *New York Times*, January 27, 2008, WK16, https://www.nytimes.com/2008/01/27/opinion/27pubed.html.

9   Deborah Sontag, "An Iraq Veteran's Descent; A Prosecutor's Choice," *New York Times,* January 20, 2008, A1, https://www.nytimes.com/2008/01/20/us/20vets.html.

10   Benedict Carey, "The Struggle to Gauge a War's Psychological Cost," *New York Times,* November 26, 2005, A1, https://www.nytimes.com/2005/11/26/health/the-struggle-to-gauge-a-wars-psychological-cost.html.

11   "In More Cases, Combat Trauma Takes the Witness Stand," *New York Times*, January 27, 2008, A1, https://www.nytimes.com/2008/01/27/us/27vets.html.

12   Lizette Alvarez and Deborah Sontag, "When Strains on Military Families Turn Deadly," *New York Times,* 15 February, 2008, https://www.nytimes.com/2008/02/15/world/americas/15iht-15vets.10076087.html.

13   Lizette Alvarez, "After the Battle, Fighting the Bottle at Home," *New York Times*, July 8, 2008, https://www.nytimes.com/2008/07/08/world/americas/08iht-08vets.14317624.html.

14   Ashley Hardway, "Intoxicated Manslaughter Charges Dropped Against Bliss Soldier," *KVIA ABC-7 El Paso*, July 25, 2008.

15   Lizette Alvarez, "Visiting Castro to Meet Both Cold Shoulder and 'Fidelmania,'" *New York Times,* October 20, 1995, A7, https://www.nytimes.com/1995/10/20/world/visiting-castro-to-meet-both-cold-shoulder-and-fidelmania.html.

16   Lizette Alvarez, "Castro Back in Fatigues in Harlem," *New York Times,* October 23, 1995, A1, https://www.nytimes.com/1995/10/23/world/the-un-at-50-castro-castro-back-in-fatigues-and-harlem.html.

17   Larry Rother, "A Little Hope Pumps up an Attitude," *New York Times,* November 19, 2005, 4003, https://www.nytimes.com/1995/11/19/weekinreview/the-world-a-little-hope-pumps-up-an-attitude.html.

18   Inter-American Commission on Human Rights, Annual Report 1994, Cuba, http://www.cidh.org/annualrep/94eng/chap.4a.htm.

19   Inter-American Commission on Human Rights.

20   Lizette Alvarez, "Giuliani? He Wouldn't Get Castro's Vote," *New York Times*, October 26, 1995, A10, https://www.nytimes.com/1995/10/26/world/giuliani-he-wouldn-t-get-castro-s-vote.html.

21   DePalma, *The Man Who Invented Fidel,* 275

22   DePalma, *The Man Who Invented Fidel,* 276

23   Jayson Blair, "Front Page Raises Issue of Journalistic Ethics," *New York Times*, September 9, 2000, B3, https://www.nytimes.com/2000/09/09/nyregion/front-page-raises-issue-of-journalistic-ethics.html.

24   "Cuban Anachronisms," *New York Times*, October 26, 1995, A24, https://www.nytimes.com/1995/10/26/opinion/cuban-anachronisms.html.

Chapter 10

1   "Editor's Note," *New York Times Magazine*, August 18, 2019.

2   "The 1619 Project," *New York Times Magazine*, https://www.nytimes.com/interactive/2019/08/14/magazine/1619-america-slavery.html.

3   Matthew Desmond, "Capitalism," *New York Times Magazine*, August 18, 2019.

4   Jeneen Interlandi, "A Broken Health Care System," *New York Times Magazine*, August 18, 2019.

5   Kevin Kruse, "Traffic," *New York Times Magazine*, August 18, 2019.

6   "The Idea of America," *New York Times Magazine,* August 18, 2019.

7   Tom Mackaman, "An Interview with Historian James Oakes on the New York Times' 1619 Project," World Socialist Web Site, November 18, 2019, https://www.wsws.org/en/articles/2019/11/18/oake-n18.html.

8   Eric London, "Historian Victoria Bynum on Inaccuracies of the *New York Times* 1619 Project," World Socialist Web Site, October 30, 2019, https://www.wsws.org/en/articles/2019/10/30/bynu-o30.html.

9   Tom Mackaman, "An Interview with Historian Gordon Wood on the New York Times' 1619 Project," World Socialist Web Site, November 28, 2019, https://www.wsws.org/en/articles/2019/11/28/wood-n28.html.

10   Tom Mackaman, "An Interview with Historian James McPherson and the New York Times' 1619 Project," World Socialist Web Site, November 14, 2019, https://www.wsws.org/en/articles/2019/11/14/mcph-n14.html.

11   "Letter to the Editor," *New York Times Magazine*, December 29, 2019.

12   "Letter to the Editor."

13   Leslie M. Harris, "I Helped Fact-Check The 1619 Project. The Times Ignored Me," Politico, March 6, 2020, https://www.politico.com/news/magazine/2020/03/06/1619-project-new-york-times-mistake-122248.

14   "Twelve Scholars Critique the 1619 Project and the New York Times Magazine Editor Responds," History News Network, January 26, 2020, https://historynewsnetwork.org/article/174140.

15   Khalil Gibran Muhammad, "Sugar," *New York Times Magazine*, August 18, 2019.

16   Edmund Lee, "Bari Weiss Resigns from New York Times Opinion Post," *New York Times,* July 14, 2020, B3, https://www.nytimes. com/2020/07/14/business/media/bari-weiss-resignation-new-york-times. html.

17   Bari Weiss, "Donald Trump and the 'Disloyal' Jews," *New York Times*, August 21, 2019, https://www.nytimes.com/2019/08/21/opinion/trump-jews.html.

18   Bari Weiss, "Europe's Jew Hatred, and Ours," *New York Times,* November 28, 2018, https://www.nytimes.com/2018/11/29/opinion/antisemitism-europe-jews.html.

19   Bari Weiss, "The Coronavirus Makes Our Old Culture Wars Seem Quaint," *New York Times*, April 22, 2020, https://www.nytimes. com/2020/04/22/opinion/coronavirus-culture-war.html.

20   Bari Weiss, "Did I Just Get Yanged?" *New York Times*, January 30, 2020, https://www.nytimes.com/2020/01/30/opinion/sunday/andrew-yang-2020.html.

21   Lee, "Bari Weiss Resigns."

22   Marc Tracy, *"James Bennet Resigns as New York Times Opinion Editor,"* *New York Times,* June 7, 2020, B1, https://www.nytimes.com/2020/06/07/business/media/james-bennet-resigns-nytimes-op-ed.html.

23   Tom Cotton, "Tom Cotton: Send in the Troops," *New York Times*, June 3, 2020, https://www.nytimes.com/2020/06/03/opinion/tom-cotton-protests-military.html.

24   Joe Pompeo, "New York Times Employees Rebel against Tom Cotton's Send-in-the-Troops Op-Ed," *Vanity Fair,* June 4, 2020, accessed December 21, 2020, https://www.vanityfair.com/news/2020/06/new-york-times-employees-rebel-against-tom-cotton-send-in-the-troops-op-ed.

25   Pompeo, "New York Times Employees Rebel."

26   Laura Hazard Owen, "'This Puts Black @nytimes Staff in Danger': New York Times Staffers Band Together to Protest Tom Cotton's Anti-Protest Op-ed," Neiman Lab, June 4, 2020, https://www.niemanlab. org/2020/06/this-puts-black-people-in-danger-new-york-times-staffers-band-together-to-protest-tom-cottons-anti-protest-editorial.

27   Susan Svrluga, "UNC Chancellor Says Confederate Monument Silent Sam Must Go—and So Will She," *Washington Post,* January 15, 2019, https://www.washingtonpost.com/education/2019/01/15/unc-chancellor-says-confederate-monument-silent-sam-must-go-so-will-she/.

28   James Bohman, "Critical Theory," in *Stanford Encyclopedia of Philosophy,* edited by Edward N. Zalta, 2019, https://plato.stanford. edu/archives/win2019/entries/critical-theory.

29   Moira Kenney, *Mapping Gay L.A.: The Intersection of Place and Politics* (Philadelphia: Temple University Press: 2001).

30   "Has Anti-Racism Become as Harmful as Racism? John McWhorter vs. Nikhil Singh," YouTube video, 1:48:14, https://www.youtube.com/watch?v=mzPKk19t3Kw.

31   Michael M. Grynbaum and Sydney Ember, "Less Defiant Trump at The Times: 'I Hope We Can All Get Along," *New York Times,* November 22, 2016, A15, https://www.nytimes.com/2016/11/22/business/media/donald-trump-new-york-times.html.

Conclusion

1   David W. Dunlap, "1896: 'Without Fear or Favor'," *New York Times,* August 14, 2015, https://www.nytimes.com/2015/09/12/insider/1896-without-fear-or-favor.html.

Bibliography

Ailsby, Christopher. *The Third Reich Day by Day*. St Paul, MN: MBI, 2001.

Anderson, Barbara A., and Brian D. Silver. "Growth and Diversity of the Population of the Soviet Union." *Annals of the American Academy of Political and Social Sciences* 510 (1990): 155-177. https://doi.org/10.117 7%2F0002716290510001012.

Carynnyk, Marco. "The New York Times and the Great Famine," *Ukrainian Weekly*, September 25, 1983, 39, no. LI, http://www.ukrweekly.com/ uwwp/the-new-york-times-and-the-great-famine/.

Conquest, Robert. "How Liberals Funked It." *Hoover Digest*, July 30, 1999. https://www.hoover.org/research/how-liberals-funked-it.

DePalma, Anthony. "Myths of the Enemy: Castro, Cuba, and Herbert L. Matthews of the New York Times." Kellogg Institute Working Paper #313, July 2004.

DePalma, Anthony. *The Man Who Invented Fidel: Castro, Cuba, and Herbert L. Matthews of the New York Times*. New York: Public Affairs, 2007.

Draper, Theodor. *Castro's Revolution: Myths and Realities*. London: Thames & Hudson, 1962, 21-22.

Elon, Amos. *The Pity of it All: A Portrait of Jews in Germany, 1743-1933*. London: Penguin, 2004.

Glaser-Schmidt, Elizabeth. "Between Hope and Skepticism: American Views of Germany, 1918-1933." In *Transatlantic Images and Perceptions: Germany and America since 1776*, edited by David Barclay, 191-216. Cambridge: Cambridge University Press, 1997.

Goodman, Amy, and David Goodman. *The Exception to the Rulers: Exposing Oily Politicians, War Profiteers, and the Media That Love Them*. New York: Hyperion, 2006.

Gruber, Helmut. "Willi Münzenberg's German Communist Propaganda Empire 1921-1933." *The Journal of Modern History* 38, no. 3 (September 1966): 278-297. https://doi.org/10.1086/239912.

Heller, Mikhail. *Utopia in Power: The History of the Soviet Union from 1917 to the Present*. London: Hutchinson, 1987.

Higham, Charles. *Trading with the Enemy: An Exposé of the Nazi–American Money Plot, 1933-1949*. London: Hale, 1983.

Jacobs, Robert. "The Bravo Test and the Death and Life of the Global Ecosystem in the Early Anthropocene." *The Asia Pacific Journal: Japan Focus* 13, no. 29 (2015). https://apjjf.org/2015/13/29/Robert-Jacobs/4343.html.

Kenney, Moira. *Mapping Gay L.A.: The Intersection of Place and Politics*. Philadelphia: Temple University Press: 2001.

Knightley, Phillip. *The First Casualty: The War Correspondent as Hero and Myth-Maker from the Crimea to Iraq*. London: Quarter, 1975.

Kurzman, Dan. *Day of the Bomb: Countdown to Hiroshima*. New York: McGraw-Hill, 1986.

Leff, Laurel. "A Tragic 'Fight in the Family': *The New York Times*, Reform Judaism and the Holocaust." *American Jewish History* 88, no. 1 (March 2000): 3–51. https://www.jstor.org/stable/23886315.

Leff, Laurel. *Buried by The Times: The Holocaust and America's Most Important Newspaper*. Cambridge: Cambridge University Press, 2005.

Lenskyj, Helen Jefferson, and Stephen Wagg, eds. *The Palgrave Handbook of Olympic Studies*. London: Palgrave Macmillan, 2012.

Lusane, Clarence. *Hitler's Black Victims: The Historical Experiences of European Blacks, Africans and African Americans during the Nazi Era*. New York: Routledge, 2003.

Matthews, Herbert. *Castro*. Harmondsworth: Penguin, 1970.

Matthews, Herbert. *The Education of a Correspondent*. New York: Harcourt, Brace & Co, 1946.

Medvedev, Roy A. *Let History Judge: The Origins and Consequences of Stalinism*. New York: Alfred A. Knopf, 1972.

Mnookin, Seth. *Hard News: The Scandals at The New York Times and Their Meaning for American Media*. New York: Random House, 2004.

Moyar, Mark. *Triumph Forsaken: The Vietnam War, 1954-1965*. New York: Cambridge University Press, 2006.

Nishiwaki, Y. "Fifty Years after Hiroshima and Nagasaki." *International Nuclear Information System*, 37, no. 2 (1996): 17-26.

Rauch, Greorg Von. *A History of Soviet Russia*. New York: Frederick Praeger, 1957.

Rosenthal, John. "France: The Al-Dura Defamation Case and the End of Free Speech." *World Politics Review,* November 3, 2006, https://www.worldpoliticsreview.com/articles/312/france-the-al-dura-defamation-case-and-the-end-of-free-speech.

Sbacchi, Alberto. "Poison Gas and Atrocities in the Italo-Ethiopian War (1935–1936)." In *Italian Colonialism*, edited by Ruth Ben-Ghiat, and Mia Fuller, 47-56. New York: Palgrave Macmillan, 2005.

Selden, Mark. "Nagasaki 1945: While Independents Were Scorned, Embed Won Pulitzer," *Yale Global Online,* July 7, 2005. https://yaleglobal.yale.edu/content/nagasaki-1945-while-independents-were-scorned-embed-won-pulitzer.

Sheehan, Neil. *A Bright Shining Lie: John Paul Vann and America in Vietnam*. New York: Vintage, 1988.

Shirer, William. *Berlin Diary*. Baltimore: Johns Hopkins Press, 2001.

Shirer, William. *The Rise and Fall of the Third Reich: A History of Nazi Germany*. New York: Simon and Schuster, 1960.

Stephenson, William. *A Man Called Intrepid*. New York: Ballantine Books, 1978.

Talese, Gay. *The Kingdom and the Power: Behind the Scenes at the New York Times: The Institution That Influences the World*. New York: Random House Trade Paperbacks, 2007.

Wyden, Peter. *Bay of Pigs*. New York: Simon and Schuster, 1979.

Wyman, David. *The Abandonment of the Jews: America and The Holocaust, 1941-1945*. New York: Pantheon, 1984.